Let us make man in
our image and likeness
(Genesis 1:26)

JACOB NEUSNER

The Incarnation of God: The Character of Divinity in Formative Judaism

FORTRESS PRESS   PHILADELPHIA

BM
610
.N48
1988

Library of Congress Cataloging-in-Publication Data

Neusner, Jacob, 1932–
  The incarnation of God

  Includes index.
  1. God (Judaism)—History of doctrines.
  2. Rabbinical literature—History and criticism.
  3 Anthropomorphism. I. Title.
  BM610.N48 1988   296.3'11   87–45901
  ISBN 0–8006–2086–0

3225J87   Printed in the United States of America   1–2086

For
Burton Mack

who wants to know, about Christianity,
exactly what I am trying to find out about Judaism,
and for the same reasons.

Colleague, friend, co-worker,
he exemplifies those academic virtues
not much in evidence, but still prized,
in the life of today's university.

I value his learning, admire his scholarship, enjoy his collegiality,
and cherish his friendship.

Contents

Preface

In this book I show that in the final stage in the formation of the canon of the Judaism of the dual Torah, a term defined in context, the incarnation of God forms a principal aspect of the character of divinity. Prior to that time, the character of divinity extended to portraits of God as (1) premise, for example, the one who created the world and gave the Torah; (2) presence, for example, supernatural being resident in the temple and present where two or more persons engage in discourse concerning the Torah; and (3) person, for example, the one to whom prayer is addressed. But only at the end do we find important allusions to the incarnation of God as well as narratives that realize in concrete terms the incarnation of God. By the incarnation of God, I mean the description of God, whether in allusion or narrative, as (1) corporeal; (2) exhibiting traits of emotions like those of human beings; (3) doing deeds that women and men do, in the way in which they do them. That forms the sum and substance of my thesis. Issues of category-formation and method are worked out in part 1. Parts 2, 3, and 4 lay out the evidence in a way I think is illuminating. In part 5 I explain how I believe the Judaism of the dual Torah accomplished the incarnation of God and what the sages of that Judaism wished to say in so representing God in whose image, after whose likeness, we all are made.

While this book stands on its own, it also may contribute toward the description of the formative history of the particular Judaism with which it deals. That Judaism—unique among Judaisms in its appeal to the authority of the dual Torah of Sinai, both oral and written—like all other Judaisms is to be described in three dimensions: (1) ethos, (2) ethics, and (3) social entity. It appeals to a world view, which I identify as its ethos; it prescribes a way of life, classified broadly as its ethics; and it addresses its own conception of a social entity, an "Israel." In that way, the Judaism at hand is like all others. For there are three components of any Judaism, deriving definition from the systemic model made up of a world view, way of life, and social entity. As I explained in *"Israel": Judaism and Its Social Metaphors,*[1] "Israel" is the name of, and forms, the social entity.

Moreover, the Judaic category represented by portraits of God, for reasons set forth in chapter 2, leads us deep into the world view of a Judaism. The systemic category of the human being "in our image, after our likeness" corresponds to the way of life. The correspondence between theological anthropology and the systemic way of life—broadly speaking, the ethics—will strike the reader as obvious when we recall that, in any Judaism, with the prevailing stress on deed along with deliberation, "we" (the "Israel" under discussion) are what "we" do. To all Judaic systems known to me, therefore, one's everyday way of life forms a definitive element in the system. If we wish to know how a Judaic system at its foundations defines its way of life, it must follow that we do well to translate the details of the here and now into the portrait of humanity "after our likeness" and of divinity: the personality of God. That accounts for the program of this book in its larger context of the description of Judaism. But not only does this book stand on its own. At this time I have no plan to address the issue of theological anthropology at all. For reasons I shall spell out elsewhere, in my view the way of life of the Judaism of the dual Torah, with its implicit theological anthropology, does not present a pressing question or define a compelling category in the larger labor of systemic description, analysis, and

---

1. (New York and Cambridge: Cambridge University Press, 1988).

interpretation.[2] I hope others will differ and prove me wrong. I know where to start and how to proceed, but at this time I am not persuaded of the urgency of the task.

About writing this book, as about almost every other project, I talked from four to fifteen times a day with Calvin Goldscheider, whose patience exceeds even that of Job, and whose simple love of colleagues exceeds that of Pinhas b. Yair. Many times I rethought and rewrote major components of the argument because of his sharp insights.

William Scott Green was spared as many inquiries only because our talks, by long-distance phone, while less numerous, lasted longer when they took place.

Ernest S. Frerichs as ever remained the ideal colleague: listening, learning, teaching, encouraging, sharing—above all, loving.

One colleague, who knows much more than I can ever learn about the theological categories to which I refer in this book, must be spared any blame for my treating as simple issues of classification—genus and species—what he knows as complex issues of theological discourse. Though he gets a fair share of credit for clarifying theological issues for me, Wendell S. Dietrich cannot bear any responsibility for neglect of my theological education. When I use as generic words he knows as particular to theology of Christianity, such as "consubstantial" and "incarnation," he at least has taught me what I am doing. He did indeed ask me all the hard questions; he is spared any onus for the theological results I present (descriptively to be sure), which he resisted with vigor and urgency.

But I do maintain that the Judaism of the dual Torah resorted to the incarnation of God. I maintain that the incarnation of God formed part of the unfolding of the inner logic of that Judaism, as it does of any Judaic system spun out of the heritage of the Hebrew Scriptures. I do hold that and, in this book, I prove it.

From Professor and Father Andrew Greeley, University of

---

2. I should imagine the place to start the study of the theological anthropology of Judaism is in *Genesis Rabbah,* from which point one may move in a number of directions.

Chicago and University of Arizona, I enjoyed the benefit of insights on matters having to do with divine incarnation and, in particular, the use of narrative, including story ("fiction"), for reflection on the full meaning of incarnation.

I have always treasured my transactions with Fortress Press and its entire staff, but I express my special thanks for Dr. Harold Rast and his ministry of kindness and love for authors in general, and for me in particular. All of us who have the privilege of working with him know what a truly great editor is, and I gladly pay my tribute to him.

Hoshannah Rabbah, 5748   JACOB NEUSNER
October 14, 1987
Program in Judaic Studies
Brown University
Providence, Rhode Island

Abbreviations

A.Z.	*Avodah Zarah*
Ar.	*Arakhin*
ARNA	*Avot de Rabbi Nathan,* version A (= *The Fathers According to Rabbi Nathan*)
b.	Babylonian Talmud (= Bavli)
B.B.	*Baba Batra*
B.M.	*Baba Mesia*
B.Q.	*Baba Qamma*
Ber.	*Berakhot*
Chron.	Chronicles
Dem.	*Demai*
Deut.	Deuteronomy
Ex.	Exodus
Ez.	Ezekiel
Gen.	Genesis
Gen. R.	*Genesis Rabbah*
Hab.	Habakkuk
Hag.	*Hagigah*
Hor.	*Horayot*
Hos.	Hosea
Is.	Isaiah
Jer.	Jeremiah
Jud.	Judges

Kel.	*Kelim*
Ket.	*Ketubot*
Lam.	Lamentations
Lev.	Leviticus
Lev. R.	*Leviticus Rabbah*
m.	Mishnah
M.Q.	*Moed Qatan*
Mak.	*Makkot*
Mal.	Malachi
Men.	*Menahot*
Mic.	Micah
Ned.	*Nedarim*
Num.	Numbers
Pe.	*Peah*
Pes.	*Pesahim*
Pesiq. Rab Kah.	*Pesiqta deRab Kahana*
Prov.	Proverbs
Ps.	Psalms
Qid.	*Qiddushin*
R.H.	*Rosh Hashshanna*
Sam.	Samuel
San.	*Sanhedrin*
Shab.	*Shabbat*
Sheb.	*Shebuot*
Sheq.	*Sheqalim*
Sifré Deut.	*Sifré to Deuteronomy*
Sifré Num.	*Sifré to Numbers*
Song	Song of Songs
Sot.	*Sotah*
Suk.	*Sukkah*
t.	Tosefta
Ta.	*Taanit*
Uqs.	*Uqsin*
y.	Yerushalmi (= The Talmud of the Land of Israel)
Zeb.	*Zebahim*
Zech.	Zechariah

Prologue

Let us make man in our image and likeness
(Gen. 1:26)

In the Judaism of the dual Torah, as in every other Judaism in the histories of Judaisms, God, who created the world and gave the Torah to Moses, encounters Israel in a vivid and personal way. While all Judaic systems record a compelling encounter with God, some portray God only as a premise, presence, and person, but not as a personality with whom human beings may identify. Others represent God as a personality, specifically as a human being whom people may know and love and emulate. The categories of premise, presence, and person hardly require much explanation. As premise, God forms (in philosophical terms) the ground of being. Otherwise uncharacterized, God may form a presence and be present in all things. As a person, again without further amplification, God is a "you," for example, to whom people address prayers. When portrayed as a personality, in any Judaism, God is represented in an incarnate way, not merely by appeal to anthropomorphic metaphors, but by resort to allusions to God's corporeal form, traits of attitude and emotion like those of human beings, capacity to do the sorts of things mortals do in the ways in which they do them, again, corporeally. In all of these ways, the incarnation of God is accomplished by treating God as a

1

personality. That is the proposition, concerning one Judaism, that I propose to prove in this book.

In writings redacted in the earlier stages in the formation of the Judaism of the dual Torah, God does not make an appearance as a vital personality with whom other personalities, human ones, transact affairs. By contrast, other documents, in particular in the later stages in the unfolding of that same canonical system, represent God in quite personal terms. These, as already suggested, are three: outer traits, inner characteristics, and capacity for concrete action done as human beings carry out their wishes. That is to say, in some of these later documents God appears in corporeal form. God exhibits traits of emotion and exemplifies virtuous attitudes. God carries out actions as human beings do—and does them in the same way. That is what I mean by God appearing as a personality, not as a mere premise of being, abstract presence, or even disembodied person.

I introduce categories deriving from an explicit principle of category-formation. I further analyze the documentary facts in accord with a much-reflected-upon principle of the classification of documents and the correct reading of their evidence. These constitute the (rather obvious) methodological contributions I propose to make in this book, as distinct from the proposition I wish to argue.

That proposition, stated in simple terms, is as follows: the final statement of the formative period of the Judaism of the dual Torah represented God in the flesh in the analogy of the human person—hence, accomplished for that Judaism, from antiquity to modern times, the incarnation of God. In that Judaism, prior to the Bavli, the faithful encountered God as abstract premise, as unseen presence, as a "you" without richly defined traits of soul, body, spirit, mind, or feeling. The Bavli's authorship for the first time in the formation of Judaism presented God as a fully formed personality, like a human being in corporeal traits, attitudes, emotions, and other virtues, in actions and the means of carrying out actions. God then looked the way human beings look, felt and responded the way they do, and did the actions that they do in the ways in which they do them. Yet, in that portrayal of the character of divinity, God always remained God. The insistent comparison of God with humanity "in our image and likeness" comes to its conclusion in one sentence that draws humanity upward and does not bring God downward. For despite its treatment of the sage as a holy man, the Bavli's characterization of God never confused God with a sage or a sage with God. Quite to the contrary, the point and purpose of that characterization reaches its climax in a story that in powerful language demands that in the encounter with the sage of all sages God be left to be God: *Silence, for that is how I have decided matters.* When we reach that point, we shall have come to the end of my account of the incarnation of God. Beyond that point, for the formation of Judaism in its classic, normative, and authoritative statement, is only silence.

The single authoritative statement in the verse cited above, which portrays the human being as formed in the model of God, supplied ample justification—just as it did, read in a different way, for Christianity in some of its diverse systems (or: "for Christianities"). It must follow, for the Priestly author, that God may be represented entirely in human form. That verse yielded an explicit statement of the matter for the Judaism of the dual Torah in its later stages, which we find in the following passage to which we return later on:

1.A. Said R. Hoshaiah, "When the Holy One, blessed be he, came to create the first man, the ministering angels mistook him [for God, since man was in God's image,] and wanted to say before him, 'Holy, [holy, holy is the Lord of hosts].'

B. "To what may the matter be compared? To the case of a king and a governor who were set in a chariot, and the provincials wanted to greet the king, 'Sovereign!' But they did not know which one of them was which. What did the king do? He turned the governor out and put him away from the chariot, so that people would know who was king.

C. "So too when the Holy One, blessed be he, created the first man, the angels mistook him [for God]. What did the Holy One, blessed be he, do? He put him to sleep, so everyone knew that he was a mere man.

D. "That is in line with the following verse of Scripture: 'Cease you from man, in whose nostrils is a breath, for how little is he to be accounted' (Is. 2:22)."

(Gen. R. VIII:X)

In light of this reading of Gen. 1:26, we may hardly find surprising the power of diverse heirs of Scripture, framers of various Judaic religious systems, to present portraits of the incarnation of God, corporeal, in affects and virtues consubstantial with humanity, doing things human beings do in the ways in which they do them.

The incarnation of God forms a commonplace for Judaisms from the formation of Scripture forward. For the Priestly author—not to mention authorship of JE, as well as the prophetic visionaries who saw God enthroned, riding horses or chariots, and the like—invited precisely that exercise of remarkable imagination. In addition, given the exegesis of the Song of Songs as a love song between God and Israel, on which basis that book found its way into the canon of Judaism, we must suppose many accepted the invitation. Nonetheless, however routine for ancient Israel the conception of the incarnation of God may have been, it did not come to full literary expression in every document of every Judaism. The history of how diverse Judaisms imagined God contains more than a single, uniform chapter about God portrayed as a human being (ordinarily, a man).

As is now clear, this book traces the appearance of the incarnation of God—God represented in human form, as a human being, corporeal, consubstantial in emotions and virtues, alike in action and mode of action—in the unfolding canon of one Judaism in late antiquity, specifically, the Judaism of the dual Torah. I want to show how in the unfolding of the canonical writings conceptions of God moved from essentially the philosophical and theological—premise, presence, even person—to the immediate, specific, and particular, and therefore the social and historical, the concrete and corporeal. In chapter 1 I explain three fundamental principles of this study: first, the basis for category-formation; second, the theory of the classification of evidence; and finally, the context and plan of historical, that is, sequential, reading of the evidence by the categories I have invented. Specifically, in that chapter I define the particular Judaism under discussion and briefly set forth the sequence and history of its canonical writings so that the historical picture I present will be readily accessible to all readers. Then I trace the evidences of the four ways, categories, in which the

canonical writings of the Judaism of the dual Torah ultimately represented God—premise, presence, person, and in the end, fully
exposed, amply etched personality. In the next three parts of the
book I analyze the pertinent evidence within the categories I have
provided and lay out the documents in accord with the classification
scheme explained in chapter 1. In this way we see the stages by
which God emerged for the Judaism of the dual Torah in its formative period as a historical personality and social being, as the God
who, in the long history of Israel's encounter with the divinity, becomes that ever-present friend, confidant, and beloved that is represented not only in the liturgies of the synagogue but in the
everyday life of the faithful. In the concluding chapter I revert to
the topic introduced at the outset, the incarnation of God in the
Judaism of the dual Torah and how the character of divinity is set
forth by that particular Judaism in its formative writings.

While this is a very simple book which is intended to make only a
very modest point, I realize that my presentation of the facts of how
the Judaism of the dual Torah accomplished the incarnation of God
may possibly surprise two sorts of readers—the only kinds I expect
in any numbers to read this book. First there are those who have
long taken for granted the utterly aniconic and nonanthropomor-
phic character of "Judaism," by which they meant the one at hand,
the one of the dual Torah. Many theologians of Judaism have built
their theological apologetic upon that single characterization of
"Judaism," meaning this kind, and I here show that that characterization is not valid. An entire philosophical movement within Judaism in medieval times proposed to explain in other than concrete
and corporeal terms the anthropomorphic representation of God in
the Hebrew Scriptures, including rich accounts of the incarnation
of God. Nineteenth- and early-twentieth-century apologists of Judaism, particularly in Reform Judaism and its associated scholarly
circles, carried forward that same insistence upon the utterly incor-
poreality of God in "Judaism," by which they meant the Judaism
represented in Scripture and in the canon of the dual Torah. So
there is ample reason to anticipate a measure of puzzlement on the
part of readers within contemporary Judaism.

Judaic and Christian believers as well as historians of religion
form the second class of readers apt to find my results puzzling.

These have deemed the Christian belief in humanity and divinity united in Jesus Christ, God incarnate, to be absolutely unique. They have further held that conception of God to be utterly incompatible with that of Judaism—any (kind of) Judaism. Christians may find in the Israelite Scriptures a rich legacy of anthropomorphism in general and evidence for the conviction of the incarnation of God in particular. They may maintain that in Jesus Christ, humanity and divinity united and incarnate, the "Old Testament" legacy has reached its natural and necessary climax. Hence finding in the Judaism that became normative (the one of the dual Torah) a continuation of that mode of meeting God (the mode of the incarnation of God) may prove as jarring for Christian as for Judaic readers. To both classes of readers I say very simply that I mean no disrespect in treating the incarnation of God as profoundly characteristic of the scriptural representation of God on the one side, and the Judaism of the written and oral Torah on the other. The conception of the incarnation of God offered in this book was idiomatic to a variety of Judaic authorships (though here I treat only the one I have specified). That the particular framing of that conception in reference to Jesus Christ, God become man, is unique to Christianity is in no way called into question. I cannot imagine a more self-evident fact of the history of religion.

We all recognize that one powerful modern theological apologetic for Judaism has contrasted Christian-pagan anthropomorphism with the "more spiritual" conception of God provided by Judaism.[1] Those who lay a heavy burden of faith upon the structure of theological apologetics will simply have to judge for themselves whether the evidence I set forth justifies my claim that, in the Bavli in particular, God is portrayed as incarnate in body and soul, attitude and deed. The Judaism of the dual Torah was, and is, a religion of the here and now—and so was, and is, its God. My definitions are not idiosyncratic, and my evidence not fictive. It is

---

1. At the end of chapter 9 I point out that Judaism confronted that very critique on the part of Zoroastrian philosophical theology in the ninth century. We seem to recapitulate familiar ground, with the parties to the argument changing roles while the arguments remain pretty much the same. I suppose that, even in theology, there is a limited number of possible arguments, but an endless range of possible parties. That is why where and when a position, always logically present at least as a potential, actually finds exponents and serves a concrete context seems to me an interesting question in the history of religion.

read accurately not only as a whole but in every detail, as a check of my translations against the original Hebrew in the standard printed texts will indicate; all stories I cite occur in the best manuscript evidence and form part of the received version of the documents. Better texts may improve details but will not change the facts as I portray them.[2]

I understand, further, that the use of the term "incarnation" may trouble those who regard it as particular ("unique") to Christianity. Theologians of Christianity invoke the principle of the absolute uniqueness of Christianity; one indicator is the conception of incarnation. No one will argue that the Christian formulation of incarnation bears traits different from other religions' formulation of that same notion, which forms a species of the genus anthropomorphism, as I shall suggest. But incarnation does define a category in the history of religion and, so far as (in the eyes of the world in general) Christianity for its part writes a chapter in that same history, it is fair to appeal to a category pertinent to more than a single case, as historians of religion in general maintain. Christians accustomed to regarding the union of divinity and humanity in the person of Jesus Christ, God incarnate, as unique will address their complaint not to me but to the definition of incarnation I have taken from the most current and standard encyclopedia I could find. Now to the definition of anthropomorphism and incarnation.

---

2. So much for critics who argue that until all manuscript evidence has been collated (which critics call "the making of a critical text") no work of description, analysis, and interpretation is possible. We who now do that work use the best texts we have; when better ones come out, we turn to them. But no claim in this book rests on the priority of one reading over some other. And to my knowledge no story cited in this book exists only in a fragment of the larger manuscript evidence for the document that now contains it. When I allege that, for example, the Bavli's authorship has included a given story, I base that allegation on the consensus of manuscript evidence presently in hand, and I do not appeal to a story that appears in one manuscript but not in some other. Critics who mount an argument based on the inadequacy of available textual evidence moreover ignore the stress, in the work done today on the history of religion for Judaism, upon the ubiquitous traits of form, including the formalization of rhetoric, the prevalence of a given (documentary) logic, the recurrence and conventionality of a given (documentary) topical program. No one known to me composes a history of religion, for Judaism, based on the premise that the texts we now have accurately and in every detail represent the original statement of the initial authorship. Quite to the contrary, it is because of the uncertainty of our textual tradition and its available representation that the entire emphasis lies on uniformities and continuities, within a document, of a given convention in rhetoric, logic, and topic.

PART ONE

Issues of Method:
Category-Formation and the
Classification of Evidence

1

Anthropomorphism and Incarnation: Defining Categories and Identifying Evidence

Anthropomorphism forms the genus of which incarnation constitutes a species. Anthropomorphism denotes forming religious concepts and ideas in human terms, in accord with the shapes and metaphors of this world and the human experience of it.[1] Essential to anthropomorphism is the appeal to (a) God in human form, as R. J. Z. Werblowsky maintains, "since otherwise one would have to deal with representations and manifestations of the divine in all possible material forms."[2] Anthropomorphism may appeal to physical or corporeal traits or may refer to what is called "mental or psychological anthropomorphism," also called anthropopathism— encompassing not human form or shape but human feelings such as love, hate, desire, anger, and the like.[3] But as Werblowsky argues, "The ultimate, residual anthropomorphism . . . is the theistic notion of God as personal, in contrast to an impersonal conception of the divine. Also, verbal imagery, no matter how metaphorical it is supposed to be, preserves this basic anthropomorphism."[4] So much for the genus.

The broad definition of the genus, anthropomorphism, leaves

---

1. Cf. R. J. Zwi Werblowsky, "Anthropomorphism," in *The Encyclopedia of Religion*, ed. Mircea Eliade (New York: Macmillan Co., 1987), 1:316–20.
2. Ibid., 317.
3. Ibid.
4. Ibid.

ample space for speciation. God may be given personal traits of definition without emerging within the representation of a human being "in our image and likeness." But that phrase does require us to speak of incarnation in particular, that is, the representation of the human being as in the image of God, hence the conception of God in incarnate form. As to the species, by incarnation I mean the representation of God in the flesh, as corporeal, consubstantial in emotion and virtue with human beings, and sharing in the modes and means of action carried out by mortals. Defined by Manabu Waida as "the act or state of assuming a physical body by a nonphysical entity such as the soul, the spirit, the self, or the divine being,"[5] incarnation here refers specifically to God. When God is represented in corporeal form, with arms, legs, cheeks, and so on, or is assigned emotions out of the repertoire of human feelings, attitudes, and virtues, or is portrayed as doing things human beings do in exactly the ways in which mortals do these deeds, such as kick, butt, laugh, clap hands, and the like, then we have a case of the incarnation of God.

The most familiar example of incarnation derives from the Christian conviction that the union of divinity and humanity took place in Jesus Christ. The incarnation of God and of other otherwise nonmaterial entities, whether in the king, emperor, imam, or other human personality, constitutes a familiar phenomenon among religious traditions, for example, in Greece, India, and Iran, as Waida shows. Critical to the differentiation of the conception of the incarnation of God from that of the mere sanctification of a human being (e.g., a holy woman or man) is the conviction that God personally takes human form, adopts a human personality. That is different from the conception of a God-like mortal or mere holy person, magician, or the like. One may readily differentiate the particularly Christian version of that conviction from the statements of the same category idiomatic to Hinduism or Buddhism.[6] But the

5. Manabu Waida, "Incarnation," in *Encyclopedia of Religion* 7:156–61. The quotation is from 156.

6. Waida refers to Geoffrey Parrinder, *Avatar and Incarnation: The Wilde Lectures in Natural and Comparative Religion in the University of Oxford* (New York: Barnes & Noble, 1970), for example. My sense is that Waida treats incarnation in a somewhat broader framework than allows for a truly precise definition of the category.

conception of God incarnate—the representation of God in the corporeal form of women or men, exhibiting human traits of heart and mind, carrying out the deeds human beings do in the way they do them—that conception constitutes on its own not only a species of the genus anthropomorphism, but also a distinct genus subject to the speciation.

The work of defining the category or genus and species now requires illustration within the context of the Judaism of the dual Torah in particular. I will give two examples of what may be classified as (merely) anthropomorphic and then a striking statement of or alluding to the incarnation of God. The concrete sources will permit a simple statement of the difference between the one and the other, within the sources subject to analysis here. In the first statement, we have a theological axiom expressed in vivid and personal language. We cannot confuse anthropomorphic rhetoric with the intent to accomplish the anthropomorphic representation of God. More than resorting to "I" and "you" is required. That is why in the following I find neither anthropomorphism in general nor incarnation in particular:

A. "The Lord, the Lord:" (Ex. 34:6):
B. [God says,] "I am he before one sins, and I am he after one sins and repents."
C. "A God merciful and gracious" (Ex. 34:6):
D. Said R. Judah, "A covenant has been made with the thirteen attributes [listed in the cited verse] that they will not be turned away empty-handed, as it says, 'Behold, I make a covenant' (Ex. 34:10)."

(b. R.H. 17b)

Imputing a statement to God is not the same as representing God in the model of a human being, for example, engaged in conversation or argument. The language of B means simply that God remains the same, despite the sin committed by a human being. The voice of B is defined at D: a theological statement given, at B, the form of a person "I." Presenting in slightly dramatic rhetoric what is a simple statement of a theological principle hardly illustrates the phenomenon of anthropomorphization, let alone incarnation. It is, at best, a kind of hypostatization.

Let us move on to a clear instance of anthropomorphism in which God is portrayed in the model or paradigm of a human being. In the following I see an explicit comparison of God's traits to those of a human being. The premise of comparison is that both exist within the same continuum of attitudes and emotions but the one is superior to the other. On that basis I invoke the conception of consubstantiality (recognizing, of course, that introducing that word will prove jarring) and allege that God and the human being are treated as emotionally comparable or, more to the point, consubstantial. God is now not wholly other but the same, if better:

A. Take note of how the trait of the Holy One, blessed be he, is different from that of mortals.

B. In the case of a mortal, when he is conquered, he is unhappy.

C. But when the Holy One, blessed be he, is conquered, he rejoices,

D. as it is said, "Therefore he said that he would destroy them, had not Moses the chosen one stood before him in the breath to turn back his wrath" (Ps. 106:23).

(b. Pes. 119a)

Here the contrast between the human and the divine trait in response to defeat treats the two as opposites but, as I said, within the same continuum. God is not wholly other—for example, without emotions or with altogether different emotions from those displayed by a human being. God and a mortal share the same emotional framework, which is why we may draw a contrast between how each one responds to the same thing. But while anthropomorphic in the strict sense, the passage may hardly be held to accomplish the incarnation of God. Whether or not God is represented as forming the corporeal image and likeness in accord with which humanity has been shaped is not a question to be settled by a passage such as the foregoing. But that passage also presents God as a person, even as a personality, with concrete traits like those of a human being, in a way in which pericope cited from b. R.H. 17b does not.

Proceeding beyond the clear limitations of the foregoing, which hardly suggests a portrayal of the incarnation of God, we now proceed to two explicit statements of how an incarnation of God reaches expression. On this basis, we may define the principal point of interest of this book. The pertinent line of the passage, deriving from Genesis Rabbah, ca. 400–450, is this:

A. Said R. Hoshaiah, "When the Holy One, blessed be he, came to create the first man, the ministering angels mistook him [for God, since man was in God's image,] and wanted to say before him, 'Holy, [holy, holy is the Lord of hosts].'" . . .

Here is a simple and straightforward statement that the angels, seeing the first man, thought that he was God. When we seek an example of representation of the incarnation of God, we can find no better statement of matters *in principle* than one which says the angels confused the first man with God. Proposing that upon seeing the first man angels perceived yet another version of God remains a rather general statement of incarnation in principle. When God and a human being—the first man—are indistinguishable, then God looks like man, walks, talks, acts, engages with others like man, and therefore, in context, is man: divinity in the form of humanity, however the relationships between the one and the other are sorted out. And that is what, in a narrowly descriptive framework, incarnation, as a species of the genus anthropomorphism, means.

But what about the concrete representation of God? The general notion of the incarnation of God reaches quite specific formulation in yet another document of the same general time, namely, the middle of the fifth century. The passage derives from a document that came to closure in the later stages of the formation of the canon of the Judaism of the dual Torah, ca. 450–500:

6.A.   Because the Holy One, blessed be he, had appeared to them at the sea like a heroic soldier, doing battle, appeared to them at Sinai like a teacher, teaching the repetition [of traditions], appeared to them in the time of Daniel like a sage, teaching Torah, appeared to them in the time of Solomon like a lover . . .

(Pesiq. Rab Kah. XII:XXIV)

The passage opens with an allusion to the incarnate forms taken by God. True, we have no detailed account of the feelings and actions of God incarnate. Such concrete accounts of the incarnation of God, as we shall see, first make their appearance in the Bavli (Talmud of Babylonia). But for the present purpose of definition it suffices to point to the statement at hand as illustration of the precise meaning of incarnation when it comes to God: the representation of God as teacher, warrior, lover (of the congregation of Israel, it is, of course, understood).

B. [it was necessary for] the Holy One, blessed be he, to say to them, "You see me in many forms. But I am the same one who was at the sea, I am the same one who was at Sinai, *I [anokhi] am the Lord your God who brought you out of the land of Egypt* (Ex. 20:2)."

The qualification of the foregoing yields no difficulty. God appears in diverse models of incarnation. It is one and the same God.[7] We come now to a restatement of the same matter:

7.A. Said R. Hiyya the Elder, "It is because through every manner of deed and every condition he had appeared to them [that he made that statement, namely:]
B. "he had appeared to them at the sea as a heroic soldier, carrying out battles in behalf of Israel,
C. "he had appeared to them at Sinai in the form of a teacher who was teaching Torah and standing in awe,
D. "he had appeared to them in the time of Daniel as an elder, teaching Torah, for it is appropriate for Torah to go forth from the mouth of sages,
E. "he had appeared to them in the time of Solomon as a youth, in accord with the practices of that generation: *His aspect is like Lebanon, young as the cedars* (Song 5:15),
F. "so at Sinai he appeared to them as a teacher, teaching Torah: *I am the Lord your God who brought you out of the land of Egypt* (Ex. 20:2)."

(*Pesiq. Rab Kah.* XII:XXIV)

When portrayed as a warrior, teacher, sage, and lover, God is represented in incarnate form. Incarnation now is fully exposed and an explicit and intentional statement of God in human form is set before us.

Permit me now to generalize on the basis of the foregoing examples, repeating first what I stated in the preface. By the incarnation of God I mean this:

---

7. A comparison here of incarnation and of the union of humanity and divinity in Jesus Christ, as Christians read matters, would begin with a simple thesis: For Christianity incarnation is limited to a single case; the species is the genus, so to speak. In the passage before us, by contrast, no one incarnation of God completes the matter. But this is only a suggestion.

The description of God, whether in allusion or narrative, as corporeal; exhibiting traits of emotions like those of human beings; doing deeds that women and men do in the way in which they do them.

If these conditions are met, then we deal with the incarnation of God. If not, we do not. Having provided passages that illustrate the incarnation of God, I point to their limitation. In our first passage God is represented as corporeal. The same is so in the second. That is why I introduced them in this initial statement. But apart from imputing an "I"–"you" dialogue to God ("You see me in many forms. But I am . . ."), the second does not present God as exhibiting the emotions of a human being or as doing deeds people ordinarily do and doing them in the way mortals carry out their plans. The passages merely validate my inquiry, which begins with the claim that in the later stages of the formative history of Judaism God emerges incarnate. Beyond the present point, we note further issues requiring attention. Neither passage before us tells us in detail (e.g., through a narrative) precisely the consequences, in the vision of faith and the eye of the believer, of God's incarnation. Both passages constitute allusions to God's corporeality and refer to God's capacity to take on human traits of mind and soul and spirit as well as of outward form.

On the model of this sort of writing, however, we could not compose a counterpart for Judaism to the Gospels of Jesus Christ as God incarnate (whether or not the evangelists meant to compose that kind of gospel I do not claim to know). But if we ask for the meaning in a concrete transaction of the incarnation of God, we come away puzzled. What we do not know is how, within the Judaism of the dual Torah, the incarnation of God yields a specific message. When people perceive God as teacher or sage or lover, what does this mean? Let me provide snippets of stories in which God and a human being engage in sustained discourse, with God emerging as a fully equal conversation partner. On the basis of a large number of stories along these lines, we might well contemplate composing the story of God on earth—a kind of gospel of God incarnate, walking among human beings, talking with them, teaching them, acting among them, just as, for the evangelists as the church received and venerated their writings, Jesus Christ, God incarnate, walked on earth, taught, and provided the example for humanity of the union of humanity and divinity. That is hardly to suggest that the Judaism of the dual Torah and the Christianity of Jesus Christ as God incarnate are to be matched. But they assuredly sustain comparison. These snippets of stories (to be presented in chapter 8 and briefly reviewed in chapter 9) show how, in concrete terms, the incarnation of Judaism in the Bavli comes to expression:

A. Said R. Joshua b. Levi, "When Moses came up on high, he found the Holy One, blessed be he, tying crowns onto the letters of the Torah. He said to him, 'Moses, don't people say hello in your town?'

B. "He said to him, 'Does a servant greet his master [first]?'" . . .

(b. Shab. 89a)

A. Said R. Isaac, "When the temple was destroyed, the Holy One, blessed be he, found Abraham standing in the Temple. He said to him, 'What is my beloved doing in my house?'

B. "He said to him, 'I have come because of what is going on with my children.'

C. "He said to him, 'Your children sinned and have been sent into exile.'" . . .

(b. Men. 53b)

K. "He said to him, 'Lord of the universe, you have now shown me his mastery of the Torah. Now show me his reward.'

L. "He said to him, 'Turn around.'

M. "He turned around and saw people weighing out his flesh in the butcher shop.

N. "He said to him, 'Lord of the universe, such is his mastery of Torah, and such is his reward?'

O. "He said to him, 'Be silent. That is how I have decided matters.'" . . .

(b. Men. 29b)

Were we to embellish these stories and string them together, for instance telling the story of God incarnate at the time of the destruction of the first or second temple, we could develop a kind of gospel. The first of the three stories would then form the basis of how God collected the band of prophets and sages, such as Moses: one day as God was working in the shop, Moses came in but failed to say hello. The second then would place God and Abraham at the destruction and allow God to explain to Abraham both why the children of Abraham had been punished and how, in the future, they would be forgiven and saved (as the story goes on to relate). The third then distinguishes God from the sage (as we shall see at the end) and treats God as unique on the one side, and utterly in charge of all matters on the other, demanding of even the wise sage silence before the divine decree. The utter ineffability of God, the inscrutable character of God's rulings, the wisdom surpassing human understanding that marks God's mind—these theological principles emerge in the gospel of God incarnate, but the gospel stands on its own and teaches its lessons without referring, beyond itself, to theological abstractions. When God is incarnate the message is immediate.

It seems to me, therefore, that out of the materials of the final stage of the canon of the Judaism of the dual Torah, we can compose something very like a gospel of God incarnate on earth. True, that gospel will not prove as smooth in its unfolding as the Gospels of Jesus Christ, God incarnate, as the church has received and read the Gospels. We have no counterpart to a fair number of the stories of the Gospels, for example, no narrative of birth, death, or resurrection. And, for the Gospels, we have no counterpart to the stories of God as a human being ruling the world; that would come in due course. But so far as Jesus is represented as teacher and master, we can find adequate counterparts for the "Holy One, blessed be he," "Lord of the world," of the dual Torah. Comparing discrete stories to the cogent and sustained narratives of the four canonical Gospels (not to mention the noncanonical ones) is meant only to suggest an angle of analysis not yet understood in the comparative study of a Judaism and a Christianity. It places the study at hand into focus.

The full statement of the incarnation of God would respond to a variety of questions, such as those asked just now. Answers to those questions, however, would be long in coming. The reason is that through the unfolding canon of formative Judaism, the representation of God in incarnate form and with a fully displayed personality emerged only in the final document, the Bavli. God figures in the canon of the Judaism of the dual Torah as premise, presence, person, and, at the end, personality. God is represented not solely in abstract terms of attributes (e.g., merciful, loving) but in concrete terms of relationships with the world, humanity, and Israel. The theological discourse of the dual Torah may be classified in four parts: first comes discourse which presupposes God as premise; second is the recognition of God as a presence; third, God appears as a person; and fourth, God personally participates in the here and now of everyday discourse. As we shall see, God forms the premise of all discourse. The Torah as God's will and word for Israel, a full and exhaustive account of matters, permits no other conception. But that essentially theological conception, justification for the authority of the Torah as sages taught it, for example, formed no more than a premise; it played slight part in the exegesis of the Torah, in the spinning out of propositions of law and doctrine. God furthermore constitutes a presence, ubiquitous in theory, hearing prayer, inhabiting a given space. Here, too, God's presence accorded with rules that did not require ad hoc application or invention any more than the principle of God's creation of the world and giving of the Torah did. In acts of prayer and certain other circumstances, God even constituted a person, a "you" to whom people spoke—again in accord with regulations and rules.

What we do not find before the redaction of the Bavli, that is, the statement of consensus of an authorship of the sixth century, is a clear account of what I may call "the particularity of God." By that phrase I mean God as a specific personality whom one might encounter in a concrete circumstance *not* defined by universal principles—for example, abstract theological truths expressed in hypostatization—nor governed by prevailing rules. From the Mishnah until the Bavli, God is portrayed in an essentially philosophical way, as premise, presence, even person, always subject to rules and conforming to regularities. Everything therefore is susceptible to explanation, little left as mystery. And, in the nature of things, the operation of reliable rules precludes the entry of uncertainty, irregularity, or particularity into regularity. But the emblem of personality is singularity. When we wish to portray a distinct personality, we appeal to distinctive traits. In the case of the personality of God, moreover, the state of the world will require an appeal to the ineffable and ultimately unknowable. For when we propose to relate the condition of existence to the character of the rules by which creation works, in accord with which the details of revelation (the Torah) are formulated, we have to appeal to God's personality to explain the unpredictable character of the here and now—beginning with God in that here and now. Only at the end, in the Bavli, do we find that personality. And, as we shall see at the end of chapter 9, one solitary story in the entire Bavli brings to full expression the tremendum of God as personality: *Be silent, that is my decree.*

But in saying so I have moved far ahead of my story. It suffices at this stage to note that Scripture presents a rich repertoire of cases of the particularity of God, a singular and textured personality with powerful desires, hatreds, even corporeal traits similar to those of humanity, distinctive attitudes like those one might find in a human being. Before the remarkable statement of the Bavli, God as a personality—whether or not incarnate in the ways in which I have suggested—never emerges in the portrayals of and references to God in the documents we shall survey. Quite to the contrary, God in rich particularity, God appearing in a distinctive way in a particular circumstance, God not as mode of alluding to principles of divine governance of the world but a personality exhibiting very distinctive traits, proves difficult to locate. In the Bavli, by contrast, we find extensive allusions to God in incarnate form on the one side, and even stories people told about things God did and said in concrete circumstances on the other. Out of the numerous and important discussions about God and references to God in the Mishnah and its successor writings through the Yerushalmi, the Talmud of the Land of Israel, in ca. A.D. 400, and even out of most of the exegetical compilations serving Scripture produced down to that same time, we cannot compose a "gospel" of God on earth. Out of the Bavli, we can begin to do just that.

To conclude, when we speak of the incarnation of God, therefore, we are talking about a very specific thing. It is the representation of God as a human being who walks and talks, cares and acts, a God who not only makes general rules but also by personal choice transcends them and who therefore exhibits a particular personality. True, that way of framing the direct encounter with the living God found its canonical place and hearing only at the end of the history of the formative stage of the Judaism of the dual Torah. But from then to the present, God as personality—not merely abstract premise, theoretical presence, even liturgical person, but as the engaged, compassionate personality and counterpart to Israel, also viewed as person and personality—endured. From then to now that God incarnate with divine love sustained passionate, God-loving Israel, the Jewish people. And that God, in whose image we all are, with love sustains us still.

2

The Character of Divinity, the Classification of Evidence

IMAGINING DIVINITY

In this book we deal with the world view of a particular Judaism, as that world view came to expression in statements about God as premise of all being, presence in the world, person who receives prayer, and personality subject to important biographical stories: one who cares and loves and feels and acts, much as human beings do. The world view subject to description here derives from the canon and expresses the ethos of a particular Judaism at its formative period, the Judaism of the dual Torah, written and oral, in late antiquity, meaning the first six centuries of the Common Era (= A.D.). A definitive statement of the proposition that God appears to humanity in diverse forms sets the stage for our inquiry:

1.A. Another interpretation of *I am the Lord your God [who brought you out of the land of Egypt]* (Ex. 20:2):

B. Said R. Hinena bar Papa, "The Holy One, blessed be he, had made his appearance to them with a stern face, with a neutral face, with a friendly face, with a happy face.

C. "with a stern face: in Scripture. When a man teaches his son Torah, he has to teach him in a spirit of awe.

D. "with a neutral face: in Mishnah.

E. "with a friendly face: in Talmud.

F. "with a happy face: in lore.

G. "Said to them the Holy One, blessed be he, 'Even though you may see all of these diverse faces of mine, nonetheless: *I am the Lord your God who brought you out of the land of Egypt'* (Ex. 20:2)."

(*Pesiq. Rab Kah.* XII:XXV)

So far we deal with attitudes. As to the iconic representation of God, the following is explicit:

2.A.   Said R. Levi, "The Holy One, blessed be he, had appeared to them like an icon that has faces in all directions, so that if a thousand people look at it, it appears to look at them as well.

B.   "So too when the Holy One, blessed be he, when he was speaking, each and every Israelite would say, 'With me in particular the Word speaks.'

C.   "What is written here is not, I am the Lord, your [plural] God, but rather, *I am the Lord your [singular] God who brought you out of the land of Egypt* (Ex. 20:2)."

That God may show diverse faces to various people is now established. The reason for God's variety is made explicit. People differ and God, in the image of whom all mortals are made, must therefore sustain diverse images—all of them formed in the model of human beings:

3.A.   Said R. Yose bar Haninah, "And it was in accord with the capacity of each one of them to listen and understand what the Word spoke with him.

B.   "And do not be surprised at this matter, for when the manna came down to Israel, each and every one would find its taste appropriate to his capacity, infants in accord with their capacity, young people in accord with their capacity, old people in accord with their capacity.

C.   "Infants in accord with their capacity: just as an infant sucks from the tit of his mother, so was its flavor, as it is said, *Its taste was like the taste of rich cream* (Num. 11:8).

D.   "Young people in accord with their capacity: as it is said, *My bread also which I gave you, bread and oil and honey* (Ez. 16:19).

E.   "Old people in accord with their capacity: as it is said, *The taste of it was like wafers made with honey* (Ex. 16:31).

F.   "Now if in the case of manna, each and every one would find its taste appropriate to his capacity, so in the matter of the Word, each and every one understood in accord with capacity.

G.   "Said David, *The voice of the Lord is [in accord with one's] in strength* (Ps. 29:4).

H.   "What is written is not, *in accord with his strength in particular,* but rather, *in accord with one's strength,* meaning, in accord with the capacity of each and every one.

I. "Said to them the Holy One, blessed be he, 'It is not in accord with the fact that you hear a great many voices, but you should know that it is I who [speaks to all of you individually]: *I am the Lord your God who brought you out of the land of Egypt'* (Ex. 20:2)."

(Pesiq. Rab Kah. XII:XXV)

The individuality and particularity of God rest upon the diversity of humanity. But it follows that the model of humanity—"in our image"—dictates how we are to envisage the face of God. And that is the starting point of our inquiry.

THE PERSONALITY OF GOD AND THE WORLD VIEW OF THE JUDAISM OF THE DUAL TORAH

When we seek through words to etch the face of God, seeking language we can grasp for what ultimately cannot be portrayed at all, we propose to represent the personality, the individuality, of God. What does God look like? How does God feel? What sort of deeds such as the ones that we mortals carry out does God do, and how does God do them? In secular language, by imagining such a portrait of corporeal and emotional traits of mind, spirit, and deed, we describe in particular terms the view of the world of a group of people. For any Judaism, the reason derives from Scripture. In speaking of God, a group appealing to Scripture with its explicit statement that humanity is "in our image and likeness" expresses its deepest perceptions of its understanding of the makeup of the world.

Here, therefore, we follow the lines of the world view of a social group of ancient Jews, one that produced and revered particular holy books and called them the one whole Torah of Moses, our rabbi. Between the first and the seventh centuries, the group, called sages and bearing the title of honor "rabbi," formed the Judaism known as the Judaism of the dual Torah, meaning both written (equivalent to what Christians know as the Old Testament) and oral (a term defined presently). Because I want to describe, analyze, and interpret the world view of that Judaism, I raise my sights upward toward God in heaven as that Judaism envisaged matters on high. For while we naturally see "world view" from the perspective set down here, from the viewpoint of this Judaism there is another view of the world, and it is God's.

Sages in their depiction of the world of creation and humanity proposed to view the world from heaven's perspective as that is set forth in the Torah of Sinai. They read the Torah as God's account, set forth from there to here, of creation and, especially, of humanity and of Israel within humanity. In their view the Torah portrayed heaven's picture of earth and of us. For our part, since we wish to describe the world view of the Judaism of the dual Torah, therefore, we have to read the sages' statements about God in accord within the same syntactic rules—only upside down, that is, in the reverse of sages' conceptions of what they said in making those statements. Speaking about the world, in sages' view, the oral Torah gave God's perspective. Speaking about God, from our secular view, sages portrayed the world as they saw it—and that at its fundamental and irreducible reality.

I ask in particular about God's personality as sages knew God. My question finds its answers in the ways by which God was portrayed, that is to say, what we may identify as the metaphors selected when sages wished to express their relationship with and view of God. For when the authorships of the canonical documents of the Judaism of the dual Torah—the written one we know as the Hebrew Scriptures, the oral one now written down in the diverse compositions of the ancient sages—spoke of God in heaven, they also set forth their viewpoint and perspective on humanity here on earth. These they took to be God's as set forth in the Torah. In explicit discourse on the personality of God and on the relationship between God and Israel, therefore, sages implicitly explained the world as they saw it. When we describe the portraits of God as person on the one side, and the reliable rules of relationship between God and humanity in general and Israel in particular on the other, we grasp the view of the world that sages' Judaic system set forth overall. That issue defines our inquiry: God as (1) premise, (2) presence, (3) person, and (4) personality in the principal writings of the Judaism of the dual Torah, read in sequence, one by one. Let us consider these four dimensions of God, the measures by which we grasp the character of divinity in the Judaism under study. These dimensions are concrete and specific; we can readily determine where and when and how we may take the measure dictated by each of them.

1. By God as premise, I refer to passages in which an authorship reaches a particular decision because that authorship believes God created the world and has revealed the Torah to Israel. We therefore know that God forms the premise of a passage because the particular proposition of that passage appeals to God as premise of all being, for example, author and authority of the Torah. Things are decided one way rather than some other on that basis. That conviction of the givenness of God who created the world and self-evidently gave the Torah defines the premise of all Judaisms before our own times. There is nothing surprising in it. But a particular indicator in so general a fact derives from the cases in which, for concrete and specific reasons in quite particular cases, sages invoke God as foundation and premise of the world. When do they decide a case or reach a decision because they appeal to God as premise, and when do they not do so?

2. God as presence stands for yet another consideration. It involves an authorship's referring to God as part of a situation in the here and now. When an authorship—for example, of the Mishnah—speaks of an ox goring another ox, it does not appeal to God to reach a decision for them and does not suggest that God in particular has witnessed the event and plans to intervene. But when an authorship—also in the Mishnah—speaks of a wife's being accused of unfaithfulness to her husband, by contrast, that authorship expects that God will intervene in a particular case, in the required ordeal, and so declare the decision for the case at hand. In the former instance, God is assuredly a premise of discourse, having revealed in the Torah the rule governing a goring ox. In the latter, God is not only premise but very present in discourse and in making a decision. God furthermore constitutes a person in certain settings, not in others.

3. One may readily envisage God as premise without invoking a notion of the particular traits or personality of God. So, too, in the case of God as presence, no aspect of the case at hand demands

that we specify particular attitudes or traits of character to be imputed to God. But there is a setting in which God is held always to know and pay attention to specific cases, and that involves God as a "you," that is, as a presence. For example, in the Mishnah (obviously not alone in that document) all discourse concerning liturgy understands that God also hears prayer, hence is not only a presence but a person, a "you," responding to what is said, requiring certain attitudes and rejecting others. In a later document, by contrast, God is not only present but a participant, if only implicitly, when the Torah is studied among disciples of sages. Here, too, we find an interesting indicator of how God is portrayed in one situation as a premise, in a second as a presence, and in a third as a person. In cases in which God is portrayed as a person, however, there are rules and regulations to which God adheres. These permit us to imagine that God is present without wondering what particular response God may make to a quite specific situation, for example, within the liturgy. We do not have to wonder because the rules tell us. Accordingly, while God is a liturgical "you," God as person still is not represented in full particularity, reaching a decision on a specific case in accord with traits of mind or heart or soul that yield out of a unique personality—different (by nature) from all other personalities—a concrete decision or feeling or action. God as person but not as personality remains within the framework established at the outset when we considered the matters of God as premise and as presence.

4. There is a final way in which God plays a part in the discourse of authorships of documents of the Judaism of the dual Torah. God emerges as a vivid and highly distinctive personality, actor, conversation partner, hero. In references to God as a personality, God is given corporeal traits. God looks like God in particular, just as each person exhibits distinctive physical traits. Not only so, but in matters of heart and mind and spirit, well-limned individual traits of personality and action alike endow God with that particularity that identifies every individual human being. When God is given attitudes but no active role in discourse, referred to but not invoked as part of a statement, God serves as person. When God participates as a hero and protagonist in a

narrative, God gains traits of personality and emerges as God like humanity: God incarnate.[1]

The authorships of the Hebrew Scriptures would not have been surprised that in the unfolding of the canonical writings of the Judaism of the dual Torah God gained corporeality and personality and so became incarnate. They had long ago portrayed God in richly personal terms: God wants, cares, demands, regrets, says, and does—just like human beings. God is not merely a collection of abstract theological attributes and thus rules for governance of reality, nor a mere person to be revered and feared. God is not a mere composite of regularities, but a very specific, highly particular personality, whom people can know, envision, engage, persuade, impress. Sages painted this portrait of a personality through narratives—stories in which God figures like other (incarnate) heroes. When, therefore, the authorships of documents of the canon of the Judaism of the dual Torah began to represent God as personality, not merely premise, presence, or person, they reentered that realm of discourse about God that Scripture had originally laid out. It was not inevitable that some sages, represented by the authorship of the Bavli, should have done so. True, for the sages (who in the first six centuries A.D. created the Judaism of the dual Torah) that legacy of Scripture's God as actor and personality constituted an available treasury of established facts about God—hence, God incarnate. But within the books and verses of Scripture sages picked and chose, and they did so with regard to God as well. At some points in the unfolding corpus, without regard to the entire range of available facts of Scripture, God was represented only as implicit premise; in others, as presence and source of action; in still others, as person. So the repertoire of Scripture tells us solely what might have been. It was only at the end, in the Bavli, that we reach what did come about: the portrayal (much as in Scripture and on the strength of Scripture's facts) of God as personality, with that same passionate love

---

1. I should claim that these categories serve to make possible the comparison of how a number of Judaisms accomplish the incarnation of God and otherwise portray God, and also the systematic comparison of some Judaisms and some Christianities. But in the present study, I mean only to set forth the four-part classification system and show how it works.

for Israel that, as Scripture's authorships had portrayed matters, had defined God in the received, written Torah.

Accordingly, in our survey of the unfolding canon, we follow the path that leads at the end to what we may call "the rebiblicization" of the portrayal of God. The point of this study, however, is not merely to observe the renewal of ancient Israel's Scripture's picture of God as incarnate, that personality who said to make us "in our image, after our likeness." Following the path to Scripture's account on its own leads us to merely formal conclusions: now they did not quote, then they did quote facts of Scripture's account of God. The fact that at a late stage in the unfolding of the Judaism of the dual Torah an authorship reverted to Scripture for its redactional structure as much as for its facts about God seems to me to require no explanation on its own and to explain nothing beyond itself.[2] Let me rather specify what for me is at stake. The fundamental mode of thought, the basic view of the world of the Judaism of the dual Torah is typified in sages' modes of thought about and portrayal of God. That is why, when we grasp how the authorships of diverse books of the canon of the Judaism of the dual Torah spelled out the character of divinity as they conceived it, we find our way deep into the inner structure of those authorships' views of the world at large. And, in time to come, we may seek to correlate their portrait of God with other important and formative components of their larger system, their Judaism.

The reason for our turning to heaven, to the character of divinity, in quest of their vision of their social world is simple. The world made by God, the dimensions of humanity in the image of God, the model for the person of virtue, the requirements of holiness at home and in society—these fundamental issues that comprise the system's world view all in the end found their generative point of definition in a single consideration. It was the will, character, personality of God in whose image the human being was

---

2. In my *Judaism. The Classic Statement. The Evidence of the Bavli* (Chicago: University of Chicago Press, 1986) I show that the authorship of the Bavli appealed to both the Mishnah (oral Torah) and Scripture (written Torah) in the formation of large-scale pericopes. Hence both components of the Torah defined sizable redactional units. That is not commonly the case with the prior Talmud, the Yerushalmi, and it is not at all the case in any earlier component of the canon of the dual Torah.

made. From God all things came, to God all things referred. No wonder, then, that if we hope to sort out the diverse components which, all together, comprised the world view of the Judaism of the dual Torah, we begin with the issue of God, specifically, God as person: God incarnate in the virtues and traits and—above all—relationships that humanity could grasp and should imitate.

Before moving onward, let me place into the correct context of systemic analysis the matter of world view in general, character of divinity in particular. The world view comprised one component of the three that, all together, made up the religious system of the Judaism of the dual Torah. That system, like any other, was made up of three parts to form one cogent statement:

1. world view, beginning with an account of God in relationship to the world, which by reference to the intersection of the super- natural and the natural worlds accounts for how things are and puts them together into a cogent and harmonious picture;
2. way of life, which expresses in concrete actions the world view and which is explained by that world view;
3. a social entity (e.g., a group with determinate traits of defini- tion) for which the world view accounts, a social entity defined in concrete terms by the way of life, and therefore which gives expression in the everyday world to the world view and is de- fined as an entity by that way of life.

A religious system, in our case, a Judaism, therefore is com- posed of three necessary components: an account of a world view, a prescription of a corresponding way of life, and a definition of the social entity that finds definition in the one and description in the other. When those three fundamental components fit to- gether as they do in diverse Judaic systems,[3] they sustain one another in explaining the whole of a social order, hence constitut- ing the theoretical statement and account provided by a system. When we describe a religious system we investigate how, in the context of their picture of the world and their life, people explain to themselves the character and calling of the social entity that

---

3. That is the argument of my *"Israel": Judaism and Its Social Metaphors* (New York and Cambridge: Cambridge University Press, 1988), chap. 11.

they comprise. This they do by appeal to metaphors for their social entity or group, world view, and way of life, and all form a cogent symbolic statement, a "system." When, as is common, people invoke God as the foundation for their world view—maintaining that their way of life corresponds to what God wants of them, projecting their social entity in a particular relationship to God—then we have a religious system. And when, finally, a religious system appeals as an important part of its authoritative literature or canon to the Hebrew Scriptures of ancient Israel or Old Testament, we have a Judaism.

In the setting of a religious system, how important a place is accorded to the character of divinity? The theological component of a religious system forms the heart of the matter. For a religious system is one that appeals to God as the principal power and as the encompassing explanation for and source of the life of the group (an "Israel"). Such a systematic explanation within the system appeals to God's plan for the world and the group within the world, accounts for the social form of the system, and spells out how the distinctive way of life of that group transforms the participants into God's people, severally and jointly. A theology of a Judaic system speaks to the very heart of the matter, explaining the origin and destiny of the "Israel" comprising the system. And the system before us, the Judaism of the dual Torah, speaks of God not in abstraction but in very concrete terms. When we grasp those terms, we understand the system's theology. As we shall see in the Judaism before us, we shall describe God as, successively, systemic premise, presence, person, and animating personality. This brief outline of the issues of theological description of systems suffices to explain the centrality of theology in systemic description. It is theology that serves as the bond for the rest. Thought about God and metaphors for God (and when it comes to God, all speech frames a metaphorical statement) form the centerpiece and shape the paradigm of religious expression in system-formation. Therefore, if we wish to find out how the system as a whole holds together, we discover in the theological component of the system that center of gravity that holds together also the matters of social entity and way of life. I see the social entity as a statement of theology expressed in the terms of sociology, and I discern the representation of the way of life as a statement, within anthropology, of theology as well. How people understood, lived with, and served God formed the definitive component of their system.

Now how, in the study and description of the theology of Judaism, are we to investigate matters? The answer to that question defines a paradigm for theological description. For reasons I shall set forth presently,[4] we have to read the documents one by one and in their affines. That allows us to see how matters look in specific documentary settings. What questions do we bring to each document? When sages speak about God, God's character, personality, presence, power, and earthly program, they answer that question. That means that a given document within the writings of the Judaism of the dual Torah must be asked to make its statement, whole and complete, of this component of its system among the three systemic elements, that is, world view, way of life, and particular address, its own "Israel." In that systemic context we also read the account of God and ask ourselves how God plays a principal part in the composition of the system as a whole.[5]

---

4. See pp. 37–44 below.

5. That work of description complete, we may move onward to the analytical inquiry. In systemic analysis, we wish to compare and contrast one documentary component and its system to the next within its canon. In the work of interpretation, we ultimately contrast and compare one Judaic system to the next. These second and third stages in the work allow us to see in context—therefore under the aspect of comparison and contrast—how a given system addresses its circumstance. We seek to know how, in response to the critical concerns of the moment, those framers compose a cogent and compelling statement. All of these questions serve equally to lead us into the system's world view, way of life, and "Israel." I do not undertake this stage of the work in the present book. It can come later on.

In my *"Israel": Judaism and Its Social Metaphors* I analyzed the social metaphors important to the Judaism of the dual Torah. In investigating the theories of Israel presented by the documentary evidence of that Judaism, I outlined the rules that govern thinking about the social entity (or social thought) of an important religious formation. What I really want to know is where, when, and why a given systemic statement will invoke one metaphor, and the conditions in which a different metaphor proves compelling. Furthermore, I pointed to the images, issues, points of self-evidence that followed in the retinue of a regnant metaphor. In asking, for the social thought of Judaic systems, why this and not that I therefore entered into processes of thought concerning the social consciousness of a given group as important statements of that consciousness come before us. Rules of this kind are proposed at the end of that book, and they generate their own hypothesis. Here we move on to the theological metaphors and the processes of thought that generated them and that they then dictated. Here the source of facts is two: Scripture on the one side; individual perception and experience, sorted out in the consensus of the social group of sages, on the other.

METAPHOR AND SYSTEMIC MEANING

In all three matters—way of life, world view, theory of a systemic social entity—the framers of a system pursue a course of thought that leads them from the known to the unknown. They follow the lead of a curiosity that draws them onward to try to explain, in terms of the familiar, an unfamiliar condition or circumstance or entity—to answer an unprecedented and urgent question. What precipitates curiosity is why are things one way rather than some other, why has this happened and not that. But system makers or framers see things fresh.[6] That, by definition, is why they frame a system of their own, presenting a canon without a past or parallel, rather than merely rehearsing one. It is the reason that religion has history, not merely structure, yielding change and development, not merely restatement. And when those framers go beyond the received, they follow paths beyond the limits of their charts. How to proceed? It is by moving forward while looking backward, which is to say, by appealing to the known in the explanation of the unknown. Searching in received models and modes of thought for what is relevant, comparing and contrasting to the known the unfamiliar and urgently at hand, the system builders engage in a thoroughly commonplace enterprise of explanation. It is one that we may call in the most general terms appeal to explanation through metaphor.[7] Comparing the unknown to the known, the framers invoke as explanation for the unfamiliar the model of what is already understood—yet (necessarily) preserving the unfamiliarity of the thing explained: *this is not exactly that, but it is sufficiently like that so that I can understand this by finding out how it is like, and unlike, that.* So far as this is like that, it follows the rules of that; so far as this is not like that, it follows the opposite of the rules of that. Such a mode of reasoning forms the substance of metaphorical thinking in religion. In the case of thought about God, the metaphors of course will derive from humanity—the "image" and the "likeness" projected not only from heaven to earth but also from earth to heaven. The

---

6. Later on (much later on) their consensus reaches form in documents that express the system as a whole.
7. I use the word "metaphor" in only a very general sense, not intending to violate the rules of literary criticism which impart to the word a variety of very specific meanings.

personality of God will then encompass metaphors for God and express thought about God, relationship to God, the systemic place and meaning of God, that, all together, comprise the system's world view.

One disaster is like some other—or not like it; one classification of person, hitherto not recorded, like some other—or unlike; and so forth. Thus, through processes of metaphor a system accommodates the challenge of the unknown—and demonstrates its formidable power to cope and overcome. Metaphors work in two stages. First, applied to an object, a circumstance, an unfamiliar kind of fish, or an unprecedented disaster, that mode of thought requires the metaphorization of the unfamiliar—but also, therefore, of what is already known. One thing stands for another, whether the known or the unknown. We confront the unknown by a search for an appropriate comparison which takes the form of metaphor: it is like this, then this guides us in understanding that. In the process of comparison and contrast made possible by the metaphor that links one thing to something else, we can make sense of the unknown. If the unknown is like the known, then it follows the rule governing the known; it may be explained in the way in which the known is understood. If the unknown is the opposite of the known, then it follows the inverse of the rule governing the known and may be explained as standing in antonymic relationship. Then all things may retain their place in a cogent whole and nothing will be allowed to form an anomaly.

Second, a metaphor serves as a model for shaping the unknown. The metaphor, whether drawn from social givens or theological knowns, whether concerning society or God, once invoked takes on its own formative and definitive power. The process of metaphorical thinking extends, moreover, to a second, equally urgent inquiry besides the one into the utterly unknown. It is to what is unknown in a different sense, namely, to the results of processes of thought that lead from the familiar to the abstract. That inquiry requires us to think not about the here and now that we can feel and touch, but about more general and abstract matters, processes, or generalizations. When we name and treat as real and concrete what are in fact abstractions and intangible processes, we impose upon ourselves the need to compare the abstract to the concrete. We once again think in a process of analogy, contrast, comparison, and (in the loose sense used here) metaphor about that thing which, to begin with, we ourselves have identified and so made up in our minds. For whatever lies beyond our immediate experience, encompassing all abstraction and process, demands to be set into relationship with what we already know. Connections that we make, abstractions that we perceive only in their concrete manifestations, processes that we can imagine but not identify in the here and now (not the blow but power, not the caress but love) form the raw material of mind.

To take the example of a group to which the social entity of a system may refer: when two or more persons perceive themselves to bear traits in common and to constitute, on account of those traits, a group, they face a range of choices in thinking about the classification and character of that social entity that they imagine they comprise. A family, a village, a neighborhood, a town—these form part of felt experience; we can walk in the streets, recognize relationship with persons we know and our relationship to whom we can name, and we can trace the outer limits of the settled area. But when people identify with others they have not met and may never meet, the process of the search for appropriate metaphors to take the place of absent experience in the everyday world begins. Then metaphors for the social group present themselves.[8] In seeing matters in this way, I am guided by the statement of Ernst Cassirer, cited by Sheldon Sacks:

If metaphor . . . is not just a certain development of speech, but must be regarded as one of its essential conditions, then any effort to understand its function leads us back . . . to the fundamental form of verbal conceiving.[9]

That brings us directly to the issue of expressing a world view by speaking about God. For reasons I have already set forth, I see in portraits of God the epitome of the world view of a system. Thought about God—by definition—moreover appeals

---

8. See Sheldon Sacks, ed., *On Metaphor* (Chicago: University of Chicago Press, 1978).
9. Ibid., v.

to metaphor. There is no language referring to God that is other than metaphoric, so far as I know, since given the nature of that being to whom we refer—defined as the Creator of the entire universe, for example—we can at best appeal to things in this world that we think stand for that being, that God beyond all this-worldly comparison or characterization. I surely break no new ground in simply treating as axiom the fact that when sages speak of God, the very definition of their speech begins with metaphor. But what sort of metaphor? That is the issue at hand: the knowledge expressed in, and transformed by, theological metaphors expressed in the canonical writings of the Judaism of the dual Torah.

METAPHORS AND THE CHARACTER OF DIVINITY: GOD THE PREMISE, PRESENCE, PERSON, AND PERSONALITY

To join the matter of metaphor with the classification scheme at hand, we turn to the sources of knowledge of God available to the sages of the Judaism of the dual Torah. Sages knew God in two ways: first, from the written Torah; second, from their own encounter with God in everyday life and in Israel's history. How they translated that knowledge into language appropriate to their larger system forms the subject of this study. As I have already explained, the metaphors they invoke fall into four classifications. First, God may form the premise of a system, to which all things refer. Second, God may constitute a presence, within a system, with which all things relate. Third, God may act as a person with whom all other persons relate, for example, to whom they speak, before whom they stand, by whom their deeds are recorded. In this sense God realizes and embodies the system in such a way that human beings may identify themselves and their traits with those required in the system. Fourth, God may take an active role in discourse, being represented in conversation and dialogue with humanity, arguing and debating, loving and rejecting, above all, caring: a personality with wants and needs. When God is represented in such a way, we of course regain access to the God of the written Torah. It is specifically in the final and classic statement of the Judaism of the dual Torah, the Bavli or Babylonian Talmud, that that reunion of Torahs, written and oral, takes place, here as in other aspects of the formative age.

All four—premise, presence, person, and personality—require modes of reflection and expression: What do we mean? Of what, and of whom, do we speak? These carry us (by definition) from the known to the unknown, hence into metaphor. All four classifications that guide this project constitute, on their own, metaphorizations of experience, whether direct or preserved in (canonical) records of prior encounters with God. In the case of (a) Judaism, the known derives from revelation, the Torah; the unknown, from the reality of the here and now. Speaking of God in a systematic way within a system, that is to say, forming and framing a theology, then moves the system builders to appeal to the known in quest for understanding of and language for the unknown, to the then in search for meaning in the now. Theology—especially in an idiom alien to the abstract mode of the theology of the philosophers—therefore presents occasions for metaphor.

THEOLOGICAL METAPHORS AND THE DESCRIPTION OF A SYSTEM'S WORLD VIEW: THE PRIORITY—AND INSUFFICIENCY—OF DOCUMENTARY DISCOURSE

Having explained the principle of category-formation that guides my inquiry and set my categories into their larger context, let me proceed to the evidence, what is at stake in my reading of it, and how I have chosen to classify it in the way that I have. The documentary components of the dual Torah require differentiation as to time, place, and circumstance of composition, and each document has, to begin with, to be read as a statement on its own and of its own system.[10] Before setting forth the principal stages in

---

10. That is not to suggest every document forms a system; it is only to ask whether a given document may be read on its own terms and in its own context. The more difficult problem concerns the unstated premises and presuppositions that diverse documents take for granted, that is, the system beyond a given document and, indeed, beyond all documents. I found that the Yerushalmi, for one

the documentary unfolding of the Judaism of the dual Torah, let me briefly explain why I follow the procedure that I do.

I conceive the correct route to systemic description of God to guide us through the documents, read one by one but in groups that share the same taxonomic traits, and finally, all together and all at once. I want to know how God functions, that is, as an active participant in discourse. Then, again, where and when does God form the premise of discourse, for example, as the (remote) authority behind the laws of the Torah? Further, under what conditions do authorships invoke God as a powerful presence in the immediacy of the here and now; as an inchoate being or as a personality, with whom concrete discourse is possible beyond all rules and incantations and liturgical formulas? These categories, of course, emerge from beyond the documents of the canon. The canon in the end must dictate its own categories within its larger imperatives, singly and all at once. This stress on the movement from documents to a larger system, implicit in all I have said, now requires clarification. For that purpose we have to go back to the beginning of matters, the established mode of describing the historical theology of (the) Judaism (of the dual Torah).

But the analysis of matters document by document does not end the work; it only defines its initial stages. We have then to move on and ask ourselves what links document to document and, of greater importance still, what premises undergird groups of documents and even the entire canon, whole and complete. Many claim—and with good theological reason—that there is a Judaism that transcends all particular authorships and circulates beyond any one document, to which in some way or other all documents in various ways and proportions are supposed to attest. And—in the view of theologians—that Judaism prior to, and encompassing all documents, each with its Judaism stated as a singular system,

---

striking instance, presupposed a world of values, indeed a realm of facts, in no place laid forth and explicitly argued yet everywhere taken for granted. While the Mishnah presents us with a closed system, a statement pretty much complete in its own terms and program, the Yerushalmi is just the opposite. When I pointed to this problem in my *Talmud of the Land of Israel.* XXXV. *Introduction. Taxonomy* (Chicago: University of Chicago Press, 1985), I could not solve the problem. I have since made very good progress toward a solution. The next chapter in this book spells out this problem, and the outlines of my solution, in some detail.

imposes its judgment upon our reading of every sentence, every paragraph, every book. But the question requires attention not only for theological reasons. Entirely objective and valid descriptive purposes, such as motivate my work, require us to pursue the same issue. Specifically, I wonder whether and how we may describe, beyond the evidence of what an authorship has given us in its *particular* piece of writing, what that authorship knew, had in mind, *in general* took for granted, and otherwise affirmed as its larger "Judaism." That each authorship took as premises positions shared with other authorships needs hardly be doubted since, we recognize, all authorships appealed to Scripture for one thing, and to the absolute givens of God's rule of the world and sanctification of Israel for another—and these are only some of the premises of all discourse. But what are the other premises, specific to any document and its authorship, shared among a variety of documents and their authorities?

The deeper agenda of this project—one that emerges within my larger program of the description, analysis, and interpretation of the formation of the Judaism of the dual Torah—now requires exposure. Let me explain in concrete, literary terms what is at stake here, that is, the matter of seeing things whole. Until now, as I have explained, I have worked on describing the principal documents of the Judaism of the dual Torah each in its own terms and context. I have further undertaken a set of comparative studies of two or more documents showing the points in common as well as the contrasts between and among them. This protracted work is represented by systematic accounts of the Mishnah, tractate *Avot*, the Tosefta, *Sifra, Sifré to Numbers*, the Yerushalmi, *Genesis Rabbah, Leviticus Rabbah, Pesiqta deRab Kahana, The Fathers According to Rabbi Nathan*, the Bavli, *Pesiqta Rabbati*, and various other writings. In all of this work I have proposed to examine one by one and then in groups of affines the main components of the dual Torah. I wished to place each into its own setting and so attempt to trace the unfolding of the dual Torah in its historical manifestation. In the later stages of the work, I attempted to address the question of how some, or even all, of the particular documents formed a general statement. I wanted to know where and how documents combined to constitute one Torah of the dual Torah of Sinai.

Time and again I have concluded that while two or more documents did intersect, the literature as a whole is made up of distinct sets of documents, and these sets over the bulk of their surfaces do not as a matter of fact intersect at all.[11] The upshot was that while I could show interrelationships among, for example, *Genesis Rabbah, Leviticus Rabbah, Pesiqta deRab Kahana,* and *Pesiqta Rabbati,* or among *Sifra* and the two *Sifrés,* I could not demonstrate that all of these writings pursued in common one plan defining literary, redactional, and logical traits of cogent discourse, or even one program comprising a single theological or legal inquiry. Quite to the contrary, each set of writings demonstrably limits itself to its distinctive plan and program and scarcely coheres with any other set. And the entirety of the literature most certainly cannot be demonstrated to form that one whole Torah, part of the still larger Torah of Sinai, that constitutes the Judaism of the dual Torah.[12]

Having begun with the smallest whole units of the oral Torah, the received documents, and then moved onward to the recognition of the somewhat larger groups comprised by those documents, I had reached an impasse. On the basis of literary evidence— shared units of discourse, shared rhetorical and logical modes of cogent statement, for example—I came to the conclusion that a different approach to the definition of the whole, viewed all together and all at once, was now required. Seeing the whole all together and all at once demanded a different approach. But *it has to be one that takes full account of the processes of formation and grants full recognition to issues of circumstance and context, the layers and levels of completed statements.*

Essentially, my problem was that I had reached the question of that religion "out there," that Judaism beyond all the texts of the dual Torah that reaches concrete expression in the bits and pieces of the documents "in here." At issue is the claim that there is a

---

11. This is the argument of my *Canon and Connection: Intertextuality in Judaism,* Studies in Judaism (Lanham, Md.: University Press of America, 1986).

12. The Orthodox Judaic hermeneutics that reads each bit and piece of rabbinic writing as interchangeable with all others and so treats as null the documents as distinct compositions has made its way into literary criticism. My treatment of that position is in my *Literature and Midrash: The Primacy of Documentary Discourse* (Lanham, Md.: University Press of America, 1987).

"Judaism out there," beyond any one document, to which in some way or other all documents in various ways and proportions are supposed to attest. And that Judaism "out there," prior to, encompassing all documents, each with its "Judaism in here," imposes its judgment upon our reading of every sentence, every paragraph, every book. People wonder whether and how we may describe, beyond the evidence of what an authorship has given us in its particular piece of writing, what that authorship knew, had in mind, took for granted, and otherwise affirmed as its larger "Judaism." If one starts with the question, "What does the authorship of this book mean to say, when read by itself and not in light of other, *later* writings?" then it would be improper to import into the description of the system of the Mishnah in particular (its "Judaism"—hence Judaism: the evidence of the Mishnah in particular) conceptions not contained within its pages.[13] Tractate *Avot*, for one instance, cites a range of authorities who lived a generation beyond the closure of the (rest of the) Mishnah and so is ordinarily dated to about A.D. 250, with the Mishnah dated to about 200. On that basis I do not know how one can impute to the Mishnah's system conceptions first attaining closure half a century later.

To describe the Mishnah, for example, as a part of "rabbinic Judaism" is to invoke the premise that we know, more or less on its own, just what this "rabbinic Judaism" is and says. It is one thing to confess that what we cannot show we do not know. And, as a matter of established fact, many conceptions dominant in the final statements of rabbinic Judaism to emerge from late antiquity play no material role whatsoever in the system of the Mishnah, or, for that matter, of Tosefta and *Avot*. It is quite another thing not to attempt to find out. And it is through the theological metaphors first, the sociological and anthropological ones later on, that I propose to

---

13. I stated explicitly at no fewer than six points in *Judaism: The Evidence of the Mishnah* (Chicago: University of Chicago Press, 1981) my recognition that diverse ideas floated about, and insisted that the authorship of the Mishnah can have entertained such ideas. But the statement that they made in the Mishnah did not contain them, and therefore was to be read without them. Alas, the few reviews that the book did receive contained no evidence that the reviewers understood that simple and repeated caveat. Jakob J. Petuchowski, in *Religious Studies Review* for July 1983, subjected the book to a savage attack of trivializing and with vast condescension imputed to the book precisely the opposite of its message.

outline what I conceive to be the main lines of that "Judaism out there" that comes to concrete expression, in various forms and circumstances, within the "Judaism in here" of particular documents. But how do we know what we wish to find out? And if the categories of theologians seem to me asymmetrical to the interests of our documents, what are the categories that should guide our inquiry by telling us what we wish to know? The claim that there is a "Judaism out there," beyond any one document, to which in some way or other all documents in various ways and proportions are supposed to attest presents the next stage in the research program facing me. I take the claim seriously. That Judaism "out there," prior to, encompassing all documents, each with its "Judaism in here" imposes its judgment upon our reading of every sentence, every paragraph, every book. But where shall we locate the working of that judgment, and how shall we know when we have found it? These are questions not yet answered by the proponents of the view that everything is everywhere, all at once: Judaism out there, prior to, encompassing all the specific, documentary Judaisms in here. It is in that context that the present inquiry finds its place. That brings us to the final methodological point requiring explanation.

THE CLASSIFICATION OF EVIDENCE [1]:
THE TWO STAGES IN THE FORMATION
OF THE JUDAISM OF THE
DUAL TORAH

It remains to explain the organization of this book as it lays out the sources of the Judaism of the dual Torah. I deal with the canonical writings in groups: In part 1, the Mishnah and its close companions, the Tosefta and tractate *Avot;* then in the same context the secondary and transitional writings, *Sifra* and the two *Sifrés.* In part 2, I take up the first of the two Talmuds, the Yerushalmi, and its close friends, *Genesis Rabbah* and *Leviticus Rabbah* with *Pesiqta de-Rab Kahana.* In part 3, we consider the final statement of the whole, the second of the two Talmuds, the Bavli. Since the Bavli remains well within the orbit of the earlier Talmud, I work in essentially two stages marked, first, by the Mishnah, second, by the Yerushalmi, with its program in its fundamental structure and morphology carried forward in the Bavli. All documentary contexts studied to date define one fact: what we know about the formative history of the Judaism of the dual Torah, oral and written, through the writings produced by sages, or rabbis, of late antiquity in the Land of Israel ("Palestine") and Babylonia (mainly the former location), shows us how the writings are to be sorted out. Those writings fall into two groups each with its own plan and program, the one produced in the second and third centuries, the second in the fourth and fifth. A brief introduction to the documents subject to review here is now in order.

The Documents of the First Stage in the Formation of Judaism

The first of these groups of writings begins with the Mishnah, a philosophical law book brought to closure at ca. A.D. 200, later on called the first statement of the oral Torah. In its wake the Mishnah drew tractate *Avot,* ca. A.D. 250, a statement concluded a generation after the Mishnah on the standing of the authorities of the Mishnah; Tosefta, ca. A.D. 300, a compilation of supplements of various kinds to the statements in the Mishnah; and two systematic exegeses of books of Scripture or the written Torah: *Sifra,* on Leviticus, *Sifré to Numbers,* and another *Sifré,* to Deuteronomy, of indeterminate date but possibly concluded by A.D. 300.

These books overall form one stage in the unfolding of the Judaism of the dual Torah, which stressed issues of sanctification of the life of Israel, the people, in the aftermath of the destruction of the Temple of Jerusalem in A.D. 70 (in which, it was commonly held, Israel's sanctification came to full realization in the bloody rites of sacrifice to God on high). I call this system a "Judaism without Christianity," because the issues found urgent in the documents representative of this phase address questions not pertinent to the Christian *défi* of Israel at all. The authorities cited in *Sifra* and the two *Sifré*s are pretty much the same names as those in the Mishnah and Tosefta. Since the three documents cite the Mishnah as well as the Tosefta verbatim, they presumably came to closure some time after the other documents. But they remain well within the circle of inquiry and exegesis drawn by the authorship of the Mishnah, and, over all, if we impute a date of ca. 300 we are not likely to be far off the mark. But that is only a guess. The more substantial reason for treating *Sifra* and the two *Sifré*s within the framework of the Mishnah is the recurrent concern of their authorships to demonstrate that teachings of the Mishnah rest upon the authority of the written Torah, Scripture, and not upon unfettered reason.

The Documents of the Second Stage in the Formation of Judaism

The second set of the same writings begins with the Talmud of the Land of Israel, or Yerushalmi, generally supposed to have come to a conclusion at ca. A.D. 400; *Genesis Rabbah,* assigned to about the next half century; *Leviticus Rabbah,* ca. A.D. 450; *Pesiqta deRab Kahana,* ca. A.D. 450–500; and finally, the Talmud of Babylonia, or Bavli, assigned to the late sixth or early seventh century, ca. A.D. 600. The two Talmuds systematically interpret passages of the Mishnah and the other documents do the same for books of the written Torah. Some other treatments of biblical books important in synagogue liturgy, particularly the Five Scrolls, for example, *Lamentations Rabbati, Esther Rabbah,* and the like, are also supposed to have reached closure at this time. This second set of writings introduces, alongside the paramount issue of Israel's sanctification, the matter of Israel's salvation, with doctrines of history on the one side and the Messiah on the other given prominence in the larger systemic statement. The Judaic system of the dual Torah, expressed in its main outlines in the Yerushalmi and associated compilations of biblical exegeses concerning Genesis, Leviticus, and some other scriptural books, culminated in the Bavli. That Talmud, the second, emerged as the authoritative document of the Judaism of the dual Torah from then to now. At the beginning of parts 1 and 2 I shall expand on these matters.

THE CLASSIFICATION OF EVIDENCE [2]: THE THREE MODES OF DISCOURSE OF THE JUDAISM OF THE DUAL TORAH: ORAL, WRITTEN, INCARNATE

It remains to explain the way in which I classify the documents of the two stages in the formation of Judaism. Because there are three distinct modes of organizing sustained discourse in the canon of the Judaism of the dual Torah, at each of the principal stages of my work I present my analysis of the representation of the character of divinity in three distinct divisions. In the analysis that follows, we shall organize our inquiry in accord with the three types of materials that form cogent statements within the larger canon of the Judaism of the dual Torah. These cogent statements are (1) those built around the exegesis of the oral Torah, (2) those that serve to amplify the written Torah, and (3) those that find cogency in the life and teaching of a given sage or group of sages.[14] To spell this out, let me explain that there were three modes of organizing large-scale discourse in the Judaism of the dual Torah. One was to make use of books or verses or themes of Scripture. A second was to follow the order of the Mishnah and compose a systematic commentary and amplification of that document. This was the way of those who created the Talmud of the Land of Israel a century or so before. A third was to organize stories about and sayings of sages. These were framed around twin biographical principles, either as strings of stories about great sages of the past or as collections of sayings and comments drawn together solely because the same name stands behind the sayings.

Why not do the same with the final stage, represented by the Bavli? The reason is simple. A tripartite corpus of inherited materials awaiting compilation into a cogent composite document found its way into the Bavli. That is why, when we come to the Bavli, we have no reason to investigate matters along three distinct lines. But prior to that time, the framers of documents had tended to resort to a single principle of organization, whether scriptural, mishnaic, or biographical. The authorship of the Bavli for its part took up materials, in various states and stages of completion, pertinent to the Mishnah or to the principles of laws that the Mishnah had originally brought to articulation. Second, they had in hand received materials, again in various conditions, pertinent to the Scripture, both as the Scripture related to the Mishnah and also as the Scripture laid forth its own narratives. Finally, they collected and arranged sayings of and stories about sages. But this third

---

14. In chap. 10 I explain and justify my representation of the sage as Torah incarnate.

principle of organizing discourse took a subordinate position, behind the other two. The framers of the Bavli organized it around
the Mishnah. But they also adapted and included vast tracts of
antecedent materials organized as scriptural commentary. These
they inserted whole and complete, not at all in response to the
Mishnah's program. And, finally, while making provision for compositions built upon biographical principles—preserving strings
of sayings from a given master (and often a given tradent of a
given master) as well as tales about authorities of the preceding
half millennium—they did nothing new.

That is to say, the ultimate authorships of the canonical documents never created redactional compositions of a sizable order
that focused upon given authorities, even though sufficient materials lay at hand to allow doing so. God's will reached Israel
through Scripture, Mishnah, sage—that is, by the evidence and
testimony of each of these three media equally. That is the premise
of the Judaism of the entire rabbinic canon, of each of the stories
that appeal to a verse of Scripture, a phrase or sentence of the
Mishnah, or a teaching or action of a sage. Recognizing the three
components of the single canon—the written Torah, the oral
Torah, and the sage as the living Torah—leads us deep into the
investigation at hand.

PART TWO

PREMISE, PRESENCE, PERSON:
THE CHARACTER OF DIVINITY
IN THE FIRST STATEMENT
OF JUDAISM, 70–300

3

Oral Torah:
The Mishnah and
the Tosefta

THE MISHNAIC PHASE IN THE FORMATION OF JUDAISM: JUDAISM WITHOUT CHRISTIANITY

The Mishnah presents a world view that speaks of transcendent things, a way of life in response to the supernatural meaning of what is done, a heightened and deepened perception of the sanctification of "Israel" in deed and in deliberation. Sanctification in this context meant two things: (1) distinguishing "Israel" in all its dimensions from the world in all its ways; (2) establishing the stability, order, regularity, predictability, and reliability of "Israel" in the world of nature and supernature in particular at moments and in contexts of danger. Danger meant instability, disorder, irregularity, uncertainty, and betrayal—experiences drawn from the just-passed encounter with Rome on the battlefield. Each topic of the system as a whole takes up a critical and indispensable moment or context of social being. Through what is said in regard to each of the Mishnah's principal topics, what the system of norms as a whole wishes to declare is fully expressed. Yet if the parts severally and jointly give the message of the whole, the whole cannot exist without all of the parts, so well joined and carefully crafted are they all. The effect of the Mishnaic system was to limit the impact upon the politics of the Jews in the Land of Israel of the disruptive events of the late first and second centuries. The crisis precipitated by the destruction of the second Temple and the failure of the second revolt, led by Bar Kokhba three generations later, to regain Jerusalem and rebuild the Temple therefore affected both the nation and the individual.

The Mishnah's system presents a cultic Judaism of sanctification, temporarily without a temple. That system emerged in a world in which (to the framers) there was no Christianity. Here we see the Judaism that flowed from the critical question framed by the destruction of the Temple. That Judaism did not find necessary a doctrine of the authority of Scripture and a systematic exegetical effort to link the principal document, the Mishnah, to Scripture. It presented no explicit doctrine of history and eschatology, for example, who the Messiah is and when the Messiah will come. The list of omissions is as interesting as the list of matters that the Mishnah's authorship did define as its principal focus. The system of the Mishnah—a Judaism for a world in which nascent Christianity played no considerable role—laid no considerable stress on the symbol of the Torah; though, of course, the Torah as a scroll, as a matter of status, and as revelation of God's will at Sinai enjoyed prominence. And it produced a document, the Mishnah, so independent of Scripture that, when the authors wished to say what Scripture said, they chose to do so in their own words and in their own way. Whatever their intent, the authorships of the documents of the first phase in the Judaism of the dual Torah clearly did not need to explain to a competing "Israel," heirs of the same Scriptures of Sinai, just what authority validated the document and how the document related to Scripture. That same system took slight interest in the Messiah and presented a teleology lacking all eschatological, therefore messianic, focus. The Mishnaic system defined all matters in relationship to all other matters in a structure given force and energy by the task of classification and taxonomy. When we listen to the silences of the Mishnah, as much as to its points of stress, we hear a single message. It is a message of a Judaism that answered a single encompassing question: What, in the aftermath of the destruction of the holy place and holy cult, remained of the sanctity of the holy caste, the priesthood, the holy land, and, above all, the holy people and its holy way of life? The answer: Sanctity persists, indelibly, in "Israel," the people, in its way of life, in its land, in its priesthood, in its food, in its mode of sustaining life, in its manner of procreating and so sustaining the nation.

PREMISE

Standing at the head of the writings that ultimately formed the canon of the Judaism of the dual Torah, the Mishnah (ca. A.D. 200) defined the focus of discourse for a continuous exegetical tradition. In sequence the Tosefta, a compilation of supplements to the Mishnah's statements (of indeterminate age but possibly ca. A.D. 300), the Yerushalmi or Talmud of the Land of Israel (ca. A.D. 400), and the Bavli or Talmud of Babylonia (ca. A.D. 600) served to amplify selected tractates of the Mishnah, organizing whatever their respective authorships wished to convey in the form of exegeses to sentences or paragraphs of the Mishnah. The Mishnah's deeply philosophical authorship concerned itself with making statements regarding the order and regularity of important components of reality, and that attitude of mind also imparted its distinctive mark upon the portrayal of the character of divinity in the first document of the new Judaism.

Let us start with a specific case and move to the more general principle concerning God as premise as spelled out in the Mishnah. The premise that God has imposed requirements upon humanity in general, and Israel in particular, encompasses the entirety of the corpus of commandments presented in the Torah, and the Mishnah sets forth the rules governing observance of those commandments.[1] From that fact it must follow that God forms the principal premise of all Mishnaic discourse, even though that premise rarely reaches explicit expression. That is moreover a statement not of theory but of everyday fact. Where the fact makes a difference can be easily specified. For instance, if one violates the law of the Torah

---

1. The argument that follows means to take up the challenge of specifying the "Judaism out there" to which documents refer but which they rarely make explicit. I believe that we may satisfactorily outline the main components of the Judaism beyond the text at hand without violating sound rules of evidence and argument.

as set forth in the Mishnah, one transgresses the expressed will of God. Here is one explicit statement of that view:

> Those [who practice usury] transgress a negative commandment: the one who lends at usury, the one who borrows, the one who guarantees the loan, and the witnesses. Sages say, "Also the scribe."
> They transgress the commandments, "Thou shall not give him your money upon usury" (Lev. 25:37), "You shall not take usury from him" (Lev. 25:36), "You shall not be to him as a creditor" (Ex. 22:25), "Nor shall you lay upon him usury" (Ex. 22:25), "You shall not put a stumbling block before the blind, but you shall fear your God. I am the Lord" (Lev. 19:14).
>
> (*m. B.M.* 5:11)

Here is an explicit statement, among many, that God through the Torah stands behind the laws of the Mishnah, and that those who violate the laws offend God, those who keep them please God. One fundamental trait of divinity is to lay forth and then guarantee rules of order and regularity in the world.

Now to proceed to a more general statement of the facts. The God of Sinai defined the foundation and premise of the Mishnah, its message and authority, even though in the Mishnah itself no one found it necessary to say so explicitly. My argument for God as the premise of all discourse in the Mishnah and, therefore, for God's ubiquitous place within the world view of the Mishnah appeals to what I take to be self-evident facts. The premise of the Mishnah's authorities is, first, that God revealed the Torah at Sinai, and second, that the Torah represents God's will for Israel. The Mishnah's "Israel" is holy because of that fact. And all else follows.

To be sure, the authorship of the Mishnah, excluding that of tractate *Avot*, never tells us the basis on which sages listed by name, and their heirs and disciples, in particular exercise authority and therefore are able to declare that matters are to be done in one way rather than in some other. Nonetheless, in some passages the document explicitly appeals to the authority of the written Torah—therefore to the will of God—and in many more does so implicitly. Of the latter fact we may be certain for two reasons. The first is that vast stretches of the Mishnah propose to spell out in detail the ways to carry out the requirements of the law of the Torah. Consequently, the Mishnah's authorship clearly proposed to perform a secondary act of explication, depending upon the primary authority of the Torah. Tractates such as *Yebamot, Pesahim,* and *Yoma* specify in rich detail the ways in which the Torah's laws are to be observed and applied. While the authorship at hand only rarely cites verses of Scripture, seeing no need for proof texts, that same authorship has as a principal task the application of the Torah's laws to everyday situations. The authority behind Scripture—God's revelation to Moses at Sinai—therefore stands behind the Mishnah, and the presence of God's will and word forms the paramount fact of the Mishnah.

But that can be the case only if it can further be shown that the authorship of the Mishnah implicitly views itself as continuous with the "Israel" to whom God spoke through Moses at Sinai. And that brings us to the second reason. The Mishnah's writers everywhere do take for granted that they address that same "Israel" that Scripture knows, and the social group known to them—meaning all the Jews subject to their witness—consists of the same social group of which the written Torah speaks. From that fact it followed, in my view, that the authority that addressed ancient *and now-contemporary* "Israel," God at Sinai in the written Torah, spoke also through the authoritative law of the Mishnah as well. That continuity from "Israel" then to "Israel" now carried with it many other ongoing facts of life; indeed, the most important of these truths out of ancient times was God's commanding voice at Sinai. Then it must be deemed a fact that the premise of all discourse in the Mishnah is that God rules "Israel," having revealed the Torah and, by extension, all authoritative law. It follows that the authorship of the Mishnah identified the Jews of their time with that same "Israel" that formed the address and the focus of the written Torah of Sinai, which God had revealed and commanded to "Israel." And if Jewry now, to whom the Mishnah's authorship spoke, constituted the same "Israel" of then, that is, of Sinai, then the rest followed: God who revealed the Torah to "Israel" at Sinai defined the premise of authority over "Israel" from that time to this, and the authorship of the Mishnah implicitly appealed to that same authority in every sentence of the rulebook that they composed.

But that God, who created the world and revealed the Torah— so identified in the received Scripture, the written Torah—forms the premise of all Mishnaic discourse may be shown not only in so indirect a way as appeal to the imputed continuity with the social entity, the ancient Israel of Sinai. That conviction is stated in so many words every time the Mishnah has someone say, "May it be pleasing before you . . ." That address to heaven, which is a commonplace in the document as a whole, contains the simple conviction that God rules and makes concrete decisions on the here and now. From that routine phrase it follows that the premise of all existence for the authorship of the Mishnah is God who governs and carries out decisions for the everyday world. Not only so, but the operative principle of the Mishnaic system that makes things relative to human intentionality presupposes God's concern with and response to that same intentionality. Imputing to God an interest in human intentionality presupposes that God is a premise, a presence, a sentient being.

We do not, moreover, have to rely merely upon a ubiquitous phrase and the attitude it bespeaks for proof of the facticity of God as premise for all things. The Mishnah makes reference to liturgical requirements, and these presuppose the premise of God who requires "Israel" to do these things (as well as the presence of God who hears the words, as we shall note presently). Saying the Hallel-psalms (Pss. 113—18), for example, was a commonplace in the liturgical year (e.g., *m. Pes.* 5:7; 10:6; among many references), and these required direct address to God who heard and answered prayers. Reciting the *Shema,* for example, as well as saying blessings over various foods (e.g., *m. Ber.* 6:1–8), reciting the grace after meals (*m. Ber.* 7:1), and performing similar rites associated with meals, such as are spelled out in tractate *Berakhot,* all invoke as their premise that God has laid down various rules which "Israel" is to obey. The recitation of blessings on other occasions made explicit the same premise—that God took full responsibility for whatever happened and that the Israelite was to take account of God's deeds by acknowledging them:

If one saw a place where miracles had been done for Israel, one says, "Blessed is the one who did miracles for our ancestors in this place." If it was a place in which idolatry had been uprooted, one says, "Blessed is the one who uprooted idolatry from our land." On the occasion of shooting stars, earthquakes, lightning, thunder, and storm, one says, "Blessed is the one whose power and might fill the world."

(*m. Ber.* 9:1)

The list of appropriate occasions for reciting such blessings covers building a house, using newly acquired clothing or goods, and the like. There are blessings that are not to be said, specifically covering events no longer subject to divine intervention, for example, praying that one's wife, already pregnant, produce a male is inappropriate since that question is no longer open. One is obligated to say a blessing even on the occasion of evil things as much as for God, acknowledging God's presence and intervention in every circumstance (*m. Ber.* 9:5). Thus, wherever in the Mishnah we turn we meet God's commandments in the Torah, with the consequence that God forms the premise of all normative statements in the document, even though references to God's presence, person, and personality prove sparse.

The notion that God forms the premise of discourse in the Tosefta, as in the Mishnah, has to be regarded as everywhere implicit. God created the world with wisdom (*t. San.* 8:9E). God of course revealed the Torah. The Torah conveys God's will and, it follows, God serves as premise for the entire law. That is not a merely theoretical appeal to God to serve as authority in the far-distant background of an ongoing legal system. Doing God's will produces one consequence, not doing God's will, a different one, for example, "When priests perform God's will, what is written concerning them? 'I have given it to them as their portion of my offerings that are made by fire' (Lev. 6:10). . . . But when they do not perform God's will . . ." (*t. Dem.* 2:8Y–CC). This, among many passages, takes for granted that the Torah expresses God's will, and that God forms the premise of the life of holy Israel. That humanity was formed in God's image defines yet another premise. The first man was created one and alone, "To show the grandeur of the King of the kings of kings, blessed be he. For with one seal he created the entire world and from a single seal all those many seals have come forth" (*t. San.* 8:5).

PRESENCE

It is one thing to find God as premise of the law. It is quite another to locate evidence of the portrayal of God as a presence within the processes of exposition and—more important— application of the law. The Hebrew word generally translated "presence," *Shekhinah,* does occur in the Mishnah, in only one passage:

> Said R. Meir, "When a human being is in distress, as to the Presence of God, what does [its] tongue say . . . ?"
>
> (*m. San.* 6:5)

The premise is that God suffers along with human beings. It follows that, in general, God is understood not merely as a philosophical premise, a source of authority, but also as a presence.

But the picture painted by the authorship of the Mishnah in general leaves a quite different impression. Like eighteenth-century Deists, the Mishnah's philosophers focus upon the government by the rule and law that God has set forth in the Torah. Taking slight, and then merely episodic, interest in God's particular and ad hoc intervention into the smooth application of the now-paramount regularities of the law, that authorship rarely represented God as an immediate—therefore ad hoc and episodic, by definition irregular—presence, let alone person. That sort of intervention by God is invoked only in one instance known to me, as I shall suggest in a moment. The Mishnah's authorship rarely decided a rule or a case by appealing to God's presence and choice particular to that rule or case.

That is to say, God not as premise but immediate presence does not very often play an everyday and active role in the Mishnah's processes and system of decision making. To take two stunning examples, in the entire division of Purities, which encompasses more than a quarter of the Mishnah in volume, I cannot point to a single passage in which God's presence forms a consideration of cleanness or uncleanness, susceptibility or insusceptibility to uncleanness, in the statement or application of a rule (excluding the tacked-on conclusion at *m. Uqs.* 3:12). The rules of susceptibility to and contracting of uncleanness as well as those of removing that uncleanness work themselves out with appeal to God's will or person. That is the case even though the division attends to laws meant by the account of the Priestly authorship of Leviticus and Numbers to protect the cult from the danger of uncleanness. A survey of the civil code presented in the tractates *Baba Qamma, Baba Mesia,* and *Baba Batra* (covering the transactions of commerce, real estate, torts, damages, labor law, and the like, that in the aggregate correspond to civil law in our own society) yields not a single appeal to God's presence or God's ad hoc intervention into a case. All things are governed by regularities and norms, such that God has no place in the everyday world of mortals' exchanges and interchanges. While God forms the prevailing premise of discourse, that fact makes slight difference in what is said. The Mishnah's is a God of philosophers.[2] The full weight of the nature of the Mishnah's portrayal of the character of divinity will make its mark only when we have taken the measure of the Bavli's. There the contrast between God as essentially a premise of all being and God as an active personality engaged in everyday transactions with specific persons will lend immediacy to these now-general observations. But even in the Mishnah an exception to the rule of God as formal premise of being highlights the rule.

The exception, which shows us how things might have been, is represented by the ordeal imposed on a woman accused of adultery (tractate *Sotah*). There, it is presupposed, God does intervene on an ad hoc basis. Since pentateuchal writings know many other cases in which God is expected to intervene, case by case (e.g., the death of the sons of Aaron at Lev. 16:1), we may wonder why the Mishnah's authorship has chosen, among all possibilities for immediate divine participation in the administration of the law, the case at hand. But that exception does prove the rule that God has defined the norms and does not thereafter intervene in their application and execution. For no other ordeal, relying upon God's engagement in a decision-making process, appears in the Mishnah's system. The Mishnah moreover rarely appeals to heavenly sanctions; commonly, in practical matters, to human ones. The penalties catalogued in tractate *Sanhedrin,* for example, encompass this-worldly recompense for this-worldly sin.

True enough, the Mishnah's system knows penalties inflicted by heaven, catalogued in the tractate on *Keritot,* grounds for extirpation or premature death. But the same authorship invokes

---

2. The contrast will underline the validity of that statement. Tractate *Avot* presents us with a divine Presence whenever two people sit and exchange Torah-teachings, for example. The Tosefta's conception of God's presence is treated presently.

heavenly intervention only by rule and law, not by case-by-case choice. The imposition of the penalty of extirpation is governed by the same regularities that dictate who must forfeit property in payment of a penalty. It is all one system. The same is so even for denial of a share in the world to come—on grounds important to heaven and assessed by heaven, namely, denying that the resurrection of the dead derives from the Torah, denying that the Torah comes from heaven—and Epicureanism. These are not matters subject to human inquisition but rather to God's knowledge. But here too there is a single law which applies throughout, and God does not have to play a role in judging specific cases, except for the one involving the accused wife. In general, therefore, God's presence in the system of the Mishnah, while everywhere a premise and an implicit fact, plays only a limited and, on the whole, a passive or inert role.

Quite to the contrary, it is the will and intention of the human being—not those of God—that form the variable. God is the norm and the given, God's will and law, revealed in the Torah, the ubiquitous fact. For the philosophers behind the Mishnah, therefore, God's presence forms part of the guaranteed and reliable structure of existence. It is the human will that is unpredictable—and that imparts to the Mishnah's system its movement, energy, dynamism. That human and not divine intentionality defines the system's principal problematic is shown, paradoxically, in its presentation of the cult on everyday occasions and of the rules for the upkeep of the cult. Here the variable is the attitude and intention of the *sacrifier,* the owner, who designates a beast as holy, on the one side, and of the *sacrificer,* the priest, who kills the beast and sprinkles the blood on the altar, on the other. God's presence at the cult, God's enjoyment of the smell of the smoke of meat burning on the holy barbeque form no point of discourse at all, though, of course, Scripture has assured them a place at the center of matters. We look in vain in the principal tractates to take up the disposition of offerings, *Zebahim* and *Menahot,* and in the ones that define what is deemed sanctified or designated for use on the altar, *Meilah* and *Temurah,* for decisive examples for God's act of intervention or a divine indication that one rule, rather than some other, applies to a given case. Validation or invalidation of an act of designation of a beast as holy or an act of sacrifice depend upon the intention of the sacrificer or the sacrificer, not upon the intervention of God. The rules are what they are and they apply as they apply.

Always present, invariably a participant in the sacrifice as principal beneficiary of the smoke of the burning meat, in the exposition of the rules of the Mishnah God is no presence in the cult. That fact is shown in a striking way by the prevailing power of fixed rules, rather than the engagement of "the sacred" in specific cases. The statement is simple: "The altar consecrates what is appropriate to the altar" (*m. Zeb.* 9:1), and does not consecrate what is inappropriate to it. What that means is that merely being placed upon the altar does not consecrate a beast (e.g., a chicken or a turtle) that is not an acceptable sacrifice. That rule imposing totally rational considerations of fixed law in the place of unpredictable intervention of power beyond all rule will have surprised Scripture, which understood that merely touching the altar imparted holiness to whatever touched it: "Whatever touches the altar shall become consecrated" (Ex. 29:37). Here there is no counterpart in the entirety of the civil law to the ordeal at which God is required to give a specification of the pertinent rule or decision for a given case. That is not to suggest as a final judgment that the Mishnah's God is to be compared to the Deists', or that God is merely the one who made the watch and wound it up to run on its own forever, more or less. In the Mishnah we deal with a system in no way comparable to that of the eighteenth-century philosophers' God. The reason is simple. In the Mishnah we deal with God not merely as the rule maker and premise of a system but as a presence. For the Mishnah's is a God who hears prayer and sometimes responds to human wishes and requests. God, moreover, is surely present in the Temple, as the Mishnah's authorship states in diverse ways, even though in the story told in tractate *Tamid* God plays no role in the picture of the conduct of the cult as it is carried out every day.

The generative force of the Mishnah's system—the active power that makes the system work, frames its questions, and dictates its answers—is the human attitude and intention. That is the point at which, ordinarily, the Mishnah also invokes God's presence. That is to say, God's presence forms the presupposition of those rules that attend to human attitude during the performance of certain religious actions, for example, the recitation of obligatory prayers. The obligation to recite the *Shema* encompasses the requirement "to direct one's heart," which is to say, to recite the required words with the intention of fulfilling one's duty to recite those words (*m. Ber.* 2:1). One's attitude is taken into account in diverse other ways, for example, not reciting the *Shema* under circumstances that will prevent one from forming the right attitude, such as when one has to bury a deceased relative (*m. Ber.* 3:1). So too, when reciting the Prayer (the Eighteen Benedictions), it must be in a sober attitude, and particular piety requires an hour of inner preparation, "that they may direct their heart toward God" (*m. Ber.* 5:1). It must follow that there is a presence to assess the recitation of the correct words with the correct attitude. That presence is not material; one fulfills the obligation even though the words are not said sufficiently loud to be heard, even by the one who says them (*m. Ber.* 2:3). But it is physical, in the sense that God is assumed to be located in one place rather than in some other. Accordingly, one recites prayers facing a particular location, namely, Jerusalem, and if one cannot do so in a physical way, at least one does so in the heart, directing the heart "toward the Holy of Holies" (*m. Ber.* 4:6). That God is conceived to be located in the Holy of Holies is underlined by the rule that one should not conduct oneself in an inappropriate way while opposite the Temple's eastern gate, which faces the Holy of Holies (*m. Ber.* 9:5). It goes without saying that God hears and answers statements made in any language, not only in Hebrew, although Hebrew is the holy and preferred language for certain formulas (*m. Sot.* 7:1).

God's presence is signified by awareness of the character of the occasion as well. For example, rules covering the recitation of prayers took account of the size and importance of those present on the occasion. If three are present, for the grace after meals one begins, "Bless the one of whose bounty we have partaken," if there are ten, "Bless our God . . . ," and onward up to ten thousand, "We will bless the Lord our God, the God of Israel, the God of hosts, who sits between the Cherubim, for the food we have eaten . . ." (*m. Ber.* 7:3). But this is a minor point. The main consideration is that God responds to the human will and expression of human intentionality. That becomes especially blatant when we turn to how God hears statements of what a human being wishes, or does not wish, joined to an act of consecration or sanctification through human words: vows, oaths, statements of sanctification and dedication, and the like. Here is where the encounter between God and the human person takes place—which is to say, at the human being's action and volition.

God hears not only prayers offered by the community but also vows and oaths taken by individuals. That is the foundation of the tractates on vows (*Nedarim*), oaths (*Shabuot*), oaths of valuation of another person such as are specified at Lev. 27:1 (*Arakhin*), and the special vow of the Nazirite (Num. 6:1–21, tractate *Nazir*). To this list we may add numerous tractates that presuppose that God (directly or through angels or other messengers) confirms the stated intention of a human being. These include, for example, *Temurah*'s rules on designating gifts to the altar or to the upkeep of the Temple house or *Terumot*'s rules (representative of an equivalent premise governing tractates *Peah, Demai, Maaserot, Maaser Sheni, Hallah,* and *Bikkurim*) on the designation of a portion of the crop for God's share and use. The mere utterance of the appropriate words invokes, for the person who says them, a vow or an oath (depending on the formula, purpose, and occasion); such a statement is then binding and imposes concrete obligations on acts of commission or omission. A vow commonly compares a secular object to a holy one, for example, imposing upon food the status of God's food upon the altar; the one who has imputed the sacred status consequently may not consume such food. God then is assumed not only to have heard but also to have taken account of the vow (or oath), which again implies immediacy and presence under all circumstances. God furthermore will consider the attitude of mind or intentionality associated with a verbal expression, so that there are vows that are not binding, for example, those of incitement, exaggeration, error, and constraint (*m. Ned.* 3:1). In such cases the statement is null; God knows the difference. The same principles in general apply to the special vow of the Nazirite.

It goes without saying that God knows not only public but also secret deeds as much as intentions. Consequently, God will settle the matter of a husband's jealousy of his wife by guiding the working of the bitter water in such a way as to show what, if anything, has actually taken place (Num. 5:11–31, tractate *Sotah*). God's involvement in the rite is direct, since the name of God is written on the scroll prepared for the rite and then blotted out in the water that the woman has to drink. The oath that is imposed, of course, contains the expected implication that God hears oaths and punishes those taken in vain. In all of these aspects, God forms a powerful presence, if a systemically inert one, guaranteeing rules but not exhibiting distinctive traits. But the philosopher's conception of God competes in the Mishnah with yet another.

The Tosefta's pertinent materials do not vastly change the picture. The presence of God, referred to by the word *Shekhinah*, makes an explicit appearance at *t. Men.* 7:8B–F, with reference to the verse, "Moses saw all the work . . . and Moses blessed them" (Ex. 39:43): "With what blessing did he bless them? He said to them, 'May the Presence of God dwell with the work of your hands . . .'" And further, "Just as you have been engaged in the work of making the tabernacle and the Presence of God has dwelled with the work of your hands, so may you have the merit of building before me the chosen house, and may the Presence of God dwell with the work of your hands." God's presence is furthermore acknowledged by the "you" of the liturgy, for example, "May your will be done in heaven above, and grant ease to those that fear you" (*t. Ber.* 3:7C, among numerous instances), so too, "May it be your will . . ." (*t. Ber.* 6:2C, among many instances). God's presence (*Shekhinah*) is further said to depart from Israel because of the sin of murder (*t. Yoma* 1:12; *Sheb.* 1:4) or for tale bearing (*t. Sot.* 14:3). The presence waited upon various persons (*t. Sot.* 4:7).

The confession for the day of atonement (*t. Yoma* 2:1; 4:14) forms another occasion for acknowledging God's presence. Rules for reciting benedictions, for example, in the prayer, are also spelled out in the Tosefta (*t. Ber.* 1:4), with some to be marked by genuflection, others not. These rules again rest on the conviction that God is present when prayers are said. But the presence of God was not the sole consideration; the convenience of the community at large made a difference. By himself, Aqiba would pray slowly and at length; with the community he cut matters (*t. Ber.* 3:5).

PERSON

God as a person whom one might envisage and even see had formed the subject of interpretation of Ezekiel's vision of the chariot (Ez. 1:4), but the framers of the Mishnah merely allude to that fact (*m. Hag.* 2:1) and do not tell us the substance of the vision of God as a physical person. God's person, not merely presence, however, forms the presupposition of all acts of the recitation of prayer, which take for granted that God not only hears prayer but also cares what the human being requests. One example is the prayer of the high priest on the day of atonement: "O God, your people, the house of Israel, have committed iniquity, transgressed and sinned before you. O God, forgive the iniquities and transgressions and sins which your people, the house of Israel, have committed . . . as it is written in the Torah of your servant, Moses, 'For on this day shall atonement be made for you to clean you, from all your sins shall you be clean before the Lord (Lev. 16:30)'" (*m. Yoma.* 6:2). God is everywhere a "you," and therefore a person. Not only so, but as a person God is assumed to respond to words and to events pretty much as human beings do. For example, when the community suffers from drought and prays for rain, God is not only asked to act as God had done in times past, "May the one who answered our ancestors at the Red Sea answer you" (*m. Ta.* 2:4), but the acts of self-mortification and deprivation are meant to impress God and to win sympathy, much as they would (it was assumed) from a mortal ruler. The one who represents the community in prayer therefore was to be an elder, who had children for whom to worry and a house empty of food (*m. Ta.* 2:2); such a one would then be wholehearted in the prayer. God would discern the sincerity and respond with sympathy. Hence God was understood as a person in whose model the human being had been made, and human beings, searching their own hearts, could understand God's.

While throughout the Mishnah we find the datum that God hears and answers prayer, for example, "When I enter [the house of study], I pray that no offense will take place on my account, and when I leave, I give thanks for my lot" (*m. Ber.* 4:2), that is not the end of the matter. Of still greater interest, God is assumed to take the form of a person, in the model of a heavenly monarch or emperor. For example, when one is reciting the prayer, one is assumed to stand before the king and that location, in God's presence, requires appropriate probity: "Even if the king greets a person, one is not to reply, and even if a snake wrapped itself around one's heel, one is not to interrupt" (*m. Ber.* 5:1). The response to the recitation of prayer derives not from concrete personal engagement by God; there is no story in the Mishnah that suggests anyone believed God talked back to the one who says the prayer. But there are explicit statements that God heard and answered prayer and so indicated on the spot:

If one who recites the Prayer makes an error, it is a bad omen for that person, and if that person recited the Prayer in behalf of the entire community, it is a bad omen for those who assigned the task to that person.

They said of R. Hanina that, when he would say a prayer over the sick, he would say, "This one will live," or, "That one will die."

They said to him, "How do you know?"

He said to them, "If my prayer flows easily in my mouth, I know that it is accepted, and if not, I know that it is rejected."

(*m. Ber.* 5:5)

God as "you" occurs not only in liturgy, but also in legal formulas recited upon specified occasions. Here, to be sure, the language as much as the context is defined by Scripture:

"I have removed . . . according to all your commandment which you have commanded me . . ." [Deut. 26:13] . . .

"Look down from your holy habitation from heaven:" "We have done what you have decreed concerning us, now you do what you have promised to us."

(*m. M.S.* 5:10–13)

The transaction is between two persons, each bound by the same rule as governs the other.

But the personhood of God as a "you" plays a role principally in the address of prayer. Scripture's portrait of God as an active personality finds no counterpart whatsoever in the Mishnah. That fact may be seen in a simple observation. The majestic presence of God in the unfolding of events, which forms the great theme of the scriptural narratives of ancient Israel's history, may define a premise of the Mishnah's world view. But at no passage in the Mishnah does an action of God serve to explain an event, nor do we find lessons as to God's purpose or will drawn from events. Events take place, truths endure, but the two form a merely assumed and implicit relationship. In passages in which important events are catalogued, for example, God's action is not at issue. Interestingly, these events are always catalogued as completed actions and in the past tense, changes of circumstance or situation, not decisions and actions of a divine monarch deciding from day to day what is to be done, then doing it:

When the first prophets died, Urim and Thummim ceased. When the Temple was destroyed, the Shamir-worm ceased . . . and faithful men came to an end, as it is written, "Help, Lord, for the godly man ceases" (Ps. 12:1). . . . During the war of Vespasian, they forbade the crowns of the bridegrooms and the wedding drum. During the war of Titus, they forbade the crowns of the brides and that a man should teach his son Greek. In the last war they forbade the bride to go forth in a litter inside the city . . . When R. Meir died, there were no more makers of parables.
(*m. Sot.* 9:12–15)

Along these same lines, when at *m. Zeb.* 14:4–8 diverse periods in the history of the cult are specified, we find no invocation of the action or purpose of God. That is not to suggest anyone imagined God had not done these things by decree. It is only to point out that the sorts of explicit conclusions drawn from historical events by the prophetic historians in Joshua, Judges, Samuel, and Kings, for example, find no counterpart in the Mishnah. God now presides as much as in the biblical narratives God ruled. But the appeal is particular to the Mishnah:

R. Phineas b. Yair said, "When the Temple was destroyed, . . . men of violence and loud tongue prevailed. No one expounds, no one seeks, no one asks. On whom may we rely? On our father in heaven . . ."
   R. Eliezer the elder says, "Since the temple was destroyed, sages diminished to the standing of school teachers, school teachers to synagogue beadles, synagogue beadles to people of no standing . . . , and none was there to seek. On whom may we rely? On our father in heaven . . ."
(*m. Sot.* 9:16)

The contrary picture of course makes its mark: "With the foot-prints of the Messiah presumptions shall increase . . ." (*m. Sot.* 9:16), once more language noteworthy for its failure to speak directly and immediately of God's intervention. The plan prevails, the person plays no explicit part. Once more God forms a premise, scarcely a person, in the unfolding of vast events of politics and history. That fact sets the stage for the most important observation, which is, in the nature of things, a negative one.

In the Tosefta's amplification of the Mishnah, God's communication with biblical figures is of course noted. God spoke with Moses, Abraham, Jacob, Samuel, and others (*t. Ber.* 1:2), but these passages take for granted merely the facts of the biblical narrative. God's attitudes compare to those of mortals: "One in whom people take delight, God takes delight" (*t. Ber.* 3:3C). God is a person with emotions such as anger and mercy, so: If when God is angry at the righteous, he has mercy on them, when he is disposed to be merciful, how much more does he have mercy on them! (*t. Ber.* 4:16J). God respects learning, of course, and is affronted when religious duties are carried out in an ignorant way (*t. Ber.* 6:18). The saying of Hillel which follows can be read as a statement imputed to God: "If you will come to my house, I shall come to your house. If you will not come to my house, I shall not come to your house, as it is said, 'In every place where I cause my name to be remembered I will come to you and bless you' (Ex. 20:24)" (*t. Suk.* 4:3B–D). If so, God is saying that those who come to the Temple will receive God in their houses, a clear indication of God as person, not merely premise or even presence.

God does not approve arrogance and favors the humble, a point repeatedly made in a review of the ancient history of creation: "The generation of the Flood acted arrogantly before the Omnipresent only on account of the good which he lavished on them . . . that is what caused them to say to God . . . The Omnipresent said to them, 'By the goodness which I lavished on them do they take pride before me? By that same good I shall exact punishment from them'" (*t. Sot.* 3:6–8), and so for the men of the Tower, Sodom, Egyptians, Samson, Absalom, Sennacherib, Nebuchadnezzar (*t. Sot.* 3:9–19). The statement attributed to God is not representative of a conversation of a vivid personality; rather it is an observation of a merely theological character, that is, the rendering in conversation form of a principle that God exacts punishment for arrogance and ingratitude, and does so through that very matter that brings up the arrogance or ingratitude. The contrary position—that God also responds to what the patriarchs and matriarchs and other saints did by favoring the descendants—is clearly spelled out as well, for example, Abraham went and got a morsel of bread for the angels (Gen. 18:5), so God gave manna in the wilderness (Num. 11:8), and so on as a counterpart construction (*t. Sot.* 4:1–19). The same principle of divine reciprocity is expressed in connection with Deut. 26:17–18, "You have declared this day concerning the Lord that he is your God." So, the passage goes on, "Said the Holy One . . . to them, 'Just as you have made me the only object of your love in the world, so I shall make you the only object of my love in the world to come'" (*t. Sot.* 7:10C). This propositional statement does not convey the characterization of the one who said it, for instance, expressing the personal traits of God. It simply states, in yet another way, the basic thesis of Tosefta *Sotah* throughout, which is the prevalence of the principle of measure for measure in the fate of Israel. So too when there is heavenly communication in both the Mishnah and the Tosefta, it is ordinarily through the medium of a heavenly echo (e.g., *t. Sot.* 13:5). God of course exacts punishment from the wicked and rewards the righteous (e.g., *t. San.* 8:3E).

PERSONALITY

If God is conceived as not merely a person but possessed of specific traits of personality, the Mishnah hardly contains evidence that its authorship could specify what those personal traits might be. True enough, one may infer from the rules that the Mishnah contains the attitudes of mind and preferences of personality of the God as premise, who even is invoked as presence. For instance, God is assumed to favor deeds of lovingkindness and study of the Torah; honoring of parents; making peace among people. Accordingly, God may be assumed, as a personality, to be generous, studious, respectful, and irenic, a picture explicitly limned in tractate *Avot.* But no *stories* portray God in one way rather than in some other. No other modes of discourse, beside stories, portray God as a personality who in some vivid and concrete way embodies the desired virtues. God is not portrayed as a distinct and individual personality, walking, talking, caring, acting as people do. Once more, only when we examine such explicit portraits of the incarnation of God shall we understand the remarkable reticence of the Mishnah about the same matters. True, we may impute such traits and others to the God that serves as premise and even presence. But the authorship of the Mishnah, unlike the diverse scriptural writers, simply did not portray God as a personality. Nor, apart from liturgical settings, does that translate its fixed premise of God as giver of the Torah into the notion of the active presence of God in the everyday and the here and now. God hears and answers prayers of the individual—setting aside the general rules of being when God chooses to do so. The way in which an authorship among the canonical documents of the Judaism of the dual Torah does portray the personality of God will show us, in due course, what has not been done in the Mishnah. What we find in later documents but not here is a drastic shift in the modes of discourse concerning God.

In only one story in the entire Mishnah do I find a hint that God has a personality, therefore approaches the condition of incarnation in some concrete setting. Imputed to God is, specifically, a rather wry sense of humor. But the matter appears with remarkable subtlety. That is in the account of how Honi, the circle-drawer, in a rather childish way required God to give rain: "He drew a circle and stood within it and said before God, 'Lord of the world, your children have turned to me, for I am like an intimate of yours. I swear by your name that I shall not leave this spot until you have pity on your children.' Rain began to fall but only in drops. He said, 'This is not the rain I wanted, but rain to fill up the cisterns. . . .' It rained violently. He said, 'Not for this kind of rain did I ask, but for rain that expresses goodwill, blessing, and grace.' Then it rained in moderation—until the Israelites had to evacuate Jerusalem and go to the Temple mount . . ." (*m. Ta.* 3:8). The picture of a rather petulant God, giving what was asked in such a way as to make fun of Honi, draws us near to a God with an interesting personality, no longer defined only by traits framed as rules, for example, merciful and just, but now characterized as acting as the occasion required.

Narrative in general finds more than slight place in the Mishnah, since the entire account of the Temple and its cult, the rites of the altar, the priesthood and their activities, is presented in essentially narrative form.[3] But narrative never serves in the Mishnah as a vehicle for discussing the personality or activity of God. Indeed, even when the opportunity to do so presents itself, the authorship of the Mishnah does not respond. The occasions that in Scripture commonly provoke God's anger—hence portraying God's personality in concrete terms—involve idolatry generating God's jealousy. The counterpart discourse in the Mishnah, *Abodah Zarah,* deals with worship of alien gods. No passage in that tractate refers to God's anger with idols or jealousy when Israelites worship idols. It is simply not a component of discourse on the subject. In the Mishnah's treatment of the matter, what is at stake is the relationship between Israelites and Gentiles, not between Israel and God, and the purpose of the law is to define permissible and impermissible transactions with Gentiles on the occasion of their celebration of their idol-gods. Secondary issues, for example, use of foods prepared by Gentiles, disposition of pieces of idols, and the like, do not change the picture of an authorship interested in outlining the boundaries between holy Israel and the Gentile world.

A simple fact remains to be noted. As in the Mishnah, so in the Tosefta, we find not a single story in which God is represented as a vivid personality.

SELF-EVIDENCE AND SELECTIVITY

The authorship of the Mishnah, like Israel in general, lived in a social world in which God formed a formidable presence everywhere. No wonder that the Mishnah's authorship found no necessity to restate on every possible occasion the premise of God's rule and authority. Quite to the contrary, in the course of setting forth the law only a few tractates explicitly refer to God, and most do not. The former classification of tractates, for example, *Berakhot, Taanit,* involves liturgy, and the bulk of the explicit allusions to

3. I cite the pertinent passages in my *Judaism: The Evidence of the Mishnah* (Chicago: University of Chicago Press, 1981), 245–50.

God—whether as premise or as person—appears quite naturally in discussion of prayer, with special attention to where, when, why, and above all, how one says prayers (including blessings, supplications, thanksgiving, and the like). The latter tractates—nearly the whole of the Mishnah—implicitly refer to God when topics such as the proper conduct of rites on the various appointed seasons, the correct procedures of the sacrificial cult, the maintenance of the priesthood and the Temple, and the protection of the Temple from contamination come to the fore.

Accordingly, when we wish to hear how the Mishnah's authorship speaks of the premise of God's rule and presence, we may point at systematic statements of an implicit character to the divisions of Agriculture (maintaining the priesthood, giving God the share of the crop that is due to the divinity), Appointed Seasons (laws governing conduct on holy occasions, such as the Sabbath and festivals), Holy Things (rules for the conduct of the everyday rites of the Temple and for the upkeep of the building), and Purities (laws on uncleanness, to begin with affecting the cult, as is specified in the Book of Leviticus). We may further discover in the division of Women, governing family life, a very systematic expression of God's acute interest in matters of the sanctification of a woman's sexuality to a particular man such that under some conditions sexual activity is punishable by heaven, while under others that same activity enjoys heaven's approval and blessing. Here, too, in the exposition of the requirements of sanctification of the woman and the sanctity of the family, I find implicit the premise of God's governance. Only the division of Damages fails to offer quite direct testimony to the same proposition, and even here we may find numerous specific statements, for example, *m. San.* 10:1, on the requirement, if one wishes to be (an) "Israel," of confessing that the resurrection of the dead constitutes a scripturally ordained truth. Statements of that order point toward the prevailing premise, and permit us to claim quite simply that God as systemic premise is never far from the surface of the law of the Mishnah, and commonly quite visible to the naked eye.

But that fact raises more questions than it settles. For it leads us to wonder how active a part God plays in the system of the Mishnah. Can the system of the Mishnah have taken shape without the premise of God? Certainly not. Does the system of the Mishnah, however, appeal to God—whether premise, whether presence— in the pursuit of solutions to its problems? Certainly not. And the exceptions to the rule are not only few but readily explained within the rules of the system, and hardly present exceptions at all. The focus of that system is on the discovery of the rules that govern a given classification of items—objects, facts, events—and (mostly in the secondary and exegetical work generated by the Mishnah) the harmonization of the prevailing rules with one another. The authorship of the Mishnah assigns to God, through the Torah, both priority and also a position of essential passivity, as a well-crafted legal system requires. A God who intervenes violates the law, and to the philosophers of the Mishnah, God guarantees the truth and regularity of the laws, deriving as they do from the Torah, but in particular cases God does not enforce those laws, nor should God have to. The very nature of the system prevents it. Allowing God under specified circumstances to hear and answer prayer need not, and does not, violate the orderly nature of the system, since the circumstances can be specified, and the required conditions met. So, in all, the emphasis on rules leaves God as mere premise, not active force in system of the Mishnah.

Shall we then compare God to the laws of gravity? Once we recognize that God defines a ubiquitous premise but never an independent variable, we see the aptness of such a metaphor. To a systematic account of the ecology of a botanical world, the laws of gravity constitute a given and an immutable fact. Without those laws, grass cannot sprout and trees cannot grow in the way in which they now do. But the laws of gravity, while necessary, are hardly sufficient—or, once conceded, even very urgent. They do not dictate many important systemic facts (though they make possible all facts) and they do not settle many of the system's interesting questions. So the laws of gravity in botany prove at once necessary and insufficient for explanation; implicit and ubiquitous, but not at all generative. Indeed, when we ask about the importance of the laws of gravity in a theory of botany—or biology or plate tectonics in geology, for that matter—we see how awry matters have become. The laws are absolutely necessary but, even when sufficient, still not very interesting. And, to come to the world view before us, we are therefore constrained to ask ourselves, Where is the God who acts? Where is the God who cares? Where is the God who rules "Israel" in accord with the Torah? In this system of philosophers with its law-abiding, philosophically acceptable God, the answer is nowhere. Later on, in a system consequent upon the Mishnah's, God would become not only necessary but also sufficient. But while without God the authorship of the Mishnah cannot have constructed their system to which God is necessary, still, since without God that authorship can have framed all of the system's most compelling propositions, God was hardly sufficient for the explanation of the system. God in the Mishnah's system is everywhere present, the ground of all being, giver and guarantor of the Torah—and a monumental irrelevance.

True, in any account of the Judaism "out there," beyond the pages of the Mishnah and yet presupposed and confessed by the authorship of the Mishnah, we must begin with God. Certainly, the world view of the Mishnah takes shape around the datum of God's creation of the world and giving of the Torah. No one can imagine otherwise. But then that Judaism "out there" scarcely intersects with the profound concerns and urgent questions of the Judaism "in here," that is, the system of the Mishnah in particular. The Judaism "out there" turns out to make very little difference in the shaping and direction of the Judaism "in here," in the formation and structure of the world view of the system at hand, and to contribute no more than the system builders can utilize—if also no less. The reason is to be specified with heavy emphasis.

It is that that Judaism "in here" portrayed by the authorship of the Mishnah has appealed to God in the ways and for the purposes dictated by the inner logic of the Mishnah's system, and God serves, and very well at that, precisely as that logic dictates. [4]

---

4. This is the same conclusion that is reached, with much labor, in the concluding chapter of *"Israel": Judaism and Its Social Metaphors* (New York and Cambridge: Cambridge University Press, 1988). The importance of systemic logic in the portraits of the character of God produced by diverse Judaisms seems to me—as a matter of theory—critical. But I do not plan at this time to undertake the sort of comparisons of systemic logic and its consequent social metaphors that occupied me in the other study. The method has been worked out in the completed study.

4

Written Torah:
Sifra, Sifré to Numbers,
and *Sifré to Deuteronomy*

PREMISE

That God's revelation of the Torah to Moses forms the premise of the surveyed passages of *Sifra,*[1] *Sifré to Numbers,*[2] and *Sifré to Deuteronomy*[3] requires no demonstration whatever. But the premise never surfaces in the surveyed passages of *Sifra* and *Sifré to Numbers. Sifré to Deuteronomy* provides a good entry into the way in which God as premise for all discourse actually makes an appearance. God's dominion over the world is of course a given, which yields such judgments as these: "Just as God grants the perfectly righteous a reward in the world to come for the performance of

---

1. Surveyed: Jacob Neusner, trans., *Sifra. The Rabbinic Commentary on Leviticus. An American Translation. 1. The Leper: Leviticus 13:1—14:57;* with Roger Brooks, *2. Support for the Poor: Leviticus 19:5-10,* Brown Judaic Studies (Atlanta: Scholars Press, 1985).

2. Surveyed: Jacob Neusner, trans., *Sifré to Numbers. An American Translation and Explanation. I. Sifré to Numbers 1—58; II. Sifré to Numbers 59—115,* Brown Judaic Studies (Atlanta: Scholars Press, 1986).

3. Surveyed: Reuven Hammer, trans., *Sifré. A Tannaitic Commentary on the Book of Deuteronomy* (New Haven and London: Yale University Press, 1986). Abstracts of that text are from Hammer's translation. Since Hammer does not provide a usable reference system of any kind and does not lay out the text in the conventional, Western modes of paragraphing and other ways of differentiating units of thought, the document has to be retranslated in an analytical manner. I plan to do so as my next major project. Hammer's introduction, furthermore, is not enlightening. A proper introduction to the document awaits an analytical translation. I shall attempt that as well.

commandments in this world, so God grants the perfectly wicked a reward in this world for any minor commandment performed in this world . . ." (*Sifré Deut.* 307). Such a statement does not involve the characterization of God, providing as it does only a theological explanation for the suffering of the righteous and the prosperity of the wicked. Along these same lines, since it is assumed that God gave the Torah to Moses, we find any number of times God's instructing Moses on this or that, for example,

Said the Holy One, blessed be he, to Moses, "Say to the Israelites, when you enter the land the abundance of food and drink and the easy life will lead you to rebel,"
    as it is said, "For when I shall have brought them into the land . . ." (Deut. 31:20).

(*Sifré Deut.* 318 [Hammer, p. 325])

Such a passage simply presupposes that God gave the Torah and paraphrases a given passage; it in no way forms part of a fresh effort to characterize God or even to impute to God traits of person. There is moreover the exegetical "I," in which a passage of Scripture is restated in the first person. A fair amount of paraphrase of Scripture yields some statements imputed to God, for example, "You caused me to feel like a male trying to give birth" (with reference to Deut. 32:18), "You forgot me through the merit of the fathers," and the like (*Sifré Deut.* 319). All that is contributed is a paraphrase of Scripture. Merely because the paraphrase takes the voice of the first person, it does not contribute to a rich picture of God as person beyond the given of Scripture. Here is yet another instance:

"How should one chase a thousand" (Deut. 32:30):
    If you do not observe my Torah, how can I keep the promise you sought from me, that one of you should be able to chase a thousand gentiles . . .
(*Sifré Deut.* 323 [Hammer, p. 334])

Hence God as premise produces a measure of first-person dialogue that paraphrases the sense of Scripture without providing more than a restatement of the passage subject to amplification.

PRESENCE

God's presence is invoked only rarely in the sampled passages of *Sifra* and *Sifré to Numbers*. That does not mean that God is not assumed to be everywhere near at hand. What it does mean is that God is rarely asked to intervene in a particular situation, and even when the scriptural narrative offers opportunities to say that God's presence has made a difference in the outcome of a story or case, the storyteller in the Midrash-compilation does not exploit the occasion. One example suffices to make that point. When *Sifré to Numbers* 7—21 takes up the verses of the ordeal of the accused wife, we look in vain for references to God's presence at the rite. That God in particular oversees the rite is the premise of all discourse, as Scripture has so defined matters. But opportunities for portraying God as present are not exploited, and God as a person participating in the rite never makes an appearance. The exposition of Num. 6:1 on the special vow of the Nazirite follows suit. At no point does God's presence, for example, at the taking of the vow, or at the violation thereof, play a role in any discussion. True, God favors Nazirites, who carry out the will of the Omnipresent (*Sifré Num.* 22:VI.2.E). But that general statement does not yield a picture of how God as person is present, has heard the vow, or expresses a response.

The same is so of the treatment of the Priestly Benediction (Num. 6:22–27). God's presence is invoked as part of a word-for-word exposition of the matter:

A. ". . . the Lord make his face to shine upon you:"
B. May he give you a glistening face.
C. R. Nathan says, "This refers to the light of God's presence, as it is said, 'Arise, shine for your light has come, and the glory of the Lord has risen upon you. For behold, darkness shall cover the earth, and thick darkness the peoples; but the Lord will arise upon you, and his glory will be seen upon you' (Is. 60:1–2).
D. "'May God be gracious to us and bless us and make his face to shine upon us' (Ps. 67:1)."

(*Sifré Num.* 41:I.1)

These are rather general remarks on the matter; we look in vain for important indications of how God's presence makes a difference in the outcome of passage.

The materials in *Sifré to Deuteronomy* do not much change the picture. God causes the wind to blow, the clouds to come up, the rains to come down, makes the world by a word (*Sifré Deut.* 38). When Israel does God's will Israel prospers, and when not they suffer distress (*Sifré Deut.* 40). God punishes Israel for disregarding the source of the prosperity they enjoyed (*Sifré Deut.* 43). We hardly need review a sizable corpus of materials to affirm that God forms a palpable presence in the document at hand. But while the exegesis of Deuteronomy invites that view, God's presence is not portrayed in any passage in which the text under study does not require the theme to enter.

PERSON

The sample of *Sifra* examined here yields no instances of God's taking a place in discourse as an "I" to a "you." But elsewhere in *Sifra* we do find a pertinent passage. God in the following passage serves as the authority for the statement at hand but is not portrayed in that rich detail that we shall find commonplace in the Bavli. We see that Scripture's comparison of God to the human being need not yield an anthropomorphic statement, let alone one involving the representation of God in incarnate form. *Sifra*'s editors include the following amplification of the statement, "You shall be holy":

"You shall be holy, because I the Lord your God am holy" (Lev. 19:18):

[God says to Israel,] "You shall be distinct [*perushim*]."

"You shall be holy, for I the Lord your God am holy:"

"If you sanctify yourselves, I shall credit it to you as if you sanctified me, and if you do not sanctify yourselves, I shall regard it as if you did not sanctify me."

(*Sifra Qedoshim Parashah* 1:1)

Here we have a scriptural passage that invites the representation of humanity in God's likeness—and does not provoke it. Scripture speaks in the name of a vivid personality, while *Sifra*'s exegetes treat God in the passage at hand as a premise, an authority, and, despite the "you" and "me," God scarcely emerges as a person with distinctive traits of personality.

God as a "you," a person who is present, is signified—in *Sifré to Numbers* as in other documents—by the word *Shekhinah*. What it means for God to be present is that God, as person, takes a place in Israel. That God's presence was in the camp, that is, the Temple, is explicitly stated at *Sifré Num.* 1:IV. This is in reference to *t. Kel. B.Q.* 1:12 introduced at 1:IX. God's presence comes among the righteous and is driven away by sin:

A. R. Simeon b. Yohai says, "Come and take note of how great is the power of sin. For before the people had laid hands on transgression, what is stated in their regard?

B. "'Now the appearance of the glory of the Lord was like a devouring fire on the top of the mountain in the sight of the people of Israel' (Ex. 24:17).

C. "Nonetheless, the people did not fear nor were they afraid.

D. "But once they had laid hands on transgression, what is said in their regard?

E. "'And when Aaron and all the people of Israel saw Moses, behold, the skin of his face shone, and they were afraid to come near him' (Ex. 34:30)."

(*Sifré Num.* 1:X.3)

God's presence went with Israel in the wilderness, as Scripture says:

A. R. Simeon b. Yohai says, "What is said is not, 'the ark of the covenant of the Lord went before them,' but rather, '*and* the ark of the covenant of the Lord went before them.'

B. "[The *and* refers to the fact that God, as well as the ark, went before them, thus:] the matter may be compared to the case of a viceroy who went before his armies, preparing the way before them so that they would take up an encampment. So the Presence of God went before Israel and prepared the way before them so that they would take up an encampment."

(*Sifré Num.* 82:II.2)

God's presence here should be understood as God as person, since God takes action and carries out an active part in the migration.

It nonetheless is difficult to find passages in *Sifré to Numbers* that represent God as a person and the relationship of the individual to God as person to person. The following, however, does portray a relationship. God as person is king, and the individual is to accept God's dominion so as to be taken into account by God and granted mercy:

A. If so, why [in the New Year liturgy] have sages placed [verses referring to] the sounding of the ram's horn for God's sovereignty first, then for remembrance second, and finally for the ram's horn blasts?

B. The sense is: first of all accept him as king over you, then seek mercy from him, so that you will be remembered by him, and how? With the ram's horn of freedom.

(Sifré Num. 77:IV.2)

Here the relationship of one "you" to another seems to me to permit us to conclude that God is conceived to be a person, not merely a premise or a presence of an abstract sort.

God as a person deeply engaged in Israel's life comes to richest expression in the view that God shares Israel's fate. Therefore, when Israel suffers so does God. When Israel goes into exile so does God. And when Israel will be redeemed God will join in the celebration. The following brings the matter to complete formulation:

A. "[And whenever the ark set out, Moses said], 'Arise, O Lord, and let your enemies be scattered, [and let them that hate you flee before you.' And when it rested, he said, 'Return O Lord to the ten thousand thousands of Israel']" (Num. 10:29–36):
B. The enemies to be scattered are those who are gathered together.
C. "And let them that hate you flee before you:" these are those who pursue [Israel].
D. "From before *you*" do they flee, but we are nothing before them. But when your presence is with us, we are a considerable force before them, and when your presence is not with us, we are as nothing before them.

(Sifré Num. 84:III.1)

The first proposition is that Israel without God's presence is nothing. Then comes the telling point that God and Israel form a union:

A. ". . . and let them that hate you flee before you:"
B. And do those who hate [come before] him who spoke and brought the world into being?
C. The purpose of the verse at hand is to say that whoever hates Israel is as if he hates him who spoke and by his word brought the world into being.
D. Along these same lines: "In the greatness of your majesty you overthrow your adversaries" (Ex. 15:7).
E. And are there really adversaries before him who spoke and by his word brought the world into being? But Scripture thus indicates that whoever rose up against Israel is as if he rose up against the Omnipresent. . . .

V. And whoever gives help to Israel is as if he gives help to him who spoke and by his word brought the world into being, as it is said, "Curse Meroz, says the angel of the Lord, curse bitterly its inhabitants, because they came not to the help of the Lord, to the help of the Lord against the mighty" (Jud. 5:23).

W. R. Simeon b. Eleazar says, "You have no more prized part of the body than the eye and Israel has been compared to it. A further comparison: if a man is hit on his head, only his eyes feel it. Accordingly, You have no more prized part of the body than the eye, and Israel has been compared to it. . . ."

EE. So you find, furthermore, that so long as Israel is subjugated, it is as if the Presence of God is subjugated with them, as it is said, "And they saw the God of Israel, and there was under his feet as it were a pavement of sapphire stone, like the very heaven for clearness" (Ex. 24:10).

FF. And so Scripture says, "In all their suffering is suffering for him" (Is. 63:9).

GG. I know only that that is the case for the suffering of the community. How do I know that it also is the case for the suffering of the individual?

HH. Scripture says, "When he calls me, I will answer him; I will be with him in trouble, I will rescue him and honor him" (Ps. 91:15). . . .

LL. R. Aqiba says, "If an available verse of Scripture had not said it, it would not have been possible to say it: Israel said before the Omnipresent, 'You have redeemed yourself.'"

MM. And so you find that everywhere [Israel] has been exiled, the Presence of God is with them, as it is said, "I revealed myself to the house of your father when they were in Egypt subject to the house of Pharaoh" (1 Sam. 2:27).

NN. When they were exiled to Babylonia, the Presence of God was with them: "On your account I was sent to Babylonia" (Is. 43:14).

OO. When they were exiled to Elam, the Presence of God was with them: "I set my throne in Elam" (Jer. 49:38).

PP. When they were exiled to Edom, the Presence of God was with them: "Who is this who comes up from Edom, in crimsoned garments from Bozrah" (Is. 63:1).

QQ. When they come back, the Presence of God will return with them, as it is said, "And the Lord your God will return your fortune" (Deut. 30:3). What is written is not will return, but *will come.*

RR. And Scripture further states, "With me from Lebanon, O bride, with me you shall come from Lebanon" (Song 4:8).

(Sifré Num. 84:IV.1)

The personhood of God seems to me fully exposed in the passage at hand, which treats people and God as a single complementary entity in the world. God's traits as a person are made explicit:

A. "And the Lord came down in a pillar of cloud and stood at the door of the tent [and called Aaron and Miriam; and they both came forward]:"
B. The trait of mortals is not the trait of the Holy One, blessed be he.
C. The trait of mortals is such that, when a mortal goes out to war, he goes out with many men, and when he goes out in peace, he goes out with only a few men.
D. But he who spoke and brought the world into being is not that way. Rather, when he goes out to war, he goes out only alone, as it says, "The Lord is a man of war, the Lord is his name" (Ex. 15:3). But when he comes in peace, he comes with thousands and ten thousands, as it is said, "With mighty chariotry, twice ten thousand, thousands upon thousands, the Lord came from Sinai into the holy place" (Ps. 68:17).

(Sifré Num. 102:III.1)

The traits of God are formed in the same terms as those of humanity, but God is the opposite of a human being.

Sifré Deut. 22 has "the holy spirit" rest on Rahab. God's person as the Holy Spirit, communicating with mortals, surely falls into the classification of a "you." Israel are God's children:

You are the children of the Lord your God (Deut. 14:1):
    R. Judah says, "If you conduct yourselves like [dutiful] children, you are his children, and if not, you are not his children."

(Sifré Deut. 96 [Hammer, p. 144])

Each Israelite is precious to God (*Sifré Deut.* 97). More interesting, God is characterized as experiencing joy and sorrow, specifically in relationship to Israel, and this is a personal trait:

"For the Lord will judge his people" (Deut. 32:35):
    When the Holy One . . . judges the nations, he rejoices in it, but when he judges Israel . . . he regrets it,
    as it is said, ". . . and repent himself for his servants" (Deut. 32:36).
    Repent always means regret, as it is said, "For I repent that I made them" (Gen. 5:6).
    And "I repent that I set up Saul as king" (1 Sam. 15:11).

(Sifré Deut. 326 [Hammer, p. 338, revised somewhat])

Along these same lines, when God takes the soul of a righteous person, it is done gently (*Sifré Deut.* 357). The fact permits imputing to God certain traits of personality and character, and so throughout.

PERSONALITY

No passage in the samples at hand speaks of God as a fully described personality. Stories vastly amplifying scriptural narratives do occur in *Sifré to Deuteronomy,* but these stories do not involve God as a protagonist. Quite to the contrary, Moses as hero is critical; a kind of straight man, God serves only as a conversation partner, framing statements to respond to the thoughts of Moses:

> Rabbi Nathan says, "Moses was saddened by the fact that one of his sons had not been appointed leader. So the Holy One, blessed be he, said to him, 'Why are you saddened because one of your sons had not been appointed? Are not your brother Aaron's sons like your own sons? The man whom I am appointing over Israel will still have to go and stand humbly at Eleazar's doorway.'"
>
> To what may this be likened? To a mortal king who had a son unworthy of the kingship. . . .
>
> The Holy One, blessed be he, said to the angel of death, "Go and bring me the soul of Moses."
>
> The angel went and stood before Moses and said to him . . .
>
> *(Sifré Deut.* 305 [Hammer, p. 294])

In this story God exhibits no traits of personality; God just says things pertinent to the issue, without producing any sort of identifiable characterization. The entire colloquy on the death of Moses is carried on with the angel; God plays no part. Results already in hand hardly require extensive restatement. The important conclusion is a negative one. God as a fully etched personality, sharing human appearance, feelings and attitudes, patterns of thought and action, does not play a significant role in the character of divinity portrayed in the documents at hand.

5

Torah Incarnate: Tractate *Avot*

THE TEXT

Located in the Mishnah (ca. A.D. 200) and serving as its first and most important apologetic, tractate *Avot* (ca. A.D. 250) strings together sayings of important authorities, from Sinai to one generation beyond the redaction of the Mishnah itself. The composition, called in English "the sayings of the founders," quite naturally rests upon the premises of the document it explains. But precisely how God appears in *Avot* is not to be predicted merely on that basis. Since the tractate is both brief and critical to the entire statement of the Judaism of the dual Torah, we shall review it in its entirety. I shall comment episodically, as required, and then summarize the result at the end.

Chapter One

1:1. Moses received the Torah at Sinai and handed it on to Joshua, Joshua to elders, and elders to prophets. And prophets handed it on to the men of the great assembly. They said three things: Be prudent in judgment. Raise up many disciples. Make a fence for the Torah.

The Mishnah's great apologia begins with remarkable reticence about the source of the Torah, but, of course, the authorship takes for granted that God gave what Moses received. Then why not say so? The obvious answer is that the important point for this authorship was not the source but the mode of transmission and what was handed on, which was the Torah; that is what is at stake in the allegation contained in the chain of tradition. God constitutes precisely what, in the Mishnah, we anticipate: the premise.

From this point onward, where God forms a presence it will be by inference, with reference to "heaven," and through similar circumlocutions and circumventions of the obvious. The presence of God makes a difference to one's attitude or intention; one relates to God through right attitude, which is one of acceptance and loyal service rather than exchange between equals, let alone coercion. In what follows, God or "heaven" defines right attitudes.

1:2. Simeon the Righteous was one of the last survivors of the great assembly. He would say: On three things does the world stand: On the Torah, and on the Temple service, and on deeds of loving kindness.

1:3. Antigonus of Sokho received [the Torah] from Simeon the Righteous. He would say: Do not be like servants who serve the master on condition of receiving a reward, but [be] like servants who serve the master not on condition of receiving a reward. And let the fear of Heaven be upon you.

The correct attitude toward God is awe, "fear of heaven" expressing that right attitude. At this point we find in an explicit statement the issue of intentionality (the reason one does the right thing) joined with the relationship to God. One should serve God with the correct intention, which is awe or fear, not as an act of condescension or choice but as one of obligation and duty. Here we find the missing link between intentionality and God, and at this point, the Mishnaic system takes within its active and generative framework what in the Mishnah itself seemed to me remote. God then is present and, further, as person also responds to and cares about the human person's attitude. God is not merely the one who gave the Torah, that is, who made the rules. God is now the one who, day to day and everywhere, sees to the correct working of the rules. And God knows and responds to the attitudes of those who obey the rules, hence, a person. The proportion and place of God in the spinning out of the sayings should not, however, be overestimated, as the long string of sayings of a juridical character, which now follows, indicates.

1:4. Yosé ben Yoezer of Zeredah and Yosé ben Yohanan of Jerusalem received [the Torah] from them. Yosé ben Yoezer says: Let your house be a gathering place for sages. And wallow in the dust of their feet, and drink in their words with gusto.

1:5.   Yosé ben Yohanan of Jerusalem says: Let your house be open wide. And seat the poor at your table ["make the poor members of your household"]. And don't talk too much with women. (He referred to a man's wife, all the more so is the rule to be applied to the wife of one's fellow. In this regard did sages say: So long as a man talks too much with a woman, he brings trouble on himself, wastes time better spent on studying the Torah, and ends up an heir of Gehenna.)

1:6.   Joshua ben Perahyah and Nittai the Arbelite received [the Torah] from them. Joshua ben Perahyah says: Set up a master for yourself. And get yourself a companion-disciple. And give everybody the benefit of the doubt.

1:7.   Nittai the Arbelite says: Keep away from a bad neighbor. And don't get involved with a bad person. And don't give up hope of retribution.

1:8A.   Judah ben Tabbai and Simeon ben Shetah received [the Torah] from them.

1:8B.   Judah ben Tabbai says: Don't make yourself like one of those who advocate before judges [while you yourself are judging a case]. And when the litigants stand before you, regard them as guilty. But when they leave you, regard them as acquitted (when they have accepted your judgment).

1:9.   Simeon ben Shetah says: Examine the witnesses with great care. And watch what you say, lest they learn from what you say how to lie.

1:10.   Shemaiah and Avtalyon received [the Torah] from them. Shemaiah says: Love work. Hate authority. Don't get friendly with the government.

1:11.   Avtalyon says: Sages, watch what you say, lest you become liable to the punishment of exile, and go into exile to a place of bad water, and disciples who follow you drink bad water and die, and the name of Heaven be thereby profaned.

Once more the entry of heaven carries in its wake instructions on correct motivation or attitude. One should follow the stated rule so as to avoid disgracing heaven. Then along with an attitude of service and obligation comes the sanction of fear or shame. God the person shares the attitudes of humanity, being anthropopathic or congruent in feelings and emotions. That premise, present now, runs through the document. It will not have surprised the authorship of the Mishnah, with its keen interest in attitude and conduct when one is at prayer, in the assumption that God pays attention to such matters as would an earthly ruler.

1:12. Hillel and Shammai received [the Torah] from them. Hillel says: Be disciples of Aaron, loving peace and pursuing grace, loving people and drawing them near to the Torah.

1:13A. He would say [in Aramaic]: A name made great is a name destroyed, and one who does not add, subtracts.

1:13B. And who does not learn is liable to death. And the one who uses the crown, passes away.

1:14. He would say: If I am not for myself, who is for me? And when I am for myself, what am I? And if not now, when?

1:15. Shammai says: Make your learning of the Torah a fixed obligation. Say little and do much. Greet everybody cheerfully.

1:16. Rabban Gamaliel says: Set up a master for yourself. Avoid doubt. Don't tithe by too much guesswork.

1:17. Simeon his son says: All my life I grew up among the sages, and I found nothing better for a person [the body] than silence. And not the learning is the thing, but the doing. And whoever talks too much causes sin.

1:18. Rabban Simeon ben Gamaliel says: On three things does the world stand: on justice, on truth, and on peace. As it is said, "Execute the judgment of truth and peace in your gates" (Zech. 8:16).

The opening chain of tradition twice makes the same important point concerning the right attitude toward heaven. God assuredly forms the implicit premise of the account of the origin and transmission of the Torah. Yet if we were to ask where and how God plays a part as fully exposed personality, I cannot point to a pertinent passage. God as presence and person comes to ample instantiation here. But that reaches the limits of metaphor: God is like a human being in feeling and attitude. Nothing in tractate *Avot* chapters 2, 3, and 4 changes that picture or augments it. Still, surveying the entire text will allow the reader to examine the way in which the Mishnah's great apologists have set forth, in their own words, the character of divinity as they wish to portray that character.

Chapter Two

2:1. Rabbi [Judah the Patriarch] says: What is the straight path which a person should choose for himself? Whatever is an ornament to the one who follows it, and an ornament in the view of others. Be meticulous in a small religious duty as in a large one, for you do not know what sort of reward is coming for any of the various religious duties. And reckon with the loss [required] in carrying out a religious duty against the reward for doing it; and the reward for committing a transgression against the loss for doing it. And keep your eye on three things, so you will not come into the clutches of transgression. Know what is above you. An eye which sees, and an ear which hears, and all your actions are written down in a book.

The eye which sees, the ear which hears, the book—these now constitute a presence, which, in the nature of things, we are justified in naming God. God then hears and knows all things that individuals do, a position that accords with the Mishnah's view that God hears and answers prayer and responds to appropriate petition.

2:2. Rabban Gamaliel, a son of Rabbi Judah the Patriarch says: Fitting is learning in the Torah along with a craft, for the labor put into the two of them makes one forget sin. And all learning of the Torah which is not joined with labor is destined to be null and causes sin. And all who work with the community—let them work with them [the community] for the sake of Heaven. For the merit of the fathers strengthens them, and the righteousness which they do stands forever. And, as for you, I credit you with a great reward, as if you had done [all the work required by the community].

"For the sake of Heaven," that is, "for God's sake," defines the correct intention or motive. What that means is pretty much coherent with the earlier appeal, namely, for the service of God, not for one's own benefit.

2:3. Be wary of the government, for they get friendly with a person only for their own convenience. They look like friends when it is to their benefit, but they do not stand by a person when he is in need.
2:4. He would say: Make His wishes into your own wishes, so that He will make your wishes into His wishes. Put aside your wishes on account of His wishes, so that He will put aside the wishes of other people in favor of your wishes. Hillel says: Do not walk out on the community. And do not have confidence in yourself until the day you die. And do not judge your companion until you are in his place. And do not say anything which cannot be heard, for in the end it will be heard. And do not say: When I have time, I shall study, for you may never have time.

Serving "for the sake of Heaven" finds its counterpart in another statement on right attitude. One should want what God wants, so that God will want what the person wants. This is immediately qualified: one should accede to God's wishes over one's own desires, which will provoke a counterpart action in heaven. Here God finds representation as, if not a personality, then a person, with wishes that respond to those of the human being. I cannot point in the Mishnah to an explicit statement of that view, though God's confirmation of human intention forms a persistent motif in the articulation of the Mishnah's law. What is therefore striking is the certainty of the authorship before us that God's feelings and emotions and desires correspond to those of humanity. One's duty, then, is to subordinate one's feelings and desires to those of God, conceived once more as the master to whom everyone relates as subordinate—but who then will respond to the will and wishes of subordinates of appropriate demeanor and conduct.

2:5. He would say: A coarse person will never fear sin, nor will an *am haares* ever be pious, nor will a shy person learn, nor will an ignorant person teach, nor will anyone too occupied in business get wise. In a place where there are no individuals, try to be an individual.

2:6. Also, he saw a skull floating on the water and said to it [in Aramaic]: Because you drowned others, they drowned you, and in the end those who drowned you will be drowned.

Here is a routine allegation about the perfect justice meted out from heaven. This has no bearing on God as person, but it does presuppose God's constant oversight of earthly transactions and the divine interest in a just and fair settlement of all debts.

2:7. He would say: Lots of meat, lots of worms; lots of property, lots of worries; lots of women, lots of witchcraft; lots of slave girls, lots of lust; lots of slave boys, lots of robbery. Lots of the Torah, lots of life; lots of discipleship, lots of wisdom; lots of counsel, lots of understanding; lots of righteousness, lots of peace. [If] one has gotten a good name, he has gotten it for himself. [If] he has gotten teachings of the Torah, he has gotten himself life eternal.

The notion of Torah-teachings as guarantor of eternal life rests on the premise of God as giver of the Torah.

2:8A.   Rabban Yohanan ben Zakkai received [the Torah] from Hillel and Shammai. He would say: If you have learned much Torah, do not puff yourself up on that account, for it was for that purpose that you were created. He had five disciples, and these are they: Rabbi Eliezer ben Hyrcanus, Rabbi Joshua ben Hananiah, Rabbi Yosé the Priest, Rabbi Simeon ben Nethanel, and Rabbi Eleazar ben Arakh.

2:8B.   He would list their good qualities: Rabbi Eliezer ben Hyrcanus—a plastered well, which does not lose a drop of water. Rabbi Joshua—happy is the one who gave birth to him. Rabbi Yosé—a pious man. Rabbi Simeon ben Nethanel—a man who fears sin, and Rabbi Eleazar ben Arakh—a surging spring.

2:8C.   He would say: If all the sages of Israel were on one side of the scale, and Rabbi Eliezer ben Hyrcanus were on the other, he would outweigh all of them.

2:8D.   Abba Saul says in his name: If all of the sages of Israel were on one side of the scale, and Rabbi Eliezer ben Hyrcanus was also with them, and Rabbi Eleazar [ben Arakh] were on the other side, he would outweigh all of them.

2:9A.   He said to them: Go and see what is the straight path to which someone should stick.

2:9B.   Rabbi Eliezer says: A generous spirit. Rabbi Joshua says: A good friend. Rabbi Yosé says: A good neighbor. Rabbi Simeon says: Foresight. Rabbi Eleazar says: Good will.

2:9C.   He said to them: I prefer the opinion of Rabbi Eleazar ben Arakh, because in what he says is included everything you say.

2:9D.   He said to them: Go out and see what is the bad road, which someone should avoid. Rabbi Eliezer says: Envy. Rabbi Joshua says: A bad friend. Rabbi Yosé says: A bad neighbor. Rabbi Simeon says: A loan. (All the same is a loan owed to a human being and a loan owed to the Omnipresent, the blessed, as it is said, "The wicked borrows and does not pay back, but the righteous person deals graciously and hands over [what is owed].") (Ps. 37:21).

2:9E.   Rabbi Eleazar says: Ill will.

2:9F.   He said to them: I prefer the opinion of Rabbi Eleazar ben Arakh, because in what he says is included everything you say.

2:10A.   They [each] said three things.

2:10B.   Rabbi Eliezer says: Let the respect owing to your companion be as precious to you as the respect owing to yourself. And don't be easy to anger. And repent one day before you die. And warm yourself by the fire of the sages, but be careful of their coals, so you don't get burned—for their bite is the bite of a fox, and their sting is the sting of a scorpion, and their hiss is like the hiss of a snake, and everything they say is like fiery coals.

2:11.   Rabbi Joshua says: Envy, desire of bad things, and hatred for people push a person out of the world.

2:12.   Rabbi Yosé says: Let your companion's money be as precious to you as your own. And get yourself ready to learn the Torah, for it does not come as an inheritance to you. And may everything you do be for the sake of Heaven.

2:13.   Rabbi Simeon says: Be meticulous about the recitation of the Shema and the Prayer. And when you pray, don't treat your praying as a matter of routine; but let it be a [plea for] mercy and supplication before the Omnipresent, the blessed, as it is said, "For He is gracious and full of compassion, slow to anger and full of mercy, and repents of the evil" (Joel 2:13). And never be evil in your own eyes.

The authorship of the Mishnah's rules about right attitude in prayer, correct intentionality for instance, will not have found these statements surprising. The imputation to God of the traits of heart and attitude set forth by the prophet seems to me of secondary importance.

2:14.   Rabbi Eleazar says: Be constant in learning of the Torah; And know what to reply to an Epicurean: And know before whom you work, for your employer can be depended upon to pay your wages for what you do.

2:15.   Rabbi Tarfon says: The day is short, the work formidable, the workers lazy, the wages high, the employer impatient.

2:16.   He would say: It's not your job to finish the work, but you are not free to walk away from it. If you have learned much Torah, they will give you a good reward. And your employer can be depended upon to pay your wages for what you do. And know what sort of reward is going to be given to the righteous in the coming time.

These sayings are consistent with those in the opening chapter about the right attitude toward God. One should be the faithful slave, who performs in good conscience and with good will, out of duty, above all, out of trust that God will be present to pay a valid reward for what one does.

Chapter Three

3:1A.   Aqabiah b. Mehallalel says, Reflect upon three things and you will not fall into the clutches of transgression: "Know (1) from whence you come, (2) whither you are going, and (3) before whom you are going to have to give a full account of yourself.

3:1 B.   "From whence do you come? From a putrid drop. Whither are you going? To a place of dust, worms, and maggots.

3:1 C.   "And before whom are you going to give a full account of yourself? Before the King of kings of kings, the Holy One, blessed be he."

We come from nowhere, we go to death, we give our account before the heavenly King, God on high. The familiar attitude that before God as person one gives a full account will have found a ready hearing among the authors of the Mishnah. The important thing is once more the linking of God as person to the correct attitude toward God as person. I think the matter may have been implicit in instructions on prayer. But it is now made explicit as a philosophy of life—a much more encompassing statement.

3:2 A.   R. Hananiah, Prefect of the Priests, says, "Pray for the welfare of the government. For if it were not for fear of it, one man would swallow his fellow alive."

3:2 B.   R. Hananiah b. Teradion says, "[If] two sit together and between them do not pass teachings of the Torah, lo, this is a seat of the scornful, as it is said, 'Nor sits in the seat of the scornful' (Ps. 1:1). But two who are sitting, and words of the Torah do pass between them—the Presence is with them, as it is said, 'Then they that feared the Lord spoke with one another, and the Lord hearkened and heard, and a book of remembrance was written before him, for them that feared the Lord and gave thought to his name' (Mal. 3:16)." I know that this applies to two. How do I know that even if a single person sits and works on the Torah, the Holy One, blessed be he, set aside a reward for him? As it is said, "Let him sit alone and keep silent, because he has laid it upon him" (Lam. 3:28).

The reference to God as Presence surely justifies our seeing God here as person, who attends upon the conversations of mortals, hears and responds to what is said. Here too we find Torah-study treated as the Mishnah treats prayer. The attitudes required for the one are now demanded for the other. The broadening of the person-hood of God takes place in this movement outward from words of prayer to words of Torah-study. Study is treated as counterpart to praying, a position not suggested by the authorship of the Mishnah.

3:3. R. Simeon says, Three who ate at a single table and did not talk about teachings of the Torah while at that table are as though they ate from dead sacrifices (Ps. 106:28), as it is said, "For all tables are full of vomit and filthiness [if they are] without God" (Ps. 106:28). But three who ate at a single table and did talk about teachings of the Torah while at that table are as if they ate at the table of the Omnipresent, blessed is he, as it is said, "And he said to me, This is the table that is before the Lord" (Ez. 41:22).

The point is the same as before, equally explicit and fresh.

3:4. R. Hananiah b. Hakhinai says, (1) He who gets up at night, and (2) he who walks around by himself, and (3) he who turns his desire to emptiness—lo, this person is liable for his life.

3:5. R. Nehunia b. Haqqaneh says, From whoever accepts upon himself the yoke of the Torah do they remove the yoke of the state and the yoke of hard labor. And upon whoever removes from himself the yoke of the Torah do they lay the yoke of the state and the yoke of hard labor.

3:6. R. Halafta of Kefar Hananiah says, Among ten who sit and work hard on the Torah the Presence comes to rest, as it is said, "God stands in the congregation of God" (Ps. 82:1). And how do we know that the same is so even of five? For it is said, "And he has founded his group upon the earth" (Amos 9:6). And how do we know that this is so even of three? Since it is said, "And he judges among the judges" (Ps. 82:1). And how do we know that this is so even of two? Because it is said, "Then they that feared the Lord spoke with one another, and the Lord hearkened and heard" (Mal. 3:16). And how do we know that this is so even of one? Since it is said, "In every place where I record my name I will come to you and I will bless you" (Ex. 20:24).

The shift from prayer to Torah-study once more accounts for the striking allegation that God is present among all those who engage in Torah-study. God is encountered as person in the Torah as much as in prayer, and this point is repeated time and again. Obviously, God is critical to these allegations. But God does not require extensive description; the person remains essentially premise, but the generative inquiry attends to other matters, particularly Torah-study. Tractate *Avot* works out its sayings mainly on the twin themes of study through discipleship and application of the Torah, serving as a handbook for disciples. To that program God is of course necessary but, as to making the points the authorship wishes to register, also insufficient. God is not represented as a sage; God is not portrayed as the model for the disciple or master; and God is not set forth as a student of the Torah. These later motifs never enter the imagination of our authorship. To state the matter very simply, God, now seen as the model and likeness by which the human emotions and attitudes take their measure, has yet to undergo that stage of metaphorization that renders God incarnate. To state matters as our sages would, we are like God as to our right attitudes, and God responds, therefore, to our desires and feelings; but we are not like God as to our very being, our shape and form, our activity and concrete life. We are incarnate in ways that God is not—at least, not yet.

3:7A.   R. Eleazar of Bartota says, Give him what is his, for you and yours are his. For so does it say about David, "For all things come of you, and of your own have we given you" (1 Chron. 29:14).

This saying presents no surprises, affirming, as it does, God's right of possession of all things.

3:7B.   R. Simeon says, He who is going along the way and repeating [his Torah-tradition] but interrupts his repetition and says, How beautiful is that tree! How beautiful is that ploughed field!— Scripture reckons it to him as if he has become liable for his life.

3:8.   R. Dosetai b. R. Yannai in the name of R. Meir says, Whoever forgets a single thing from what he has learned—Scripture reckons it to him as if he has become liable for his life, as it is said, "Only take heed to yourself and keep your soul diligently, lest you forget the words which your eyes saw" (Deut. 4:9). Is it possible that this is so even if his learning became too much for him? Scripture says, "Lest they depart from your heart all the days of your life." Thus he becomes liable for his life only when he will sit down and actually remove [his learning] from his own heart.

3:9A.   R. Haninah b. Dosa says, For anyone whose fear of sin takes precedence over his wisdom, his wisdom will endure. And for anyone whose wisdom takes precedence over his fear of sin, wisdom will not endure.

3:9B.   He would say, Anyone whose deeds are more than his wisdom— his wisdom will endure. And anyone whose wisdom is more than his deeds—his wisdom will not endure.

3:10A. He would say, Anyone from whom people take pleasure—the Omnipresent takes pleasure. And anyone from whom people do not take pleasure, the Omnipresent does not take pleasure.

God's attitudes prove congruent with those of a human being. God then is comparable, once more seen as a person, not merely a premise of being, and our feelings are like God's feelings.

3:10B. R. Dosa b. Harkinas says, (1) Sleeping late in the morning, (2) drinking wine at noon, (3) chatting with children, and (4) attending the synagogues of the ignorant drive a man out of the world.

3:11. R. Eleazar the Modite says, (1) He who treats Holy Things as secular, and (2) he who despises the appointed times, (3) he who humiliates his fellow in public, (4) he who removes the signs of the covenant [that is, the mark of circumcision] of Abraham, our father (may he rest in peace), and (5) he who exposes aspects of the Torah not in accord with the law, even though he has in hand learning in the Torah and good deeds, will have no share in the world to come.

3:12. R. Ishmael says, (1) Be quick [in service] to a superior, (2) efficient in service [to the state], and (3) receive everybody with joy.

3:13. R. Aqiba says, (1) Laughter and lightheadedness turn lewdness into a habit. (2) Tradition is a fence for the Torah. (3) Tithes are a fence for wealth. (4) Vows are a fence for abstinence. (5) A fence for wisdom is silence.

3:14A. He would say, Precious is the human being, who was created in the image [of God]. It was an act of still greater love that it was made known to him that he was created in the image [of God], as it is said, "For in the image of God he made man" (Gen. 9:6).

3:14B. Precious are Israelites, who are called children to the Omnipresent. It was an act of still greater love that it was made known to them that they were called children to the Omnipresent, as it is said, "You are the children of the Lord your God" (Deut. 14:1).

3:14C. Precious are Israelites, to whom was given the precious thing. It was an act of still greater love that it was made known to them that to them was given that precious thing with which the world was made, as it is said, "For I give you a good doctrine. Do not forsake my Torah" (Prov. 4:2).

God's love—like the love of a human being—takes form in God's informing humanity, in particular Israel, of that love. Once more God is given personhood, with traits remarkably like those of the human being who forms the model or the ideal of our authorship. The step yet to be taken will turn the shared psychological traits into a common incarnate being, God as not merely presence but engaged personality. That will be a while in coming. And when it did come, God would play a far more central role in the exposition of diverse authorships than we find assigned to God in tractate *Avot*. From here to the end of the document, the focus remains where our authorship wants it, which is on study of the Torah, discipleship, relationship of deed and deliberation, issues important to circles of sages. To the discourse that follows, God is necessary but insufficient.

3:15.   Everything is foreseen, and free choice is given. In goodness the world is judged. And all is in accord with the abundance of deed[s].

3:16A.   He would say, (1) All is handed over as a pledge, (2) And a net is cast over all the living. (3) The store is open, (4) the storekeeper gives credit, (5) the account-book is open, and (6) the hand is writing.

3:16B.   (1) Whoever wants to borrow may come and borrow. (2) The charity-collectors go around every day and collect from man whether he knows it or not. (3) And they have grounds for what they do. (4) And the judgment is a true judgment. (5) And everything is ready for the meal.

3:17A.   R. Eleazar b. Azariah says, If there is no learning of the Torah, there is no proper conduct. If there is no proper conduct, there is no learning in the Torah. If there is no wisdom, there is no reverence. If there is no reverence, there is no wisdom. If there is no understanding, there is no knowledge. If there is no knowledge, there is no understanding. If there is no sustenance, there is no Torah-learning. If there is no Torah-learning, there is no sustenance.

3:17B.   He would say, Anyone whose wisdom is greater than his deeds—to what is he to be likened? To a tree with abundant foliage, but few roots. When the winds come, they will uproot it and blow it down, as it is said, "He shall be like a tamarisk in the desert and shall not see when good comes, but shall inhabit the parched places in the wilderness" (Jer. 17:6). But anyone whose deeds are greater than his wisdom—to what is he to be likened? To a tree with little foliage, but abundant roots. For even if all the winds in the world were to come and blast at it, they will not move it from its place, as it is said, "He shall be as a tree planted by the waters, and that spreads out its roots by the river, and shall not fear when heat comes, and his leaf shall be green, and shall not be careful in the year of drought, neither shall cease from yielding fruit" (Jer. 17:8).

3:18. R. Eleazar Hisma says, The laws of bird-offerings and of the beginning of the menstrual period—they are indeed the essentials of the Torah. Calculation of the equinoxes and reckoning the numerical value of letters are the savories of wisdom.

Chapter Four

4:1. Ben Zoma says, Who is a sage? He who learns from everybody, as it is said, "From all my teachers I have gotten understanding" (Ps. 119:99). Who is strong? He who overcomes his desire, as it is said, "He who is slow to anger is better than the mighty, and he who rules his spirit than he who takes a city" (Prov. 16:32). Who is rich? He who is happy in what he has, as it is said, "When you eat the labor of your hands, happy will you be, and it will go well with you" (Ps. 128:2). ("Happy will you be—in this world, and it will go well with you—in the world to come.") Who is honored? He who honors everybody, as it is said, "For those who honor me I shall honor, and they who despise me will be treated as of no account" (1 Sam. 2:30).

4:2. Ben Azzai says, Run after the most minor religious duty as after the most important, and flee from transgression. For doing one religious duty draws in its wake doing yet another, and doing one transgression draws in its wake doing yet another. For the reward of doing a religious duty is a religious duty, and the reward of doing a transgression is a transgression.

4:3. He would say, Do not despise anybody and do not treat anything as unlikely. For you have no one who does not have his time, and you have nothing which does not have its place.

4:4A. R. Levitas of Yavneh says, Be exceedingly humble, for the future of humanity is the worm.

4:4B. R. Yohanan b. Beroqa says, Whoever secretly treats the Name of Heaven as profane publicly pays the price. All the same are the one who does so inadvertently and the one who does so deliberately, when it comes to treating the name of Heaven as profane.

Divine justice is given a concrete form. God responds to the way in which "the name of heaven" is treated.

4:5A. R. Ishmael, his son, says, He who learns so as to teach—they give him a chance to learn and to teach. He who learns so as to carry out his teachings—they give him a chance to learn, to teach, to keep, and to do.

4:5B. R. Sadoq says, Do not make [Torah-teachings] a crown in which to glorify yourself or a spade with which to dig. So did Hillel say, He who uses the crown perishes. Thus have you learned: Whoever derives worldly benefit from teachings of the Torah takes his life out of this world.

Right attitude toward heaven defines right attitude toward Torah-study, and correct intentionality once more forms the centerpiece of the whole.

4:6.   R. Yose says, Whoever honors the Torah himself is honored by people. And whoever disgraces the Torah himself is disgraced by people.

4:7.   R. Ishmael, his son, says, He who avoids serving as a judge avoids the power of enmity, robbery, and false swearing. And he who is arrogant about making decisions is a fool, evil, and prideful.

4:8.   He would say, Do not serve as a judge by yourself, for there is only One who serves as a judge all alone. And do not say, "Accept my opinion." For they have the choice in the matter, not you.

4:9.   R. Jonathan says, Whoever keeps the Torah when poor will in the end keep it in wealth. And whoever treats the Torah as nothing when he is wealthy in the end will treat it as nothing in poverty.

4:10.   R. Meir says, Keep your business to a minimum and make your business the Torah. And be humble before everybody. And if you treat the Torah as nothing, you will have many treating you as nothing. And if you have labored in the Torah, [the Torah] has a great reward to give you.

4:11A. R. Eleazar b. Jacob says, He who does even a single religious duty gets himself a good advocate. He who does even a single transgression gets himself a powerful prosecutor. Penitence and good deeds are like a shield against punishment.

4:11B. R. Yohanan Hassandelar says, Any gathering which is for the sake of Heaven is going to endure. And any which is not for the sake of Heaven is not going to endure.

4:12.   R. Eleazar b. Shammua says, The honor owing to your disciple should be as precious to you as yours. And the honor owing to your fellow should be like the reverence owing to your master. And the reverence owing to your master should be like the awe owing to Heaven.

By this point the implications scarcely require articulation. One's right attitude toward heaven takes shape in the model of the right attitude of a slave toward the master; awe, obedience, duty. In such a pattern God as person is fully present.

4:13A. R. Judah says, Be meticulous about learning, for error in learning leads to deliberate [violation of the Torah].

4:13B.   R. Simeon says, There are three crowns: the crown of the Torah, the crown of priesthood, and the crown of sovereignty. But the crown of a good name is best of them all.

4:14.   R. Nehorai says, Go into exile to a place of the Torah, and do not suppose that it will come to you. For your fellow-disciples will make it solid in your hand. And on your own understanding do not rely.

4:15A.   R. Yannai says, We do not have in hand [an explanation] either for the prosperity of the wicked or for the suffering of the righteous.

4:15B.   R. Matya b. Harash says, Greet everybody first, and be a tail to lions. But do not be a head of foxes.

4:16.   R. Jacob says, This world is like an antechamber before the world to come. Get ready in the antechamber, so you can go into the great hall.

4:17.   He would say, Better is a single moment spent in penitence and good deeds in this world than the whole of the world to come. And better is a single moment of inner peace in the world to come than the whole of a lifetime spent in this world.

4:18.   R. Simeon b. Eleazar says, (1) Do not try to make amends with your fellow when he is angry, or (2) comfort him when the corpse of his beloved is lying before him, or (3) seek to find absolution for him at the moment at which he takes vow, or (4) attempt to see him when he is humiliated.

4:19.   Samuel the Small says, "Rejoice not when your enemy falls, and let not your heart be glad when he is overthrown, lest the Lord see it and it displease him, and he turn away his wrath from him" (Prov. 24:17).

4:20.   Elisha b. Abuyah says, He who learns when a child—what is he like? Ink put down on a clean piece of paper. And he who learns when an old man—what is he like? Ink put down on a paper full of erasures.

4:21A.   R. Yose b. R. Judah of Kefar Habbabli says, He who learns from children—what is he like? One who eats sour grapes and drinks fresh wine. And he who learns from old men—what is he like? He who eats ripe grapes and drinks vintage wine.

4:21B.   Rabbi [Judah the Patriarch] says, Do not look at the bottle but at what is in it. You can have a new bottle of old wine, and an old bottle which has not got even new wine.

4:22A.   R. Eleazar Haqqappar says, Jealousy, lust, and ambition drive a person out of this world.

4:22B.   He would say, Those who are born are [destined] to die, and those who die are [destined] for resurrection. And the living are [destined] to be judged—so as to know, to make known, and to confirm that (1) he is God, (2) he is the one who forms, (3) he is the one who creates, (4) he is the one who understands, (5) he is the one who judges, (6) he is the one who gives evidence, (7) he is the one who brings suit, (8) and he is the one who is going to make the ultimate judgment.

4:22C. Blessed be he, for before him are no (1) guile, (2) forgetfulness, (3) respect for persons, or (4) bribe-taking, for everything is his. And know that everything is subject to reckoning. And do not let your evil impulse persuade you that Sheol is a place of refuge for you. For (1) despite your wishes were you formed, (2) despite your wishes were you born, (3) despite your wishes do you live, (4) despite your wishes do you die, and (5) despite your wishes are you going to give a full accounting before the King of kings of kings, the Holy One, blessed be he.

God as person, not merely premise or presence, is richly present here. For now we are told what God is and does, the things one expects from the living and acting God: the ultimate judge. God as the perfect judge, who does not take bribes or respond to cajoling, who demands obedience and duty, emerges as a fully described person. One step remains, and that is the description of God in the concrete terms in which one describes a personality. None of the sayings in chapter 5 seems to me to contribute materially to our inquiry. All of them repeat the main points of emphasis, organizing ideas in a different way from the earlier chapters but saying the same thing.

PREMISE, PRESENCE, PERSON, AND PERSONALITY IN THE FIRST PHASE OF THE JUDAISM OF THE DUAL TORAH

It was at prayer that the authorship of tractate *Avot* encountered God as person, not merely as premise or even as presence. Still more generally, God as person cared for the sources of human action and understood proper from improper motivation. But what God does not do in the tractate is play an active part in the everyday encounter of sages and heaven. By that I mean that these sages did not report on God's discourse with them, what God said to them and what they said to God; they did not tell stories about God's doings. True, they took for granted that God spoke to the prophets and that the Torah contained God's Word. But they do not represent conversations between personalities, human and divine, and they do not—at this stage in the unfolding of the canon—record encounters between God as an active personality and a human being, presumably a sage. Only when we have surveyed documents that do record God's conversations with sages and resort to sustained narratives to portray God's dealings with people shall we have a clear picture of what it means to render God as not solely presence and person but fully incarnate personality. At that point we shall also see why it is necessary to resort to a mode of discourse not present in our tractate, specifically to narrative and, within narrative, storytelling. When God is premise, presence, and even (implicit) person, sayings suffice. We make reference to a premise, allude to a presence, respond to a person. When it comes to portraying a fully vital personality, by contrast, for the authorships at hand (and, I am inclined to think, for all authorships) the incarnate God requires narrative, especially story, for a full and whole portrait. And that God will make a full appearance in the Judaism of the dual Torah. But not yet.

PART THREE

From Person to Personality:
The Character of Divinity
in the Second Phase of
the Judaism of the
Dual Torah, 400–500

6

Oral Torah: The Yerushalmi

THE TALMUDIC PHASE IN THE FORMATION OF JUDAISM: JUDAISM DESPITE CHRISTIANITY

While authorships of canonical documents in the first of the two stages in the formation of the Judaism of the dual Torah exhibit no sign of interest in, or response to, the advent of Christianity, the second stage confronts the challenge of Christianity's political ascendancy. From the Yerushalmi forward, points of stress and emphasis respond to and counter the challenge of Christianity. The point of difference, of course, is that from the beginning of the legalization of Christianity in the early fourth century to the establishment of Christianity at the end of that same century, Jews in the Land of Israel found themselves facing a challenge that, prior to Constantine, they had found no compelling reason to consider. The specific crisis came when the Christians pointed to the success of the church in the politics of the Roman state as evidence that Jesus Christ was king of the world, and that his claim to be Messiah and King of Israel had now found vindication. When the emperor Julian, 361–63, apostasized and renewed state patronage of paganism, he permitted the Jews to begin to rebuild the Temple—part of his large plan of humiliating Christianity. His prompt death on an Iranian battlefield supplied further evidence for heaven's choice of the church and the truth of the church's allegations concerning the standing and authority of Jesus as the Christ. That is why the Judaic documents that reached closure in the century after these events, from 400 onward, attended to those questions of salvation (e.g., doctrine of history and of the Messiah, authority of the sages' reading of Scripture as against the Christians' interpretation, and the like) that had earlier not enjoyed extensive consideration. In all, this second Judaism, which I characterize as a Judaism despite Christianity, met the challenge of the events of the fourth century.

The second phase of the formation of the Judaism of the dual Torah is marked by the completion of the Yerushalmi and associated writings. Sages worked out in the pages of the Yerushalmi and in the exegetical compilations of the age a Judaism intersecting with the Mishnah's but essentially asymmetrical with it. That Talmud presented a system of salvation, but one focused on the salvific power of the sanctification of the holy people. The first of the two Talmuds, the one closed at the end of the fourth century, set the compass and locked it into place. The Yerushalmi is not like the Mishnah, which provides a full and exhaustive account of its system and its viewpoint. Whatever we know about the Mishnah's system is in that book itself. Indeed the Yerushalmi and the Mishnah are really not comparable to one another. The Yerushalmi is continuous with the Mishnah. But the character of the document, therefore also the world to which its evidence pertains, presents us with a mirror image of the Mishnah. The Mishnah, is ca. A.D. 200, described an orderly world in which Israelite society is neatly divided among its castes, arranged in priority around the center that is the temple, systematically engaged in a life of sanctification remote from the disorderly events of the day.

While the Yerushalmi aims principally at the exegesis and amplification of the laws of the Mishnah, it also points toward a matrix beyond its text. On the one hand, the Yerushalmi's authorship's interest in the Mishnah's statements is purposeful. Transcending the Mishnah's facts, it expresses the speculative concerns of philosophical lawyers wholly within the framework of the Mishnah's modes of thought. But these same exegetes—both the ones who are named and the still more influential ones who speak through the Yerushalmi's single voice—speak implicitly within the frame-work of a larger world view, not exhausted by the Mishnah. So they bring to the Mishnah a program defined outside of the Mish-nah and expressing concerns of a segment of society beyond their own immediate circle. To begin with, the Yerushalmi's discussions are not limited to the contents of the Mishnah. Discourse encom-passes a world of institutions, authorities, and effective power that predominates quite beyond the imagination of the Mishnah's framers. Furthermore, the Talmud's picture of that world essen-tially ignores the specifications, for these same matters, of the Mishnah's law.

To take one striking example, the Mishnah's government for Is-rael rests upon a high priest and a king, with administrative courts ascending to the authority of the Temple mount. The Yerushalmi does not even pretend that such a world exists, knowing instead a set of small-claims courts and petty bureaus of state over which rabbis, defined as judges, lawyers, and masters of disciples in the law, preside. At the head of it all is a patriarch, not a priest anointed for the purpose. That example provides an instance of the curious discontinuity between the Mishnah's view of the world and of the society of Israel on the one side, and that of the Yerushalmi, contin-uous with the Mishnah and framed as little more than an exegesis of that code, on the other side. When I speak of a second phase in the unfolding of the documents of the Judaism of the dual Torah, that discontinuity serves to clarify my meaning.

The Mishnah took as its critical issue the matter of whether and how "Israel" remained a holy people, because that issue proved acute in the period of the Mishnah's framers' systematic work, the mid-second century. The Mishnah therefore is a document worked out in a world in which Christianity made no impact, so far as Is-rael's sages were concerned. Their minds were elsewhere. When, we recall, in the aftermath of the destruction in A.D. 70, sages worked out a Judaism without a temple and a cult, they produced the Mishnah, a system of sanctification focused on the holiness of the priesthood, the cultic festivals, the temple, and its sacrifices as well as on the rules for protecting that holiness from levitical un-cleanness—four of the six divisions of the Mishnah on a single theme. The Mishnah's system stresses the issue of sanctification, pure and simple. The Talmud of the Land of Israel, by contrast, reached closure approximately a century after the political triumph of Christianity. In the aftermath of the conversion of the Roman Empire to Christianity and the confirmation of the triumph of Christianity in the generation beyond Julian "the apostate," 361–63, when sages worked out, in the pages of the Talmud of the Land of Israel and in the exegetical compilations of the era, a Judaism intersecting with the Mishnah's but essentially asymmetrical with it, it was a system for salvation but one focused on the salvific power of the sanctification of the holy people. Given the political changes of the age, their implications for the meaning and end of history as Israel would experience it, the fresh emphasis on salvation, the introduction of the figure of the Messiah as a principal teleological force, and the statement of an eschatological teleology for the system as a whole constitute answers to urgent questions. The questions were raised by Christian theologians, the answers provided by the Judaic sages. The former held that the Christian triumph confirmed the Christhood of Jesus, the rejection of Israel, the end of Israel's hope for salvation at the end of time. The latter offered the Torah in its dual media, the affirmation of Israel as children of Abraham, Isaac, and Jacob, the coming of the Messiah at the end of time. The questions and answers fit the challenge of the age.

The political triumph of Christianity brought about changes of a fundamental character. Those changes effected upon the received system marked dramatic shifts in the modes of symbolization of the canon, of the system as a whole, and of the purpose and goal of the system. Each of the important changes in the documents first redacted at the end of the fourth century dealt with a powerful challenge presented by the triumph of Christianity in Constantine's age. That is the basis on which I maintain that the Judaism of the dual Torah took as its set of urgent questions the issue defined by Christianity as it assumed control of the Roman Empire, and that it provided as self-evidently valid answers a system deriving its power from the Torah, read by sages, embodied by sages, exemplified by sages, as the reply. A very rapid survey of the principal points in the political challenge of triumphant Christianity suffices.

The first change revealed in the unfolding of the sages' canon pertains to the use of Scripture. The change at hand specifically is in making books out of the collection of exegeses of Scripture. That represents an innovation because the Mishnah, and the exegetical literature that served the Mishnah, did not take shape around the order of biblical passages, even when relevant, let alone the explanation of verses of Scripture. The authorship of the Mishnah and its principal heirs followed their own program, which was a topical one. They arranged ideas by subject matter. But in the third, and especially in the later fourth centuries, other writings entering the canon took shape around the explanation of verses of Scripture, not a set of topics. What this meant was that a second mode of organizing ideas, besides the topical mode paramount for the Mishnah, the Tosefta, the Yerushalmi (and the Bavli later on), now made its way. With Christianity addressing the world (including the Jews) with a systematic exegetical apologetic, beginning of course with Matthew's and the other Gospels' demonstration of how events in the life of Jesus fulfilled, as a living exegesis, the prophecies of the shared Scripture, a Judaic response took the form of a counterpart exegesis. When, in the Mishnah, sages found a systematic exegesis of Scripture unnecessary, it was because they saw no need, there being no reading contrary to theirs that presented a challenge to them. But the Christians did compose a powerful apologetic out of the systematic exegesis of the shared Scripture and, confronting that challenge when Christianity made further indifference impolitic and impossible, sages replied with their compositions.

By the fourth century the church had reached a consensus on the bulk of the New Testament canon, having earlier accepted the Old Testament as its own. Accordingly, the issue of Scripture had come to the fore, and in framing the question of Scripture the church focused sages' attention on that larger matter of systematic exegesis. When, for example, Jerome referred to the Jews' having a "second" Torah, one that was not authoritative, and when a sequence of important fathers of the church produced exegeses of Scripture in profoundly christological terms, the issue was raised. It would be joined when sages speaking on their own and to their chosen audience went through pretty much the same processes. This they did by explaining the standing of that "second Torah," and by producing not merely counterpart exegeses to those of the Christians but counterpart compilations of such exegeses.

The generative symbol of the literary culture of the sages, the Torah, stands for the system as a whole. From the Yerushalmi onward, the symbol of the Torah took on the meaning that, when Judaism had reached its final form at the end of this period, would prove indicative. It was the doctrine that when Moses received the Torah at Mount Sinai, it came down with him in two media, written and oral. The written Torah was transmitted, as its name says, through writing and is now contained in the canon of Scripture. The oral Torah was transmitted through the process of formulation for ease in memorization and then through the memories of sages and their disciples from Moses and Joshua to the most current generation. That doctrine of the dual Torah, that is of the Torah in two media, came about in response to the problem of explaining the standing and authority of the Mishnah. But the broadening of the symbol of the Torah first took shape around the figure of the sage. That symbolism accounted for the sages' authority. Only later on, in the fourth century in the pages of the Yerushalmi, did the doctrine of the dual Torah reach expression. So in the unfolding of the documents of the canon of Judaism, the generative symbol of Torah reveals a striking change. Beginning as a rather generalized account of how sages' teachings relate to God's will, the symbol of Torah gained concrete form in its application to the dual Torah, written and oral, Scripture and Mishnah. Within the unfolding of the canonical writings such a shift represents a symbolic change of fundamental character.

When we speak of *torah* in rabbinical literature of late antiquity, we no longer denote a particular book on the one side, or the contents of such a book on the other. Instead, we connote a broad range of clearly distinct categories of noun and verb, concrete fact and abstract relationship alike. "Torah" stands for a kind of human being. It connotes a social status and a sort of social group. It refers to a type of social relationship. It further denotes a legal status and differentiates things and persons, actions and status, points of social differentiation and legal and normative standing as well as "revealed truth." In all, the main points of insistence of the whole of Israel's life and history come to full symbolic expression in that single word. If people wanted to explain how they would be saved, they would use the word "Torah." If they wished to sort out their parlous relationships with Gentiles, they would use the word "Torah." Torah stood for salvation and accounted for Israel's this-worldly condition and the hope, for both individual and nation alike, of life in the world to come. For the kind of Judaism under discussion, therefore, the word "Torah" stood for everything. The Torah symbolized the whole, at once and entire.

The ultimate position was that there were two forms or media in which the Torah reached Israel: one Torah in writing, the other Torah handed on orally, that is, in memory. This final step, fully revealed in the Yerushalmi, brought the conception of Torah to its logical conclusion. Torah came in several media, written, oral, incarnate. So what the sage said was in the status of the Torah, was Torah, because the sage was Torah incarnate. The abstract symbol now had become concrete and material once more. We recognize the many diverse ways in which the Talmud stated that conviction. Every passage in which knowledge of the Torah yields power over this world and the next, capacity to coerce the natural and supernatural worlds alike to the sage's will, rests upon the same viewpoint. The Yerushalmi's theory of the Torah thus carries us through several stages in the processes of the symbolization of the word "Torah." First transformed from something material and concrete into something abstract and beyond all metaphor (the opposite of the process affecting "Israel"), the word "Torah" finally emerged once more in a concrete aspect, now as the encompassing and universal mode of stating the whole doctrine, all at once, of Judaism in its formative age.

The teleology of a system answers the questions of purpose and goal. It explains why someone should do what the system requires. It may also spell out what will happen if someone does or does not do what the system demands. The Mishnah and its successor-documents, *Avot* and the Tosefta, present one picture of the purpose of the system as a whole, a teleology without eschatological focus. The two Talmuds, along with some intermediate documents, later laid forth a different picture, specifically, an eschatological teleology. The documents do cohere. The Talmuds, beginning with the Yerushalmi, the former of the two, to be sure carried forward not only the exegesis of the Mishnah but also the basic values of the Mishnah's system. But they did present substantial changes too, and that is the main point for our purpose.

The philosophers of the Mishnah did not make use of the Messiah myth in the construction of a teleology for their system. They found it possible to present a statement of goals for their projected life of Israel which was entirely separate from appeals to history and eschatology. Since they certainly knew and even alluded to longstanding and widely held convictions on eschatological subjects, beginning with those in Scripture, the framers thereby testified that, knowing the larger repertoire, they made choices different from others before and after them. Their document accurately and ubiquitously expresses these choices, both affirmative and negative. The appearance in the Talmuds of a messianic eschatology fully consonant with the larger characteristic of the rabbinic system—with its stress on the viewpoints and proof texts of Scripture, its interest in what was happening to Israel, its focus upon the national-historical dimension of the life of the group— indicates that the encompassing rabbinic system stands essentially autonomous of the prior, Mishnaic system. True, what had gone before was absorbed and fully assimilated. But the talmudic system, expressed in part in each of the non-Mishnaic segments of the canon and fully spelled out in all of them, is different in the aggregate from the Mishnaic system.

The Mishnah had presented an ahistorical and, in the nature of things, noneschatological teleology and did not make use of the Messiah theme to express its teleology. By contrast, the Talmuds provide an eschatological and therefore a Messiah-centered teleology for their system. Theirs is the more familiar teleology of Judaism, which, from the Talmud of the Land of Israel onward, commonly explains the end and meaning of the system by referring to the end of time and the coming of the Messiah. The teleology of Judaism as it was expressed in the Talmuds of both the Land of Israel and Babylonia thus takes an eschatological shape in its appeal to the end of history. Once people speak of the end of time—the eschaton—moreover, they commonly invoke the figure of a messiah, or the Messiah, who will bring on the end and preside over what happens then. The Judaism that emerged from late antiquity therefore took shape as a profoundly eschatological and messianic statement. The Mishnah's authorship constructed a system of Judaism in which the entire teleological dimension reached full exposure while hardly invoking the person or functions of a messianic figure of any kind. The Mishnah's non-eschatological teleology would then present a striking contrast to that of the Yerushalmi, which framed the teleological doctrine around the person of the Messiah. The issue of eschatology, framed in mythic terms, further draws in its wake the issue of how history comes to full conceptual expression: the symbolization of things that happen into events, the interpretation of the symbol as history, that is, theology. The Mishnah's framers presented no elaborate theory of events, a fact fully consonant with their systematic points of insistence and encompassing concern. One by one events do not matter. The philosopher-lawyers exhibited no theory of history either. Their conception of Israel's destiny in no way called upon historical categories of either narrative or didactic explanation to describe and account for the future. The small importance attributed to the figure of the Messiah as a historical-eschatological figure, therefore, fully accords with the larger traits of the system as a whole. If, as in the Mishnah, what is important in Israel's existence was sanctification, an ongoing process, and not salvation, understood as a one-time event at the end, then no one would find reason to narrate history.

Few then would form the obsession about the Messiah so characteristic of Judaism in its later, rabbinic mode. The figure of the Messiah looms large in both documents. The teleology of the system portrayed in them rests upon the premise of the coming of the Messiah. If one does so and so, the Messiah will come, and if not, the Messiah will tarry. So the compilers and authors of the two Talmuds laid enormous emphasis upon the sin of Israel and the capacity of Israel through repentance both to overcome sin and to bring the Messiah. "The attribute of justice" delays the Messiah's coming. The Messiah will come this very day, if Israel deserves. The Messiah will come when there are no more arrogant ("conceited") Israelites, when judges and officers disappear, when the haughty and judges cease to exist, "Today, if you will obey" (Ps. 95:7). How the characterization of God was affected by these important historical turnings will now form the center of our interest.

PREMISE

The inquiry at hand is not a theological one, concerning principles of God's dominion. If we want to know how in a concrete way God is portrayed, information concerning the principles of divine justice, mercy, and the like, is beside the point. The hypostatization of those principles or traits of divinity does not carry us close to the representation of God as a person. It forms merely a chapter in the systematic presentation of the system's premises. That God gave the Torah of course forms a premise of all discourse, but God's person or personality in giving the Torah is not set forth. So too, it is taken for granted that God, as ruler of all, assigned traits to this one or to that, for example, "The Holy One, blessed be he, gave to Israel three good qualities: modesty, kindness, and caring" (*y. San.* 6:7.II.Z). Along these same lines God, or heaven, is responsible for sending rain:

He came down to them and asked, "Why have the rabbis troubled themselves to come here today?"
  They said to him, "We want you to pray for rain."
  He said to them, "Now do you really need my prayers? Heaven has already done its miracle."

(y. Ta. 1:4.I.AA)

Obviously, the premise is that God has done the miracle of making rain without the wonder-worker's intervention. But the passage does not invoke the presence or person of God in particular; it makes exactly the opposite point, that there is nothing distinctive about the event. Countless passages of such a character restate the simple fact that God forms the premise of all discourse in the Yerushalmi, as in the other writings of the canon of the Judaism of the dual Torah.

But, overall, that fact does not yield rich statement of God as premise. For instance, God's act of revealing the Torah is not augmented or amplified. Rather, we find the passive, for example, "All those forty days that Moses served on the mountain, he studied the Torah but forgot it. In the end it was given to him as a gift" (*y. Hor.* 3:4.I.E). God of course not only gave the Torah but also enforced its laws. That premise of all discourse hardly has to be proven. Just punishment for sin, just reward for merit—these are ordinary facts of life under God's rule. God rules over land and sea, but we have no stories about God's doing so, in person, in any one case (cf., e.g., *y. A.Z.* 4:1.III.H): "An earthly king rules only on dry land but not on the sea, but the Holy One . . . is not so. He is ruler by sea and ruler by land" (*y. A.Z.* 4:1.III.L).

In the following passage, God serves as the origin of all great teachings, but as we have seen, that fact bears no consequences for the description of God as a person or personality:

E. "Given by one shepherd"—
F. Said the Holy One, blessed be he, "If you hear a teaching from an Israelite minor, and it gave pleasure to you, let it not be in your sight as if one has heard it from a minor, but as if one has heard it from an adult,
G. "and let it not be as if one has heard it from an adult, but as if one has heard it from a sage,
H. "and let it not be as if one has heard it from a sage, but as if one has heard it from a prophet,
I. "and let it not be as if one has heard it from a prophet, but as if one has heard it from the shepherd,
J. "and there is as a shepherd only Moses, in line with the following passage: 'Then he remembered the days of old, of Moses his servant. Where is he who brought out of the sea the shepherds of his flock? Where is he who put in the midst of them his holy Spirit?' (Is. 63:11).
K. "It is not as if one has heard it from the shepherd but as if one has heard it from the Almighty.
L. "Given by one Shepherd"—and there is only One who is the Holy One, blessed be he, in line with that which you read in Scripture: "Hear, O Israel: the Lord our God is one Lord" (Deut. 6:4).

(*y. San.* 10:1.IX)

In studying the Torah, sages and disciples clearly met the living God and recorded a direct encounter with and experience of God through the revealed Word of God. But in a statement such as this, alluding to but not clearly describing what it means to hear the Word of the Almighty, God at the end of the line simply forms the premise of revelation. There is no further effort at characterization. The exposition of the work of Creation (*y. Hag.* 2:1.II) refers to God's deeds, mainly by citing verses of Scripture, for example, "Then he made the snow: 'He casts forth his ice like morsels' (Ps. 147:17)," and so on. So too God has wants and desires, for example, what God wants is for Israel to repent, at which time God will save Israel (*y. Ta.* 1:1.X.U), but there is no effort to characterize God.

PRESENCE

God is understood to establish a presence in the world. This is accomplished both through intermediaries such as a retinue of angels and also through the hypostatization of divine attributes, for example, the Holy Spirit, the Presence of *Shekhinah,* and the like. The Holy Spirit makes its appearance, for example, "They were delighted that their opinion proved to be the same as that of the Holy Spirit" (*y. Hor.* 3:5.III.PP; *y. A.Z.* 3:1.II.AA; etc.). God is understood to enjoy a retinue, a court (*y. San.* 1:1IV.Q); God's seal is truth. These and similar statements restate the notion that God forms a living presence in the world. Heaven reaches decisions and conveys them to humankind through the working of chance, for example, a lottery:

To whoever turned up in his hand a slip marked, "Elder," he said, "They have indeed chosen you in Heaven." To whoever turned up in his hand a blank slip, he would say, "What can I do for you? It is from Heaven."
(*y. San.* 1:4.V.FF–GG)

The notion that the lottery conveys God's will, therefore represents God's presence in the decision-making process, will not have surprised the authorship of the Book of Esther. It is one way in which God's presence is given concrete form. Another, also supplied by Scripture, posited that God in the very presence intervened in Israel's history, for example, at the Sea of Reeds:

When the All-Merciful came forth to redeem Israel from Egypt, he did not send a messenger or an angel, but the Holy One, blessed be he, himself came forth, as it is said, "For I will pass through the Land of Egypt that night" (Ex. 12:12)—and not only so, but it was he and his entire retinue.
(*y. San.* 2:1.III.O)

The familiar idea that God's presence went into exile with Israel recurs (*y. Ta.* 1:1.X.E.). But I do not know of a single passage in the entire Yerushalmi in which it is claimed that God's personal presence at a historical event in the time of sages changed the course of events. The notion that God's presence remained in exile leaves God without personality or even ample description.

Where God does take up a presence, it is not uncommonly a literary device, with no important narrative implications. For example, God is assumed to speak through any given verse of Scripture. Therefore the first person will be introduced in connection with citing such a verse, as at *y. San.* 5:1.IV.E, "[God answers,] 'It was an act of love which I did . . . [citing a verse,] "for I said, 'The world will be built upon merciful love'"' (Ps. 89:2)." Here, since the cited verse has an "I," God is given a presence in the colloquy. But it is a mere formality. So too we may say that God has made such and such a statement, which serves not to characterize God but only to supply an attribution for an opinion:

It is written, "These are the words of the letter which Jeremiah . . . sent from Jerusalem to the rest of the elders of the exiles" (Jer. 29:1).
Said the Holy One, blessed be he, "The elders of the exile are valuable to me. Yet more beloved to me is the smallest circle which is located in the Land of Israel than a great sanhedrin located outside of the Land."
(*y. Ned.* 6:9.III.CCCC)

All we have here is a paraphrase and restatement of the cited verse.

Where actions are attributed to God, we have of course to recognize God's presence in context, for example, "The Holy One, blessed be he, kept to himself [and did not announce] the reward that is coming to those who carry out their religious duties, so that they should do them in true faith [without expecting a reward]" (*y. Qid.* 1:7.IX.B). But such a statement hardly constitutes evidence that God is present and active in a given circumstance. It rather forms into a personal statement the principle that one should do religious duties for the right motive, not expecting a reward—a view we found commonplace in tractate *Avot*. So too statements of God's action carry slight characterization, for example, "Even if 999 aspects of the argument of an angel incline against someone, but a single aspect of the case of that angel argues in favor, the Holy One . . . still inclines the scales in favor of the accused" (*y. Qid.* 1:9.II.S). It remains to observe that when we find in the Yerushalmi a sizable narrative of intensely important events, such as the destruction of Betar in the time of Bar Kokhba (*y. Ta.* 4:5.X), God scarcely appears except, again, as premise and source of all that happens. There is no characterization, nor even the claim that God intervened in some direct and immediate way, though I do not believe we can imagine anyone thought otherwise. That simple affirmation reaches expression, for instance, in the observation in connection with the destruction of the Temple, "It appears that the Holy One, blessed be he, wants to exact from our hand vengeance for his blood" (*y. Ta.* 4:5.XIV.Q). That sort of intrusion hardly suggests a vivid presence of God as part of the narrative scheme, let alone a characterization of God as person.

PERSON

Sages in the Yerushalmi may have made up conversations between biblical heroes and God, but when it came to their own day, such conversations took the form of prayers. As to the former:

At that very moment, David said to the Holy One, blessed be he, "Master of the Universe, shall your presence descend upon the earth? May your presence rise up from among them! . . ." [David is urging God to remain over the earth and not among gossip-mongers on earth.]

(*y. Pe.* 1:1.XXV.C [trans. Roger Brooks])

In this case, a conversation between God and David is made up; I cannot point in the Yerushalmi to equivalent conversations involving sages.

But of course God does occur as a "you" throughout the Yerushalmi, most commonly, of course, in a liturgical setting. As in the earlier documents of the oral part of the Torah, so in the Yerushalmi, we have a broad range of prayers to God as "you," illustrated by the following:

R. Ba bar Zabeda in the name of Rab: "[The congregation says this prayer in an undertone:] 'We give thanks to you, for we must praise your name. "My lips will shout for joy when I sing praises to you, my soul also which you have rescued" (Ps. 71:23). Blessed are you, Lord, God of praises.'"

(*y. Ber.* 1:4.VIII.D [trans. Tzvee Zahavy])

Since the formula of the blessing invokes "you," we find nothing surprising in the liturgical person imagined by the framers of various prayers. God's ad hoc intervention, as an active and participating personality, in specific situations is treated as more or less a formality, in that the rules are given and will come into play without ordinarily requiring God to join in a given transaction:

When one enters the study hall, what does he say? "May it be your will, Lord my God, God of my fathers, that I shall not be angry with my colleagues and they not be angry with me; that we not declare what is clean to be unclean and vice versa; that we not declare what is permitted to be forbidden and vice versa; lest I find myself put to shame in this world and in the world to come."

(*y. Ber.* 4:2.I.A [trans. Tzvee Zahavy])

Here we see yet another fine instance in which God is a "you," but in which that "you" does not intervene in a particular case or engage in a concrete and ad hoc transaction. "May it be your will . . . ," a standard liturgical formula, is never followed by a tale showing how, on a specific occasion, God showed that that was indeed the divine will (or the opposite). God was encountered as a very real presence, actively listening to prayers, as in the following:

See how high the Holy One, blessed be he, is above his world. Yet a person can enter a synagogue, stand behind a pillar, and pray in an undertone, and the Holy One, blessed be he, hears his prayers, as it says, "Hannah was speaking in her heart; only her lips moved, and her voice was not heard" (1 Sam. 1:13). Yet the Holy One, blessed be he, heard her prayer.

(*y. Ber.* 9:1.VII.E)

When, however, we distinguish God as person, "you," from God as a well-portrayed active personality, liturgical formulas give a fine instance of the one side of the distinction. In the Yerushalmi's sizable corpus of such prayers, individual and community alike, we never find testimony to a material change in God's decision in a case based on setting aside known rules in favor of an episodic act of intervention, and, it follows, thought on God as person remains continuous with what has gone before. Sages, like everyone else in Israel, believed that God hears and answers prayer. But that belief did not require them to preserve stories about specific instances in which the rules of hearing and answering prayer attested to a particular trait of personality or character to be imputed to God. A specific episode or incident never served to highlight the characterization of divinity in one way, rather than in some other, in a manner parallel to Scripture's authorships' use of stories to portray God as a sharply etched personality.

For yet another example of God as person in a liturgical passage, *y. Ta.* 2:11.G–H (among many instances) uses the imperative: "[They sound the horns] as if to say, 'Consider us as if we cry like a beast before you.'" But in the personification of God, referred to in context as "Lord of the world," we find very few sustained conversations in which God takes an active role in discourse. An example of the essentially passive character of God as "you" is in the following:

R. Simeon b. Yohai taught, "The book of Deuteronomy went up and spread itself out before the Holy One, blessed be he, saying before him, 'Lord of the world! You have written in your Torah that any covenant, part of which is null is wholly nullified. Now lo, Solomon wishes to uproot a Y of mine.' Said to him the Holy One, blessed be he, 'Solomon and a thousand like him will be null, but not one word of yours will be nullified.'"

(*y. San.* 2:6.II.AA–DD)

Here, as is commonly the case, the depiction of God follows the logic of the story. God has no particular traits imputed by the narrative, rather serving as a conversation partner for the Book of Deuteronomy. Still, God is portrayed as a person, not merely a presence.

One aspect of personhood is capacity to carry out deeds, and in the document at hand God is represented as doing things, past, present, and future, for example:

R. Berekhiah in the name of R. Abba bar Kahan: "In the future, the Holy One, blessed be he, is going to set the place of the righteous closer to his throne than the place of the ministering angels. The ministering angels will ask them and say to them, 'What has God wrought?' (Num. 23:23). That is, what did the Holy One, blessed be he, teach you?"

Said R. Levi bar Hayyuta, "Did he not do so in this world? . . ."

(*y. Shab.* 6:9.II.HH–II)

God's doing this or that forms part of a larger portrait of God as a person capable of carrying out purposive deeds. When, presently, we meet God as a fully etched personality, God will be shown to do the deeds human beings do in the way that human beings do them. At this point, by contrast, even a very long catalogue of the great deeds of God cannot yield much of a picture of God as a "you," a person people may know and love.

Not only so, but the representation in the Yerushalmi of God as a person does not fully work out the potential of a given subject that invites it. For example, God is angry—so Scripture says—on account of idolatry. Yet in the Yerushalmi's exposition of the pertinent chapters of *Abodah Zarah,* for example, chapter 3, I find not a single story of God's anger embodied in a picture of God as a person, let alone as a personality. The matter is left as a prevailing attitude or principle. When God does appear, it is as an essentially passive participant, for example, the conversation partner who asks, "Why?" or who confirms what the protagonist proposes, as in the following:

I. But the Holy One, blessed be he, said to Elijah, "This Hiel is a great man. Go and see him [because his sons have died]."
J. He said to him, "I am not going to see him."
K. He said to him, "Why?"
L. He said to him, "For if I go and they say things which will outrage you, I shall not be able to bear it."
M. He said to him, "Then if they say things which outrage me, whatever you decree against them I shall carry out."

(y. San. 10:2.III)

Here God is person and not abstract principle or premise, but not a vividly etched personality. The conversation consists of an exchange of conventional theological positions, not a transaction between two distinctive personalities, each entering into a one-time exchange with the other. Another example of the same phenomenon is as follows:

O. It is written, "Then the word of the Lord came to Isaiah: 'Go and say to Hezekiah, Thus says the Lord, the God of David your father: I have heard your prayer, I have seen your tears; behold I will add fifteen years to your life'" (Is. 38:4–5).
P. [Isaiah] said to him, "Thus I've already told him, and how thus do I say to him?
Q. "He is a man occupied with great affairs, and he will not believe me."
R. [God] said to him, "He is a very humble man, and he will believe you. And not only so, but as yet the rumor has not yet gone forth in the city."

S.   "And before Isaiah had gone out of the middle court, [the word of the Lord came to him]" (2 Kings 20:4).

(*y. San.* 10:2.VI)

Here once again God is a mere conversation partner, a straight man once more, pointing to facts already established in context and not doing more than moving the narrative along by word or deed. When God serves as the protagonist of a story and leads the conversation, and when God's part in the conversation is particular to that context and not simply the proclamation of well-known theological principles, then we shall meet God as a fully spelled out and individual personality: divinity in the form of humanity. But it is not in the present compilation, so far as I have been able to discover. Yet another case is in the same context:

Q.   Now all the ministering angels went and closed the windows, so that the prayer of Manasseh should not reach upward to the Holy One, blessed be he.

R.   The ministering angels were saying before the Holy One, blessed be he, "Lord of the world, a man who worshipped idols and put up an image in the Temple—are you going to accept him back as a penitent?"

S.   He said to them, "If I do not accept him back as a penitent, lo, I shall lock the door before all penitents."

T.   What did the Holy One, blessed be he, do? He made an opening [through the heavens] under his throne of glory and listened to his supplication.

U.   That is in line with the following verse of Scripture: "He prayed to him, and God received his entreaty ('TR) and heard his supplication and brought him again [to Jerusalem into his kingdom]. [Then Manasseh knew that the Lord was God]" (2 Chron. 33:13).

(*y. San.* 10:2.VII)

Here we have a more concrete characterization of a deed done by God, which shows God's character as merciful. Yet another passage shows the same tendency:

Said R. Phineas, "'Good and upright is the Lord. Therefore he instructs sinners in the way' (Ps. 25:8). Why is he good? Because he is upright. And why upright? Because he is good. 'Therefore he instructs sinners in the way' by teaching them the way to repentance."

They asked Wisdom, "As to a sinner, what is his punishment?"

She said to them, "Evil pursues the evil" (Prov. 13:21).

They asked prophecy, "As to a sinner, what is his punishment?"
She said to them, "The soul that sins shall die" (Ez. 18:20).
They asked the Holy One, blessed be he, "As to a sinner, what is his punishment?"
He said to them, "Let the sinner repent, and his sin will be forgiven for him, as it is said, 'Therefore he instructs sinners in the way' (Ps. 25:8). He shows sinners the way to repentance."

(*y. Mak.* 2:6.IV)

This is a further excellent example of how God as person represents a mere hypostatization, without concrete and particular traits. When God is represented as a "you," it turns out (thus far) to form a mere formality of rhetoric.

Imputing thoughts or public statements to God therefore does not much change the picture:

Said R. Levi, "What is the meaning of slow to 'anger'?
"The matter may be compared to a king who had two tough legions. He said, 'If they live here with me in the capital, if the city-folk anger me, they will immediately put them down with brute force. I shall send them a long way away, so that if the city folk anger me, while I am yet summoning the legions, the people will appease me and I shall accept their plea.'
"Likewise, the Holy One, blessed be he, said, 'Anger and wrath are angels of destruction. Lo, I shall send them a long way away, and if Israel angers me, while I am summoning and bringing them to me, Israel will repent and I shall accept their repentance.'"

(*y. Ta.* 2:1.XI.I–K)

God may further serve as an active voice, but only in the paraphrase of an available verse of Scripture:

Said R. Judah b. Pazzi, "[God said,] 'That [dew] which I gave as a bequest which may be nullified to Abraham, I give [to his descendants as a gift which can never be nullified], "May God give you of the dew of heaven" (Gen. 27:28).'"

Here we have assigned to God simply an amplification of the cited verse of Scripture. Yet another case in which God speaks without emerging as a well-etched personality is the following:

Said R. Samuel bar Nahman, "Said the Holy One, blessed be he, to David, 'David, I shall count out for you a full complement of days. I shall not give you less than the full number. Will Solomon, your son, not build the Temple in order to offer sacrifices in it? But more precious to me are the just and righteous deeds which you do than the offerings which will be made in the Temple.'"

(y. Sheq. 2:6.VI.D)

Numerous examples will not vastly change the picture. God is represented as a person, but not as much of a personality. God's rulings, rather than God's attitudes or emotions or deeds in a concrete narrative, are simply restated in dialogue form. That establishes God as a person, but does not then provide a rich characterization at all.

While God makes a statement in the first person, in fact it is nothing more than a restatement of the point of the parable and does not, therefore, constitute a characterization of God in some particular framework. The reason I think so is that if the story-teller had spoken in the third person, that is, instead of "I" using simply "the Holy One," in no way would the course of the story have shifted. The point of the story lies in imputing to the divinity the trait of patience, not in describing a patient personality in some particular framework. Not only so, but even when parables are drawn they commonly illustrate principles or traits, rather than serving to characterize a highly individual personality. For example, in the following parable God is shown to be more loyal as a patron than a human counterpart. But this turns out merely to illustrate a point Scripture has made and hardly serves to etch in words a vivid personality:

R. Yudan in the name of R. Isaac gave four discourses: "A person had a human patron. One day they came and told the patron, 'A member of your household has been arrested.'
    "He said to them, 'Let me take his place.'
    "They said to him, 'Lo, he is already going out to trial.'
    "He said to them, 'Let me take his place.'
    "They said to him, 'Lo, he is going to be hanged.'
    "Now where is he, and where his patron?
    "But the Holy One, blessed be he, [will save his subjects just as he] saved Moses from the sword of Pharaoh. This is in accord with what is written, 'He delivered me from the sword of Pharaoh' (Ex. 18:4)."

(y. Ber. 9:1.VIII.B–C [trans. Tzvee Zahavy])

The passage goes through a sequence of examples deriving from Scripture of the same fact, namely, God's personal salvation of the saints. God is further portrayed as loyal and humble, identifying with Israel even in their poverty, ignorance, and humiliation (*y. Ber.* 9:1.XI, for one important example). But at no point in the exposition do we find either an immediate case, deriving from sages' own time, or more to the point, a clear characterization of God in specific and vivid terms. God acts, as Scripture has made clear, and evidence of God's will and person all derive from Scripture. For instance, while everyone believed God answers prayers, where evidence of that fact is adduced it is from Scripture's cases:

Said R. Judah b. Pazzi, "Even if a woman in labor is already seated in the delivery chair, God can change the sex of the foetus, in accord with the verse, 'Behold like clay in the hand of the potter, so you are in my hand, O house of Israel' (Jer. 18:6)."

Rabbi in the name of the house of Yannai: "Originally Dinah was a male. After Rachel prayed, she was changed into a female. So it says, 'Afterwards she bore a daughter and called her Dinah' (Gen. 30:21). It was after Rachel prayed that Dinah was changed into a female."

(*y. Ber.* 9:3.VI.B–C [trans. Tzvee Zahavy])

The evidence is then expounded wholly within the framework of principles established by biblical facts, without a further effort to transform these facts into the portrait of a living personality. God emerges as a person, vital and alive in the life of Israel, but in no way incarnate in everyday encounters, stories of a personality people might know and engage in conversation.

The difference between the Yerushalmi's authorships' representation of God as premise, presence, and person and the Bavli's strikingly richer presentation of divinity as a personality will be clearer when we see how, in allusions but especially in stories of a cogent character, God may appear as a fully developed individual. Then the rather lifeless portraits at hand will indeed stand in striking contrast. A mere reference, "You are the Lord, a loving and merciful God, who answers in time of trouble" (*y. Ta.* 2:2.VI.E), hardly constitutes a detailed picture of a personality. Nor do we find a personality in the following: "Said the Holy One, blessed be he, 'If I leave Israel as is, they will be swallowed up among the nations. Lo, I shall join my great name to them, so that they may live'" (*y. Ta.* 2:6.I.B). It is merely an "I" or a "you" attached to a theological trait—quite a different thing from an incarnate God whom people can know and encounter. When God tells a human being to shut up and listen, when God instructs a sage on how to conduct himself properly, when God argues like a sage in a highly individual way, then we shall see what it means for the character of divinity to take on personality. In none of these cases does the presentation of God as a person yield a description of the individual and personal traits of that person; what we are given is a person without a personality, that is, the embodiment of abstract theological principles or powers.

PERSONALITY

For reasons amply spelled out above, I find in the Yerushalmi no sustained narratives that etch in a story the traits of a vivid personality.

CONCLUSION

What we do not find in the Yerushalmi carries heavier weight than what we have surveyed. Our rapid search for the characterization of the divinity has yielded a decidedly familiar repertoire. Whatever types of descriptions of God present themselves in the Mishnah and Tosefta make their appearance here. Nothing in the Yerushalmi will have struck prior authorships as surprising or fresh.

7

Written Torah: *Genesis Rabbah, Leviticus Rabbah,* and *Pesiqta deRab Kahana*

THE ORAL TORAH AND THE EXEGESIS OF THE WRITTEN TORAH

When sages in the canonical documents of the Judaism of the dual Torah read and expounded Scripture, it was to spell out how one thing stood for something else, that is, that fundamentally parabolic reading of Scripture. Scripture served as an example and an illustration of propositions sages intended to demonstrate. The verses that are quoted in rabbinic Midrash ordinarily shift from the meanings they convey to the implications they contain, so speaking about something, anything, other than what they seem to be saying. The as-if frame of mind brought to Scripture renews Scripture, with the sage seeing everything with fresh eyes. And the result of the new vision was a reimagining of the social world envisioned by the document at hand, I mean the everyday world of Israel in its Land in that difficult time of the fourth and fifth centuries in particular. For what the sages now proposed in *Genesis Rabbah, Leviticus Rabbah,* and *Pesiqta deRab Kahana* (among other writings) was a reconstruction of existence along the lines of the ancient design of Scripture as they read it. What that meant was that, from a sequence of one-time and linear events, everything that happened was turned into a repetition of known and already-experienced paradigms, hence, once more, a mythic being. The source and core of the myth, of course, derived from Scripture—Scripture reread, renewed, reconstructed along with the society that revered Scripture.

Reading one thing in terms of something else, the builders of the document systematically adopted for themselves and adapted to their own circumstances the reality of the Scripture, its history and doctrines. They transformed that history from a sequence of one-time events, leading from one place to some other, into an ever-present mythic world. No longer was there one Moses, one David, one set of happenings of a distinctive and never-to-be-repeated character. Now whatever happened of which the thinkers propose to take account must enter and be absorbed into that established and ubiquitous pattern and structure founded in Scripture. It is not that biblical history repeats itself. Rather, biblical history no longer constitutes history as a story of things that happened once, long ago, and pointed to some one moment in the future. Rather it becomes an account of things that happen every day—hence, an ever-present mythic world. That is why, in Midrash in the Judaism of the dual Torah, Scripture as a whole does not dictate the order of discourse, let alone its character. In this document they chose a verse here, a phrase there. In the more mature Midrash-compilations, such as *Leviticus Rabbah* and *Pesiqta deRab Kahana,* these then presented the pretext for propositional discourse commonly quite out of phase with the cited passage.

The framers of the Midrash documents saw Scripture in a new way, just as they saw their own circumstance afresh. Specifically, they rejected their world in favor of Scripture's, reliving Scripture's world in their own terms. That, incidentally, is why they did not write history, an account of what was happening and what it meant. It was not that they did not recognize or appreciate important changes and trends reshaping their nation's life. They could not deny that reality. In their apocalyptic reading of the dietary and leprosy laws, as we shall see in *Leviticus Rabbah,* they made explicit their close encounter with the history of the world as they knew it. But they had another mode of responding to history. It was to treat history as if it were already known and readily understood. Whatever happened had already happened. Scripture dictated the contents of history, laying forth the structures of time, the rules that prevailed and were made known in events. Self-evidently, these same thinkers projected into Scripture's day the realities of their own, turning Moses and David into rabbis, for example. But that is how people think in that mythic, enchanted world in which, to begin with, reality blends with dream, and hope projects onto future and past alike how people want things to be.

When sages turned to historical events, reading them as other than what they seemed, as they looked out upon the world of today, they quite naturally appealed to Scripture's account of ancient Israel as the model and paradigm for all of history. The one-time events of the generation of the flood, Sodom and Gomorrah, the patriarchs and the sojourn in Egypt, the exodus, the revelation of the Torah at Sinai, the golden calf, the Davidic monarchy and the building of the Temple, Sennacherib, Hezekiah, and the destruction of northern Israel, Nebuchadnezzar and the destruction of the Temple in 586, the life of Israel in Babylonian captivity, Daniel and his associates, Mordecai and Haman—these events occur over and over again in Midrash-compilations. They turn out to serve as paradigms of sin and atonement, steadfastness and divine intervention, and equivalent lessons. We find, in fact, a fairly standard repertoire of scriptural heroes or villains on the one side, and conventional lists of Israel's enemies and their actions and downfall on the other. The boastful, for instance, include the generation of the flood, Sodom and Gomorrah, Pharaoh, Sisera, Sennacherib, Nebuchadnezzar, the wicked empire (Rome)—contrasted to Israel, "despised and humble in this world." The four kingdoms recur again and again, always ending, of course, with Rome, with the repeated message that after Rome will come Israel. But Israel has to make this happen through its faith and submission to God's will. Lists of enemies ring the changes on Cain, the Sodomites, Pharaoh, Sennacherib, Nebuchadnezzar, Haman.

Accordingly, the mode of thought brought to bear upon the theme of history remains that of natural philosophy, namely, list making, with data exhibiting similar taxonomic traits drawn together into lists based on common monothetic traits or definitions. These lists then through the power of repetition make a single enormous point. They prove a social law of history. The catalogues of exemplary heroes and historical events serve a further purpose. They provide a model of how contemporary events are to be absorbed into the biblical paradigm. Since biblical events exemplify recurrent happenings, sin and redemption, forgiveness and atonement, they lose their one-time character. At the same time and in the same way, current events find a place within the ancient, but eternally present, paradigmatic scheme. So no new historical events, other than exemplary episodes in lives of heroes, demand narration because through what is said about the past what was happening in the times of the framers of Midrash in the Judaism of the dual Torah would also come under consideration. This mode of dealing with biblical history and contemporary events produces two reciprocal effects. The first is the mythicization of biblical stories, their removal from the framework of ongoing, unique patterns of history and sequences of events, and their transformation into accounts of things that happen all the time. The second is that contemporary events, too, lose all of their specificity and enter the paradigmatic framework of established mythic existence. So (1) the Scripture's myth happens every day, and (2) every day produces reenactment of the Scripture's myth. What that means in the actual encounter with the living God, how the divinity is characterized, we shall now examine.

PREMISE

In the exegesis of the written Torah presented in the fifth-century writings, God's traits, not cast in the form of stories of a person and the deeds such a person does, remain abstract and therefore constitute premises of the system as a whole, as in the following:

1.A. "If I were hungry, I would not tell you, for the world and all that is in it are mine. [Shall I eat the flesh of your bulls or drink the blood of he-goats? Offer to God the sacrifice of thanksgiving and pay your vows to the Most High. If you call upon me in time of trouble, I will come to your rescue and you shall honor me]" (Ps. 50:12–15):

   B. Said R. Simon, "There are thirteen traits of a merciful character that are stated in writing concerning the Holy One, blessed be he.

C.   "That is in line with this verse of Scripture: The Lord passed by
     before him and proclaimed, The Lord, the Lord, God, merciful
     and gracious, long-suffering and abundant in goodness and truth;
     keeping mercy unto the thousandth generation, forgiving iniquity,
     transgression, and sin, who will by no means clear the guilty (Ex.
     34:6–7).

D.   "Now is there a merciful person who would hand over his food to a
     cruel person [who would have to slaughter a beast so as to feed
     him]?

E.   "One has to conclude: If I were hungry, I would not tell you."

                                                      (*Pesiq. Rab Kah.* VI:I.1)

In this statement, God does not take on fleshly human traits at all,
there being no comparison of God to a mortal king, no appeal to
correct behavior here on earth, merely an effort to prove a proposition on the basis of abstract traits imputed to the divinity. But the
appeal to such premises of the divine personality as mercy and
goodness may readily yield stories about God as a person who
practices such attributes in deed.

   In stating their premises concerning the divinity, therefore,
sages easily passed the unmarked border between the statement of
an abstract principle and the presentation of such a principle in
very concrete form. In seeking metaphors and analogies by which
to express their encounter with God, sages appealed first of all to
the comparison of God and the human being, turning, within
humanity, to that quality or trait they deemed appropriate for a
metaphor for God. That part of the human being they identified
with God was the soul. The soul of the human being then is compared to God and teaches us about God:

A.   Why did the soul of David praise the Holy One, blessed be he (*b. Ber.*
     10a)?

B.   David said, "Just as the soul fills the body, so the Holy One, blessed be
     he, fills the whole world, as it is written, 'Do I not fill the entire
     heaven and earth? says the Lord' [Jer. 23:24]. So let the soul, which
     fills the body, come and praise the Holy One, blessed be he, who fills
     the world.

C.   "The soul supports the body, the Holy One [blessed be he] supports
     the world, for it is written, 'Even to your old age I am he, and to gray
     hairs [I will carry you]' [Is. 46:4]. So let the soul, which supports the
     body, come and praise the Holy One, blessed be he, who supports
     the world.

D. "The soul outlasts the body, and the Holy One, blessed be he, outlasts the world: 'They will perish, but you do endure, they will all wear out like a garment. [You change them like a garment and they pass away, but you are the same, and your years have no end]' [Ps. 102:26–27]. So let the soul, which outlasts the body, come and praise the Holy One, blessed be he, who outlasts the world.

E. "The soul in the body does not eat, and as to the Holy One, blessed be he, there is no eating so far as he is concerned, as it is written, 'If I were hungry, I would not tell you, for the world and all that is in it is mine' [Ps. 50:12]. Let the soul in the body, which does not eat, come and praise the Holy One, blessed be he, before whom there is no eating.

F. "The soul is singular in the body, and the Holy One, blessed be he, is singular in his world, as it is said, 'Hear, O Israel, the Lord our God is a singular Lord' [Deut. 6:4]. Let the soul, which is singular in the body, come and praise the Holy One, blessed be he, who is singular in his world.

G. "The soul is pure in the body, and the Holy One, blessed be he, is pure in his world: 'You who are of eyes too pure to behold evil' [Hab. 1:13]. Let the soul, which is pure in the body, come and praise the Holy One, blessed be he, which is pure in his world.

H. "The soul sees but is not seen, and the Holy One, blessed be he, sees but is not seen, as it is written, '[Am I a God at hand, says the Lord, and not a God afar off?] Can a man hide himself in secret places so that I cannot see him? says the Lord. Do I not fill heaven [and earth? says the Lord]' [Jer. 23:23–24]. Let the soul, which sees but is not seen, come and praise the Holy One, blessed be he, who sees but is not seen. . . .

(*Lev. R.* IV:VIII.1)

It is not a long step from the comparisons at hand to the amplification of God's person and personality in human terms. In stating the premises of their system, the sages of the dual Torah, through their compositions of scriptural verses and comments, resorted to traits of personality, not only of the soul, in spelling out their portrait of the divinity. We shall shortly see that some authorships in the fifth century took that step, if only in a preliminary way, leading us directly and in a straight path to the Bavli's full and unashamed incarnation of God.

While the fact that God created the world forms the premise of all discourse, that given receives substantial attention, quite naturally, in the opening parts of *Genesis Rabbah*, which attend to Genesis 1—2. Here we find a considerable program of exposition of traits or qualities of the divinity pertinent to the act of creation as portrayed in Scripture. For example, God is distinguished by modesty, by contrast to a mortal king:

A. ["In the beginning God created . . ." (Gen. 1:1):] R. Yudan in the name of Aqilas: "This one it is appropriate to call God. [Why so?]
B. "Under ordinary circumstances a mortal king is praised in province even before he has built public baths for the population or given them private ones. [God by contrast created the world before he had received the praise of humanity, so it was not for the sake of human adulation that he created the world.]"

(Gen. R. I:XII.1)

A. Simeon b. Azzai says, "'And your modesty has made me great' (2 Sam. 22:36). A mortal person mentions his name and afterward his title, for example, 'Mr. So-and-so, the prefect,' 'Mr. Such-and-such, and whatever title he gets.' But the Holy One, blessed be he, is not that way.
B. "Rather, only after he had created what was needed in his world did he make mention of his name, thus, 'In the beginning, created . . . ,' and only afterward: 'God.'"

(Gen. R. I:XII.2)

The process of presenting God in human garb finds illustration in this passage. Traits people admire—generosity of spirit, modesty—are imputed to God.

An important premise of the Judaism of the dual Torah is that God knows the future and governs all things that happen. Two distinct issues are joined: first, the deeds of wicked and righteous individuals; second, the history of the nations and of Israel. Both classifications of future history are amply displayed before God:

A. R. Abbahu and R. Hiyya the Elder:
B. R. Abbahu said, "At the beginning of the act of creating the world, the Holy One, blessed be he, foresaw the deeds of the righteous and of the wicked.
C. "'And the earth was unformed' refers to the deeds of the wicked.
D. "'And God said, "Let there be light"' refers to the deeds of the righteous.
E. "But I do not know which of the two God prefers, the deeds of this sort or the deeds of that.
F. "On the basis of what is written, namely, 'And God looked upon the light, seeing that it was good,' one has to conclude that God prefers the deeds of the righteous to the deeds of the wicked."

(Gen. R. II:V.1)

A. Said R. Hiyya the Elder, "At the beginning of the creation of the world the Holy One, blessed be he, foresaw that the Temple would be built, destroyed, and rebuilt.

B. "'In the beginning God created' [refers to the Temple] when it was built, in line with the following verse: 'That I may plant the heavens and lay the foundations of the earth and say to Zion, You are my people' (Is. 51:16).

C. "'And the earth was unformed'—lo, this refers to the destruction, in line with this verse: 'I saw the earth, and lo, it was unformed' (Jer. 4:23).

D. "'And God said, "Let there be light"'—lo, it was built and well constructed in the age to come.

E. "That is in line with this verse: 'Arise, shine, for your light has come, and the glory of the Lord is risen upon you' (Is. 60:1)."

(Gen. R. II:V.2)

If God foresees all things, then how to account for the suffering of the righteous in general, and Israel in particular? It is a mark of God's special favor and love:

A. "The Lord tries the righteous, [but the wicked and him who loves violence his soul hates" (Ps. 11:5)]:

B. Said R. Jonathan, "A potter does not test a weak utensil, for if he hits it just once, he will break it. So the Holy One, blessed be he, does not test the wicked but the righteous: 'The Lord tries the righteous' (Ps. 11:5)."

C. Said R. Yose bar Haninah, "When a flax maker knows that the flax is in good shape, then the more he beats it, the more it will improve and glisten. When it is not of good quality, if he beats it just once, he will split it. So the Holy One, blessed be he, does not try the wicked but the righteous: 'The Lord tries the righteous' (Ps. 11:5)."

D. Said R. Eleazar, "The matter may be compared to a householder who has two heifers, one strong, one weak. On whom does he place the yoke? It is on the one that is strong. So the Holy One, blessed be he, does not try the wicked but the righteous: 'The Lord tries the righteous' (Ps. 11:5)."

(Gen. R. XXXIV:II.1)

Recitation of God's great deeds, how God made the world and ordered social life, presents the premise of a God of one sort rather than some other. But there is no clear characterization of God, for example, in the following:

A. R. Simeon b. Haleputa said, "The greatness of peace is shown by the fact that, when the Holy One, blessed be he, created his world, he made peace between the creatures of the upper world and the ones of the lower world."

(Lev. R. IX:IX.8)

That statement does not contribute to the representation of God as a person, though it establishes a component of the premise of God's program and plan for the world. Along these same lines we find this curious item:

A. R. Berekhiah and R. Helbo and Ulla Bira'ah and R. Eleazar in the name of R. Haninah: "The Holy One, blessed be he, is destined to dance at the head of the line of the righteous in the time to come."

(Lev. R. XI:IX.1)

Here, too, we speak of deeds, not personality or character. So, too, to be like God means to do God's sort of deeds, such as planting trees:

J. From the very beginning of the creation of the world, the Holy One was occupied first of all only in the planting of trees . . .
K. So you too, when you enter the Land of Israel, you should first of all be occupied in the planting of trees.

(Lev. R. XXV:III.1)

These and numerous other references to things God has done or will do form a sizable statement of premises as to God's character. But in the versions of those statements at hand, the authorships found it possible to convey their meaning without a process of personalization, appealing to human traits, metaphors, analogies. When we consider how the same authorships framed discourse on God's character through narrative, we see a more concrete and human portrait, if not yet God incarnate.

PRESENCE

God as a presence, without imputed traits of personality or character, emerges in a restatement of Isaiah's vision of God's presence:

1.A. R. Jacob b. R. Zabedi in the name of R. Abbahu opened [discourse by citing the following verse:] "'And it shall never again be the reliance of the house of Israel, recalling their iniquity, [when they turn to them for aid. Then they will know that I am the Lord God]' (Ez. 29:16).

B. "It is written, 'Above him stood the seraphim: [each had six wings, with two he covered his face, and with two he covered his feet, and with two he flew]' (Is. 6:2).

C. "'With two he flew'—singing praises.

D. "'With two he covered his face'—so as not to gaze upon the Presence of God.

E. "'And with two he covered his feet'—so as not to let them be seen by the face of the Presence of God.

F. "For it is written, 'And the soles of their feet were like the sole of a calf's foot' (Ez. 1:6).

G. "And it is written, 'They made for themselves a molten calf' (Ex. 32:8).

H. "So [in covering their feet, they avoided calling to mind the molten calf,] in accord with the verse, 'And it shall never again be the reliance of the house of Israel, recalling their iniquity'" (Ez. 29:16).

(*Lev. R.* XXVII:III.1)

In this amplification of the pertinent passages, the authorship at hand simply restates the notion of God as a presence without identifiable traits. Another statement of the same chaste vision alludes to the Presence, without imparting to the divine Presence particular traits:

A. "Then Jacob called his sons and said, 'Gather yourselves together, that I may tell you what shall befall you in days to come:' . . .

G. "Jacob: 'Then Jacob called his sons and said, "Gather yourselves together, that I may tell you what shall befall you in days to come. Assemble and hear, O sons of Jacob, and hearken to Israel, your father. Reuben, you are my first-born."'

H. "This teaches that he came to reveal the time of the end to them, but it was hidden from him."

I. The matter may be compared to the case of the king's ally, who was departing this world, and his children surrounded his bed. He said to them, "Come and I shall tell you the secrets of the king." Then he looked up and saw the king. He said to them, "Be most meticulous about the honor owing to the king."

J. So our father Jacob looked up and saw the Presence of God standing over him. He said to them, "Be most meticulous about the honor owing to the Holy One, blessed be he."

(*Gen. R.* XCVIII:II.7)

Here we find no effort to treat God as a person, rather an allusion to God's majestic presence as an ineffable reality.

God as a "you" does not always yield discourse of dialogue, since the "you" may serve as a convention or standard literary expression, without yielding an account of how two persons actually relate to one another. The "you" in the following presents no more than a convention, without a pretense that God is more than a presence in the world:

A. Said R. Tanhuma, "'For you are great and do wonderful things' (Ps. 86:10).
B. "Why so? Because: 'You alone are God' (Ps. 86:10).
C. "You by yourself created the world.
D. "'In the beginning God created' (Gen. 1:1)."

(Gen. R. I:III.3)

In this composition, the "you" forms a mere routine paraphrase, not serving to establish a person as participant in an exposition. God appears as faceless presence when the same convention leads an authorship to frame, in terms of a purposive person, the thinking that led to a given action. In the following, no real, carefully drawn, individual person is involved:

A. "[When Isaac was old, and his eyes were dim,] so that he could not see, [he called Esau his older son, and said to him, 'My son,' and he answered, 'Here I am']" (Gen. 27:1).
B. R. Eleazar b. Azariah said, "'. . . so that he could not see' the wickedness of the wicked person.
C. "Said the Holy One, blessed be he, 'Should Isaac go out to the market and have people say, "Here is the father of that wicked man.
D. "'It is better that I make his eyes dim, so he will stay home.'
E. "So it is written, 'When the wicked rise, men hide themselves' (Prov. 28:28). . . .'"

(Gen. R. LXV:X.1)

In passages such as these, the narrators invoke God's presence in the world but say pretty much what they wished as a matter of principle to say. We have no characterization or individuation, and God is not compared in some concrete way to a mortal king or other mortals. Nothing in these passages will have surprised the framers of the Mishnah and other documents in the first phase of the Judaism of the dual Torah.

Nor will those authorships have found surprising the conviction that the one place in which God forms a continual presence is in the synagogue and study house at the time of prayer or Torah-study:

1.A. R. Yudan in the name of R. Isaac, "All the time that the Israelites delay [and observe an extra festival] in their synagogues and study houses, the Holy One, blessed be he, delays [and leaves] his Presence with them.

B. "What is the verse of Scripture that indicates it?

C. "May we urge you to stay? Let us prepare a kid for you (Jud. 13:15)."

(*Pesiq. Rab Kah.* XXVIII:VIII.1)

2.A. R. Haggai in the name of R. Isaac: "So long as the Israelites join together in synagogues and school houses, the Holy One, blessed be he, joins his Presence together with them.

B. "What is the verse of Scripture that indicates it?

C. "I have most assuredly joined together with [interpreting in a different way the letters usually translated, hoped in] the Lord and he turned to me (Ps. 40:2)."

(*Pesiq. Rab Kah.* XXVIII:VIII.2)

The entire repertoire of passages in which God forms a presence in the life of Israel remains well within the familiar framework. God is a presence in the world, not merely the one who, beyond time, created the world and revealed the Torah. But God's presence in the world, in statements of the present classification, does not yield a picture of God as a person.

PERSON

God's person forms the counterpart to Israel's person. The two, when equally hypostatized, are deemed counterparts forming a relationship of deep love for one another. God indeed attains personhood in relationship to Israel, God's twin:

A. Said R. Hiyya bar Abba, "How do we know that the Holy One is called 'the heart of Israel'?

B. "On the basis of this verse: Rock of my heart and my portion is God forever (Ps. 73:26)."

(*Pesiq. Rab Kah.* V:VI.2)

The amplification of the foregoing yields the picture of God as Israel's kin and lover, so both parties—the abstraction "Israel," along with the abstraction divinity—take on the traits of personhood:

A. ". . . My beloved is knocking" refers to Moses: And Moses said, "Thus said the Lord, 'At about midnight I shall go out in the midst of Egypt'" (Ex. 11:4).

B. "Open to me": said R. Yose, "Said the Holy One, blessed be he, 'Open to me [a hole] as small as the eye of a needle, and I shall open to you a gate so large that troops and siege-engines can go through it.'"

C. ". . . my sister": [God speaks:] "My sister—in Egypt, for they became my kin through two religious duties, the blood of the Passover-offering and the blood of circumcision."

D. ". . . my dearest"—at the sea, for they showed their love for me at the sea. And they said, "The Lord will reign forever and ever" (Ex. 15:19).

E. ". . . my dove"—my dove at Marah, where through receiving commandments they become distinguished for me like a dove.

F. ". . . my perfect one"—my perfect one at Sinai, for they became pure at Sinai: And they said, "All that the Lord has spoken we shall do and we shall hear (Ex. 24:7)."

G. R. Yannai said, "My twin, for I am no greater than they, nor they than I."

H. R. Joshua of Sikhnin said in the name of R. Levi, "Just as in the case of twins, if one of them gets a headache, the other one feels it, so said the Holy One, blessed be he, 'I am with him in trouble' (Ps. 91:15)."

I. ". . . for my head is drenched with dew." "The heavens dropped dew" (Jud. 5:4).

J. . . . my locks with the moisture of the night: Yes, the clouds dropped water (Jud. 5:4).

K. When is this the case? In this month: This month is for you the first of the months (Ex. 12:2).

(Pesiq. Rab Kah. V:VI.3)

The notion of God and Israel as twins, the one formed as the counterpart of the other, thus involves the hypostatization of both parties to the transaction. But in the documents at hand, God's personhood does not yield sharply etched traits of personality. God appears as a person but not as a story's protagonist. God is a conversation partner, but does not set the terms of discourse. God rather states what is needed, forming the source for the resolution of the tension of a story. So God is merely a person, a party to discourse, but not endowed with individual traits of character and personality.

Nonetheless, we do find in the Midrash-compilations at hand clear statement of God as "you," and, as anticipated, that statement takes place in the setting of a liturgy:

A. "And God made the two great lights" (Gen. 1:16):

B. "Yours is the day, yours also is the night" (Ps. 74:16).

C. [Israel speaks:] "To you [God], the day gives praise, to you the night gives praise."

D. "Just as the day falls into your dominion, so the night falls into your dominion. When you do miracles for us by day, then 'Yours is the day.' And when you do miracles for us by night, then, 'Also yours is the night.'

E. "When you do miracles for us by day, we say a song of praise before you by day. When you do miracles for us by night, we say before you a song of praise by night.

F. "You did miracles for us by day, so we sang a psalm before you by day: 'Then sang Deborah and Barak the son of Abinoam on that day' (Jud. 5:1).

G. "You did miracles for us by night, so we sang a psalm before you by night: 'You shall have a song as in the night when a feast is hallowed' (Is. 30:29).

H. "For you it is fully right to recite a song by day and by night.

I. "Why so? For: 'You have established light and sun' (Ps. 74:16)," and "you made the two great lights" (Gen. 1:16).

(*Gen. R.* VI:II.1)

What we have falls into the classification of a liturgical poem. We have no pretense at exegesis, let alone at a syllogistic argument. Rather the entire composition, certainly unitary and harmonious, presents a statement of religious feeling and would surely find a comfortable place in synagogue worship. The rhetoric of ritual is most clearly seen at the repetition, with a slight change, of 1.C, D, and E. We both go over what has been said and also add a slight change, a characteristic of ritual, hence, in the present context, of liturgy.

God is given sizable statements, which provide the appearance of God as a "you." Invented dialogue may serve to give personality to a character. But in the documents at hand these statements form theological treatises, not characterizations of an individual person as in the following invented dialogue:

A. Said R. Berekhiah, "When God came to create the first man, he saw that both righteous and wicked descendants would come forth from him. He said, 'If I create him, wicked descendants will come forth from him. If I do not create him, how will the righteous descendants come forth from him?'

B. "What did the Holy One, blessed be he, do? He disregarded the way of the wicked and joined to himself his quality of mercy and so created him.

C. "That is in line with this verse of Scripture: 'For the Lord knows the way of the righteous, but the way of the wicked shall perish' (Ps. 1:6).

D. "What is the sense of 'shall perish'? He destroyed it from before his presence and joined to himself the quality of mercy, and so created man."

2.A. R. Hanina did not explain the cited verse in this way. Rather, [he said,] "When the Holy One, blessed be he, proposed to create the first man, he took counsel with the ministering angels. He said to them, 'Shall we make man' (Gen. 1:26)?

B. "They said to him, 'What will be his character?'

C. "He said to them, 'Righteous descendants will come forth from him,' in line with this verse: 'For the Lord knows the way of the righteous' (Ps. 1:6), meaning, the Lord reported concerning the ways of the righteous to the ministering angels.

D. "'But the way of the wicked shall perish' (Ps. 1:6), for he destroyed it [to keep it away] from them.

E. "He reported to them that righteous descendants would come forth from him, but he did not report to them that wicked descendants would come forth from him. For if he had told them that wicked descendants would come forth from him, the attribute of justice would never have given permission for man to be created."

(Gen. R. VIII:IV.1)

Here we find no effort to assign a personality to God. To be sure, God's act of creation represented a demonstration of his merciful and loving character. That is the critical proposition against anyone who holds that the Creator-God was evil. The passage obviously is unitary and provides two parallel exercises in the reading of Ps. 1:6 into the base verse of Gen. 1:26. While we do not have an explicit statement that the former serves to elucidate the latter, the point is clear. The positioning of the discourse makes good sense, since we continue to follow the question, with whom did God take counsel when he said, "Shall we make man?" Here again the invented discourse does little to portray a fully exposed personality:

A. Said R. Simon, "When the Holy One, blessed be he, came to create the first man, the ministering angels formed parties and sects.

B. "Some of them said, 'Let him be created,' and some of them said, 'Let him not be created.'

C. "That is in line with the following verse of Scripture: 'Mercy and truth fought together, righteousness and peace warred with each other' (Ps. 85:11).

D. "Mercy said, 'Let him be created, for he will perform acts of mercy.'

E. "Truth said, 'Let him not be created, for he is a complete fake.'

F. "Righteousness said, 'Let him be created, for he will perform acts of righteousness.'

G. "Peace said, 'Let him not be created, for he is one mass of contention.'

H. "What then did the Holy One, blessed be he, do? He took truth and threw it to the ground. The ministering angels then said before the Holy One, blessed be he, 'Master of the ages, how can you disgrace your seal [which is truth]? Let truth be raised up from the ground!'

I. "That is in line with the following verse of Scripture: 'Let truth spring up from the earth' (Ps. 85:2)."

J. All the rabbis say the following in the name of R. Haninah, R. Phineas, R. Hilqiah in the name of R. Simon: "'Very' [at Gen. 1:31], 'And God saw everything that he had made, and behold it was very good,' refers to man.

K. "The sense is, 'And behold, man is good.'"

L. R. Huna the elder of Sepphoris said, "While the ministering angels were engaged in contentious arguments with one another, keeping one another preoccupied, the Holy One, blessed be he, created him.

M. "He then said to them, 'What good are you doing [with your contentions]? Man has already been made!'"

(*Gen. R.* VIII:V.1)

If we bypass J–K as an obvious interpolation, the entire passage forms a sustained and unitary statement. The message is that in creating man, God expressed God's special love for him. The location presents no problems, since the question that the passage—by being located here—answers is the same one with which we have been dealing: with whom did God take counsel? But the answer is more important than the question, here as earlier, since it produces a syllogism not provoked by the question at all. The stress is that the ministering angels opposed the creation of man; because of their divisive character God was able to do it anyhow. Even though, in these representative passages, God is given a full complement of statements, none of this has any bearing on the representation of God as a personality. The sizable representation in *Genesis Rabbah* of God as person in dialogue with others (e.g., Abraham, Noah, and the like) in no way changes the basic picture. For example, the representation of God in the following presents us with a mere conversation partner. It is Abraham, the story's protagonist, who is fully characterized and who emerges as a personality etched in words, while God simply functions as a kind of one-person chorus:

A. "And he said, 'Take, I pray you, your son, your only son, Isaac, whom you love, and go to the land of Moriah, and offer him there as a burnt offering upon one of the mountains of which I shall tell you'" (Gen. 22:3):

B. He said to him, "Take, I pray you," meaning, "By your leave."

C. ". . . your son."

D. He said to him, "Which son?"

E. He said to him, ". . . your only son."

F. "This one is the only son of his mother, and that one is the only son of his mother."

G. ". . . whom you love."

H. "Where are the dividing walls within the womb? [I love them both.]"

I. "Isaac."

J. Why did he not tell him to begin with? It was so as to make Isaac still more precious in his view and so as to give him a reward for each exchange.

(Gen. R. LV:VII.1)

A. Said R. Aha, "[Abraham said to God,] 'Are there jokes even before you? Yesterday you said to me, "For in Isaac shall seed be called to you" (Gen. 21:12). And then you went back on your word and said, "Take your son" (Gen. 22:2). And now: "Do not lay your hand on the lad or do anything to him."' [What's next?]

B. "Said the Holy One, blessed be he, to him, 'Abraham, "My covenant I will not profane" (Ps. 89:35). "And I will establish my covenant with Isaac" (Gen. 17:21).

C. "'True, I commanded you, "Take now your son" (Gen. 33:2). "I will not alter what has gone out of my lips" (Ps. 89:35). "Did I ever tell you to kill him? No, I told you, 'Bring him up.'

D. "'"Well and good! You did indeed bring him up. Now take him down."'"

(Gen. R. LVI:VIII.1)

The underlying polemic favors God's faithfulness and reliability. While important traits, they derive from a broader theological program. God does not emerge from these dialogues as a fully exposed personality. God remains a person bearing certain abstract traits.

In accounting for God's love of Israel, that same theological program is once more translated into dialogue between two persons, Moses and God. But here, too, God's personhood does not yield traits of individuation. The passage can have been worked out without recourse to the "you" that allows us to experience within the narrative God's presence and personhood.

A. Returning to the matter (GWPH): "Speak to the children of Israel" (Lev. 1:2).

B. R. Yudan in the name of R. Samuel b. R. Nehemiah: "The matter may be compared to the case of a king who had an undergarment, concerning which he instructed his servant, saying to him, 'Fold it, shake it out, and be careful about it!'

C. "He said to him, 'My lord, O king, among all the undergarments that you have, [why] do you give me such instructions only about this one?'

D. "He said to him, 'It is because this is the one that I keep closest to my body.'

E. "So too did Moses say before the Holy One, blessed be he, Lord of the Universe: 'Among the seventy distinct nations that you have in your world, [why] do you give me instructions only concerning Israel? [For instance,] "Command the children of Israel" [Num. 28:2], "Say to the children of Israel" [Ex. 33:5], "Speak to the children of Israel"' [Lev. 1:2].

F. "He said to him, 'The reason is that they stick close to me, in line with the following verse of Scripture: "For as the undergarment cleaves to the loins of a man, so have I caused to cleave unto me the whole house of Israel"'" (Jer. 13:11).

G. Said R. Abin, "[The matter may be compared] to a king who had a purple cloak, concerning which he instructed his servant, saying, 'Fold it, shake it out, and be careful about it!'

H. "He said to him, 'My Lord, O king, among all the purple cloaks that you have, [why] do you give me such instructions only about this one?'

I. "He said to him, 'That is the one that I wore on my coronation day.'

J. "So too did Moses say before the Holy One, blessed be he, Lord of the Universe: 'Among the seventy distinct nations that you have in your world, [why] do you give instructions to me only concerning Israel? [For instance,] "Say to the children of Israel," "Command the children of Israel," "Speak to the children of Israel."'

K. "He said to him, 'They are the ones who at the [Red] Sea declared me to be king, saying, 'The Lord will be king'" (Ex. 15:18).

L. Said R. Berekhiah, "[The matter may be compared] to an elder, who had a hood [signifying his office as Elder], concerning which he instructed his disciple, saying to him, 'Fold it, shake it out, and be careful about it!'

M. "He said to him, 'My lord, Elder, among all the hoods that you have, [why] do you give me such instructions only about this one?'

N. "He said to him, 'It is because that is the one that I wore on the day on which I was officially named an Elder.'

O. "So too did Moses say before the Holy One, blessed be he, Lord of the Universe: 'Among the seventy distinct nations that you have in your world, [why] do you give instructions to me only concerning Israel?'

P. "He said to him, '[It is because] they accepted my dominion on them at Mount Sinai, saying, "Whatever the Lord has spoken we shall do and we shall hear"'" (Ex. 24:7).

(*Lev. R.* II:IV.1)

The invented dialogue does not succeed in endowing God with a particular personality or character. God to be sure appears as a person, but the purpose is to permit the abstract traits under discussion to attain personalization. Yet another important example of the same tendency to resort to narrative for the dramatic presentation of what are, in fact, merely theological principles derives from the following. Here we have God as a partner in dialogue with the nations of the world.

1.A. "O my people, what have I done to you, in what have I wearied you? Testify against me" (Mic. 6:3).

B. Said R. Aha, "'Testify against me' and receive a reward, but 'Do not bear false witness' [Ex. 20:13] and face a settlement of accounts in the age to come."

(*Lev. R.* XXVII:VI.1)

2.A. Said R. Samuel b. R. Nahman, "On three occasions the Holy One, blessed be he, came to engage in argument with Israel, and the nations of the world rejoiced, saying, 'Can these ever [dare] engage in an argument with their creator? Now he will wipe them out of the world.'

B. "One was when he said to them, 'Come, and let us reason together, says the Lord' [Is. 1:18]. When the Holy One, blessed be he, saw that the nations of the world were rejoicing, he turned the matter to [Israel's] advantage: 'If your sins are as scarlet, they shall be white as snow' [Is. 1:18].

C. "Then the nations of the world were astonished, and said, 'This is repentance, and this is rebuke? He has planned only to amuse himself with his children.'

D. "[A second time was] when he said to them, 'Hear, you mountains, the controversy of the Lord' [Mic. 6:2], the nations of the world rejoiced, saying, 'How can these ever [dare] engage in an argument with their creator? Now he will wipe them out of the world.'

E. "When the Holy One, blessed be he, saw that the nations of the world were rejoicing, he turned the matter to [Israel's] advantage: 'O my people, what have I done to you? In what have I wearied you? Testify against me' [Mic. 6:3]. 'Remember what Balak king of Moab devised' [Mic. 6:5].

F. "Then the nations of the world were astonished, saying, 'This is repentance, and this is rebuke, one following the other? He has planned only to amuse himself with his children.'

G. "[A third time was] when he said to them, 'The Lord has an indict-ment against Judah, and will punish Jacob according to his ways' [Hos. 12:2], the nations of the world rejoiced, saying, 'How can these ever [dare] engage in an argument with their creator? Now he will wipe them out of the world.'

H. "When the Holy One, blessed be he, saw that the nations of the world were rejoicing, he turned the matter to [Israel's] advantage. That is in line with the following verse of Scripture: 'In the womb he [Jacob = Israel] took his brother [Esau = other nations] by the heel [and in his manhood he strove with God. He strove with the angel and prevailed, he wept and sought his favor]'" (Hos. 12:3–4).

(*Lev. R.* XXVII:VI.2)

3.A. Said R. Yudan b. R. Simeon, "The matter may be compared to a widow who was complaining to a judge about her son. When she saw that the judge was in session and handing out sentences of punish-ment by fire, pitch, and lashes, she said, 'If I report the bad conduct of my son to that judge, he will kill him now.' She waited until he was finished. When he had finished, he said to her, 'Madam, this son of yours, how has he behaved badly toward you?'

B. "She said to him, 'My lord, when he was in my womb, he kicked me.'

C. "He said to her, 'Now has he done anything wrong to you?'

D. "She said to him, 'No.'

E. "He said to her, 'Go your way, there is nothing wrong in the matter [that you report].'

F. "So, when the Holy One, blessed be he, saw that the nations of the world were rejoicing, he turned the matter to [Israel's] advantage:

G. "'In the womb he took his brother by the heel' [Mic. 12:3].

H. "Then the nations of the world were astonished, saying, 'This is repentance and this is rebuke, one following the other? He has planned only to amuse himself with his children.'"

(*Lev. R.* XXVII:VI.3)

I include the parable to show the rather general character of the passage. The same message is delivered in a variety of media—a syllogism at no. 1, invented dialogue between God and human beings at no. 2, a parable at no. 3—and the focus is on the mes-sage. The personhood of God does not require personalization, and God does not receive traits of an individual and profoundly personal character; God here has no personality whatever. But in the Midrash-compilations of the fifth century, the process of the incarnation of God is well under way, as we shall see presently, so that what is lacking by the end of these documents is only a fully formed personality.

PERSONALITY

While, as we shall see in a moment, God does appear in the exegetical compilations as fully incarnate, nonetheless, in the Midrash-compilations of the fifth century we find not a single saying or story in which God is given a distinctive personality or in concrete narrative portrayed as an incarnate person engaged with human beings in everyday transactions.

THE INCARNATION OF GOD:
THE INITIAL STATEMENT

The exegetical compilations that join the Yerushalmi in marking the beginning of the second state in the unfolding of the Judaism of the dual Torah do present us with a clear picture of the processes that would yield for that Judaism an incarnate God: that God like whom, in whose image and likeness, we are made. The initial statement in the writings surveyed here imputes to God profoundly human actions and concerns. And that marks the first step in the appearance, in the formative stage of this Judaism, of God incarnate. For the incarnation of God may take many forms. But the simplest is to appeal to God's doing the things human beings do. The process of humanization need not appeal to a highly distinct person, let alone a fully etched personality, since in the following God's deeds amply characterize the divinity:

A. Said R. Abbahu, "The Holy One, blessed be he, took the cup of blessing [for the benediction of the marriage of Adam and Eve] and said the blessing for them."
B. Said R. Judah b. R. Simon, "Michael and Gabriel were the best men of the first man."
C. Said R. Simlai, "We have found that the Holy One, blessed be he, says a blessing for bridegrooms, adorns brides, visits the sick, buries the dead, and says a blessing for mourners.
D. "What is the evidence for the fact that he says a blessing for bridegrooms? As it is said, 'And God blessed them' (Gen. 1:28).
E. "That he adorns brides? As it is written, 'And the Lord God built the rib . . . into a woman' (Gen. 2:22).
F. "Visits the sick? As it is written, 'And the Lord appeared to him' (Gen. 18:1).
G. "Buries the dead? As it is written, 'And he buried him in the valley' (Deut. 34:6)."

H. R. Samuel bar Nahman said, "Also he concerns himself for the mourner. It is written, 'And God appeared to Jacob again, when he came from Paddan-aram, and blessed him' (Gen. 35:9).

I. "What was the blessing that he said for him? It was the blessing for mourners."

(*Gen. R.* VIII:XIII.1)

When I speak of God's doing the things human beings do in the way in which human beings do them, this is what I mean. The discourse moves from exegetical to syllogistic, with a set of proof texts validating the view that God engages in a set of meritorious actions. The particular ethical actions emphasized by sages therefore follow the model that God has provided; hence, just as rites are (merely) natural, so acts of supererogatory virtue fostered by sages, acts that produce merit, are treated as divine. What is stunning is the clear notion that God does the things virtuous mortals do, and these things are spelled out in homely terms indeed. But matters go still further.

God not only acts like a human being. God also takes the form of a human being. God is incarnate in that God and mortals look exactly alike. This comes to expression in three stunning ways. First of all, we find the picture of God surrounded by the best looking of all the angels:

A. Another interpretation of the verse: With mighty chariotry, twice ten thousand, thousands upon thousands, [the Lord came from Sinai into the holy place] (Ps. 68:17):

B. Said R. Eleazar b. Pedat, "What is the meaning of the clause twice ten thousand? It refers to the ones that were the most attractive and praiseworthy among them.

C. "Nonetheless, the Lord is among them, meaning, outshining them all.

D. "Said the community of Israel, My beloved is all radiant and ruddy, [distinguished among ten thousand] (Song 5:10).

E. "If a mortal king goes forth to the piazza, how many are as elegant as he is, how many are as powerful as he is, how many are as well groomed as he is, how many are as handsome as he is.

F. "But the Holy One, blessed be he, is not that way. But when he came to Sinai, he took with him the most elegant and praiseworthy ministering angels that were among them."

G. Said R. Judah bar Simon, "What verse of Scripture makes that point? [The Lord came from Sinai and dawned from Seir upon us, he shone forth from Mount Paran, he] came from the ten thousands of holy ones, [with flaming fire at his right hand] (Deut. 33:2).

H. "And he was himself the noteworthy sign among the myriads of holy ones. That must be at the moment that he came to Sinai."

(Pesiq. Rab Kah. XII:XXII.5)

God comes as Israel's lover. Of still greater importance, here for the first time, we find a clear claim that God and the human being look exactly alike, a passage we have already met in the beginning of this book:

A. Said R. Hoshaiah, "When the Holy One, blessed be he, came to create the first man, the ministering angels mistook him [for God, since man was in God's image,] and wanted to say before him, 'Holy, [holy, holy is the Lord of hosts].'

B. "To what may the matter be compared? To the case of a king and a governor who were set in a chariot, and the provincials wanted to greet the king, 'Sovereign!' But they did not know which one of them was which. What did the king do? He turned the governor out and put him away from the chariot, so that people would know who was king.

C. "So too when the Holy One, blessed be he, created the first man, the angels mistook him [for God]. What did the Holy One, blessed be he, do? He put him to sleep, so everyone knew that he was a mere man.

D. "That is in line with the following verse of Scripture: 'Cease you from man, in whose nostrils is a breath, for how little is he to be accounted' (Is. 2:22)."

(Gen. R. VIII:X.1)

Since man—Adam—is in God's image, the angels did not know man from God. Only that man sleeps distinguishes man from God. I cannot imagine a more daring affirmation of humanity. The theme derives from the verse that states, ". . . in our image, after our likeness" (Gen. 1:26), but this passage is not cited in the present construction. Clearly VIII:X simply carries forward the concluding entry of VIII:IX, in which the relevant verse is cited. We have, then, no mere anthology on the cited verse. We have a profoundly polemical statement about the true character and condition of Adam-man. Accordingly, "In our image" yields two views: first, that the complete image of man is attained in a divine union between humanity—man and woman—and, further, that what makes man different from God is that man sleeps and God does not sleep. Given the premise of the base verse and the issues inherent in the allegation that man is in God's image, the treatment here proves extraordinary.

Third, we have a clear claim that God turns into the model of a mortal king and assumes the incarnate traits of such a king:

1.A. Bar Qappara opened discourse by citing the following verse: "In that day the Lord God of hosts called to weeping and mourning, to baldness and girding with sackcloth; [and behold, joy and gladness, slaying oxen and killing sheep, eating meat and drinking wine. 'Let us eat and drink for tomorrow we die.' The Lord of hosts has revealed himself in my ears: 'Surely this iniquity will not be forgiven you until you die,' says the Lord of hosts] (Is. 15:12–14).

B. "Said the Holy One, blessed be he, to the ministering angels, 'When a mortal king mourns, what does he do?'

C. "They said to him, 'He puts sack over his door.'

D. "He said to them, 'I too shall do that. I will clothe the heavens with blackness [and make sackcloth for their covering] (Is. 50:3).'

E. "He further asked them, 'When a mortal king mourns, what does he do?'

F. "They said to him, 'He extinguishes the torches.'

G. "He said to them, 'I too shall do that. The sun and moon will become black [and the stars stop shining] (Joel 4:15)'

H. "He further asked them, 'When a mortal king mourns, what does he do?'

I. "They said to him, 'He goes barefooted.'

J. "He said to them, 'I too shall do that. The Lord in the whirlwind and in the storm will be his way and the clouds [the dust of his feet] (Nahum 1:3).'

K. "He further asked them, 'When a mortal king mourns, what does he do?'

L. "They said to him, 'He sits in silence.'

M. "He said to them, 'I too shall do that. He will sit alone and keep silence because he has laid it upon himself (Lam. 3:28).'

N. "He further asked them, 'When a mortal king mourns, what does he do?'

O. "They said to him, 'He overturns the beds.'

P. "He said to them, 'I too shall do that. I beheld the seats of thrones [having been overturned, now] were placed right side up (Dan. 7:9).'

Q. "He further asked them, 'When a mortal king mourns, what does he do?'

R. "They said to him, 'He tears his [royal] purple garment.'

S. "He said to them, 'I too shall do that. The Lord has done that which he devised, he tore his word (Lam. 2:17).'"

T. What is the meaning of the phrase, he tore his word?

U. R. Jacob of Kefar Hanan said, "He tears his purple garments."

V. [Resuming the earlier account,] "He further asked them, 'When a mortal king mourns, what does he do?'

W. "They said to him, 'He sits and laments.'

X. "He said to them, 'I too shall do that. How lonely sits the city [that was full of people! How like a widow has she become, she that was great among the nations! She that was a princess among the cities has become a vassal. She weeps bitterly in the night, tears on her cheeks, among all her lovers she has none to comfort her; all her friends have dealt treacherously with her, they have become her enemies] (Lam. 1:1–2).'"

(Pesiq. Rab Kah. XV:III.1)

Again, we have an explicit claim, powerfully concrete and corporeal, that God does the things human beings do in the ways, and for the motives, that human beings do them. When, therefore, I speak of the incarnation of God in formative Judaism, the passage before us amply spells out what I mean. Here God assumes incarnate qualities as a mortal king. But drawing the consequences for a fully formed personality of the comparability of God and the human being would come only in the final document of the Judaism of the dual Torah in its formative age.

8

Torah Incarnate:
The Fathers According
to Rabbi Nathan

PREMISE

In *The Fathers According to Rabbi Nathan,* the sage becomes a figure of flesh and blood, not merely the name on which to hang a saying. But God does not gain a personality, remaining a premise and presence bearing, to be sure, implicit personhood. What is interesting in *The Fathers According to Rabbi Nathan* (ARNA) is that the framers of that document, a kind of Talmud to tractate *Avot* or *The Fathers,* vastly enriched discourse by adding important stories about sages. But as to God they did not follow suit and tell stories about God as personality. In *The Fathers According to Rabbi Nathan* the sage, a mere name in tractate *Avot,* became a figure of flesh and blood, with a large body of stories supplying important sages with pieces of biographies and, consequently, personalities. But I see no counterpart treatment of God. If we compare the program of the two documents we see how the shift has taken place. The structural program of *The Fathers* is transparent: (1) a list of names, together with (2) wise sayings. Some of these wise sayings are subjected to secondary explication or amplification; most are not but are left as simple gnomic statements. So the authorship of *The Fathers* has chosen to present us with lists of names joined to sayings, some of them amplified, most not. The types of materials in *The Fathers According to Rabbi Nathan* and their order permit comparison to *The Fathers.* The document contains amplifications of sayings in *The Fathers* as well as materials not related to anything in the original document. Where the authorship of the later document has chosen (1) to cite and amplify sayings in the earlier one, that exercise comes first. There may be additional amplification (2) in the form of (a) proof texts drawn from Scripture, or (b) parables, (c) other sorts of stories, sometimes involving named sages, that illustrate the same point, and (d) sequences of un-adorned sayings, not in *The Fathers,* that make the same point. These come later in a sequence of discourses in *The Fathers According to Rabbi Nathan.*

Given a saying of an apophthegmatic character, such as those that occur in tractate *Avot, whether or not that saying is drawn from The Fathers,* the authorship of *The Fathers According to Rabbi Nathan* will do one the following things:

1. give a secondary expansion, including an exemplification, of the wise saying at hand;
2. cite a proof text of Scripture in that same connection;
3. provide a parable to illustrate the wise saying (as often as not instead of the proof text).

These three exercises in the structuring of their document—selecting materials and organizing them in a systematic way—the authors of *The Fathers According to Rabbi Nathan* learned from the framers of *The Fathers.* In addition they contributed two further principles of structuring their document:

4. add a sizable composition of materials that intersect with the foregoing, either by amplifying on the proof text without regard to the wise saying served by the proof text or by enriching discourse on a topic introduced in connection with the base saying;
5. tack on a protracted story of a sage and what he said and did, which story may or may not exemplify the teaching of the apophthegm at hand.

The two sorts of material fall into a single category, which is an essentially autonomous body of material pertinent to a given theme or topic—hence, topical appendix is the appropriate name of the classification of materials. The point of the discourse to which they are tacked on, however, rarely affects the selection and arrangement of the materials in the appendix or makes an appearance in the composition constituted by said appendix. They work out their own internal proposition and in no way give evidence that the authorship responsible for them has in hand the proposition that, in *The Fathers According to Rabbi Nathan,* forms their host setting. The stories about Yohanan ben Zakkai's escape from Jerusalem, Eliezer's and Aqiba's beginnings, for example, were made up on their own and not in connection with the passage in *The Fathers According to Rabbi Nathan* in which they now find their position.

This brings us to the topic at hand: points in *The Fathers According to Rabbi Nathan* at which God serves as an articulated premise of discourse. I see only the following:

ARNA I:VI.1

A. Make a fence for the Torah.

B. And make a fence around your words,

C. just as [1] the Holy One, blessed be he, made a fence around his words, and [2] the first man made a fence around his words. [3] The Torah made a fence around its words. [4] Moses made a fence around his words. And so too [5] Job as well as [6] the prophets and [7] writings and [8] sages—all of them made a fence around their words.

ARNA I:VII.1

A. What is the fence that [1] the Holy One, blessed be he, made around his words?

B. Lo, [Scripture] says, *And all the nations will say, On what account did the Lord do thus to this land* (Deut. 29:24).

C. This teaches that it was entirely obvious before him who by his word brought the world into being that the generations to come were destined to say this.

D. Therefore the Holy One, blessed be he, said to Moses, "Moses, write it that way, and leave it for the coming generations to say, *It was because they abandoned the covenant of the Lord* (Deut. 29:24), *And they went and worshipped other gods and bowed down to them, gods which they had not known and which had not been assigned to them* (Deut. 29:25)."

E. Lo, in this way you learn that the Holy One, blessed be he, paid out the reward of his creatures [Goldin:] to the letter [lit: through peace].

This seems to me a perfectly standard statement, yielding no fresh and important propositions. We move on to the matter of the representation of God as presence, which, we recall, was one of the important traits of *The Fathers*.

PRESENCE

The amplification of the sayings in *The Fathers* about God's presence when the Torah is studied bears no effort to describe what God's presence entails, or how one is to know that God is at hand. What we have is simply a restatement with some further details of the established point:

ARNA VIII:III.1

A. In the case of three disciples in session and occupied with study of the Torah, the Holy One, blessed be he, credits it to them as if they formed a single band before him,

B. as it is said, *He who builds his upper chambers in the heaven and has founded his band upon the earth, he who calls for the waters of the sea and pours them out upon the face of the earth, the Lord is his name* (Amos 9:6).

C. Thus you have learned that in the case of three disciples in session and occupied with study of the Torah, the Holy One, blessed be he, credits it to them as if they formed a single band before him.

ARNA VIII:III.2

A. In the case of two disciples in session and occupied with study of the Torah, their reward is received on high,

B. as it is said, *Then they who feared the Lord spoke one with another, and the Lord heard . . . and a book of remembrance was written before him for those who feared the Lord and who gave thought to his name* (Mal. 3:16).

C. Who are those referred to as "they who feared the Lord"?

D. They are the ones who reach a decision, saying, "Let us go and free those who are imprisoned and redeem those who have been kidnapped for ransom," and the Holy One, blessed be he, gave sufficient power in their hands to do so, and they go and do it right away.

E. And who are those referred to as "they who gave thought to his name"?

F. They are the ones who reckon in their hearts, saying, "Let us go and free those who are imprisoned and redeem those who have been kidnapped for ransom," and the Holy One, blessed be he, did not give sufficient power in their hands to do so, so an angel came and beat them down to the ground.

ARNA VIII:III.3

A. In the case of an individual disciple in session and occupied with study of the Torah, his reward is received on high,

B. as it is said, *Though he sit alone and keep silence, surely he has laid up [a reward] for him* (Lam. 3:28).

C. The matter may be conveyed in a parable: to what is it comparable?

D. To someone who had a young child, whom he left at home when he went out to the market. The son went and took a scroll and set it between his knees and sat and meditated on it.

E. When his father came back from the market place, he said, "See my little son, whom I left when I went out to the market place. What has he done on his own! He has studied and taken the scroll and set it between his knees, going into session and meditating on it."

F. So you have learned that even an individual disciple who has gone into session and occupied with study of the Torah, receives his reward received on high.

I see no considerable expansion of a fairly obvious proposition. In the following, we have a rather enigmatic statement which bears the sense that God wants people to come to the temple (God's house) or to the synagogue or study house:

ARNA XII:VIII.1

A. He would say, "If you will come to my house, I shall come to your house. To the place which my heart loves, there my feet lead me."

B. If you will come to my house, I shall come to your house: how so?

C. This refers to people who get up early in the morning and stay late in the evening to attend the sessions of synagogues and study houses.

D. The Holy One, blessed be he, blesses them for the world to come.

E. That accords with the following verse: *In every place where I cause my name to be mentioned I will come to you and bless you* (Ex. 20:21).

F. To the place which my heart loves, there my feet lead me.

G. How so? This refers to people who leave [at home] their silver and gold and go up for the pilgrim-festival to greet the face of the Presence of God in the sanctuary.

H. The Holy One, blessed be he, protects them in their camps [at home, so no one will steal their money], as it is said, *Neither shall any one covet your land when you go up to appear before the Lord your God* (Ex. 34:24).

ARNA XII:IX.1

A. He would say, "If I am here, all are here. If I am not here, who is here? Turn it over again and again, because everything is in it, and in all ways, in accord with the pain is the gain."

The sense of the foregoing is not self-evident. We lack a clear statement of what God's being "here" means, or how it would be envisioned.

God's presence in the world, it was held, had taken place in easy stages. God had descended by ten stages, and then had ascended by ten stages in the aftermath of the disappointing fate of the Torah in the world:

ARNA XXXIV:VIII.1

A. There were ten descents that the Presence of God made into the world.

B. One into the Garden of Eden, as it says, *And they heard the sound of God walking in the garden* (Gen. 3:5).

C. One in the generation of the tower of Babylon, as it is said, *And the Lord came down to see the city and the tower* (Gen. 11:5).

D. One in Sodom: *I shall now go down and see whether it is in accord with the cry that has come to me* (Gen. 18:21).

E. One in Egypt: *I shall go down and save them from the hand of the Egyptians* (Ex. 3:8).

F. One at the sea: *He bowed the heavens also and came down* (2 Sam. 22:10).

G. One at Sinai: *And the Lord came down onto Mount Sinai* (Ex. 19:20).

H. One in the pillar of cloud: *And the Lord came down in a pillar* (Num. 11:25).

I. One in the Temple: *This gate will be closed and will not be open for the Lord, God of Israel, has come in through it* (Ez. 44:2).

J. And one is destined to take place in the time of Gog and Magog: *And his feet shall stand that day on the mount of Olives* (Zech. 14:4).

ARNA XXXIV:IX.1

A. In ten upward stages the Presence of God departed, from one place to the next: from the ark cover to the cherub; from the cherub to the threshold of the temple-building; from the threshold of the temple to the two cherubim; from the two cherubim to the roof of the sanctuary; from the roof of the sanctuary to the wall of the temple court; from the wall of the temple court to the altar; from the altar to the city; from the city to the temple mount; from the temple mount to the wilderness.

B. from the ark cover to the cherub: *And he rode upon a cherub and flew* (2 Sam. 22:11).

C. from the cherub to the threshold of the temple-building: *And the glory of the Lord mounted up from the cherub to the threshold of the house* (Ez. 10:45).

D. from the threshold of the temple to the two cherubim: *And the glory of the Lord went forth from off the threshold of the house and stood over the cherubim* (Ez. 10:18).

E. from the two cherubim to the roof of the sanctuary: *It is better to dwell in a corner of the housetop* (Prov. 21:9).

F. from the roof of the sanctuary to the wall of the temple court: *And behold the Lord stood beside a wall made by a plumbline* (Amos 7:7).
G. from the wall of the temple court to the altar: *I saw the Lord standing beside the altar* (Amos 9:1).
H. from the altar to the city: *Hark, the Lord cries to the city* (Mic. 6:9).
I. from the city to the temple mount: *And the glory of the Lord went up from the midst of the city and stood upon the mountain* (Ez. 11:23).
J. from the temple mount to the wilderness: *It is better to dwell in a desert land* (Prov. 21:19).
K. And then to on high: *I will go and return to my place* (Hos. 5:15).

I see nothing in this account of God's presence and its movements to suggest that God is going to be subject to description as a person let alone a personality. The striking initiatives we noted in the Midrash-compilations have no counterpart in the document devoted to the telling of stories about sages.

PERSON

God occurs as a person when dialogue is given to God as a means of stating a doctrine, a familiar mode of discourse. The following provides a good example:

ARNA XXXII:II.1

A. R. Eleazar b. Parta says, "Lo, Scripture says, *My spirit shall not judge man in this world* (Gen. 6:3).
B. "Said the Holy One, blessed be he, I shall not judge them until I double the reward that is coming to them [Goldin: until I have given them their reward in full], as it is said, *They spend their days in prosperity, but then they go down to Sheol* (Job 21:13)."

All we have is a statement in the first person of the doctrine of divine retribution. There is no effort at characterizing God in these terms. The following persist in the same pattern.

ARNA XXXII:II.2

A. R. Yose the Galilean says, "Lo, Scripture says, *My spirit shall not judge man in this world* (Gen. 6:3).
B. "Said the Holy One, blessed be he, 'I shall not treat as equivalent the impulse to do evil and the impulse to do good.'
C. "When is that the case? Before the decree has been sealed, but once the decree has been sealed, both of them are equal as to transgression."

ARNA XXXII:II.4

A. R. Simeon b. Eleazar says, "Lo, Scripture says, *My spirit shall not punish man in this world* (Gen. 6:3).

B. "Said the Holy One, blessed be he, 'I shall not judge them until I have paid the reward that is coming to the righteous.'

C. "When is this the case? In this world.

D. "But as to the world to come, *His breath goes forth, he returns to the dust in that very day* (Ps. 146:4)."

ARNA XXXII:II.5

A. R. Aqiba says, "Lo, Scripture says, *My spirit shall not judge man in this world* (Gen. 6:3).

B. "Said the Holy One, blessed be he, 'They did not come to a correct judgment of themselves, that they are mortal, but they behaved arrogantly toward the heights,'

C. "as it is said, *Yet they said to God, Depart from us, we do not want the knowledge of your ways* (Job 21:14)."

ARNA XXXII:II.6

A. R. Meir says, "Lo, Scripture says, *My spirit shall not judge man in this world* (Gen. 6:3).

B. "Said the Holy One, blessed be he, 'That generation has said, "The Lord will not judge, there is no judge in the world, God has abandoned the world."'"

ARNA XXXII:II.7

A. Rabbi says, "Lo, it says, *My spirit shall not judge man in this world* (Gen. 6:3).

B. "Said the Holy One, blessed be he, 'They did not call sanhedrins into session on earth, lo, I shall call into session a sanhedrin in heaven.'"

In all of these instances, God is given language to speak, but the language is not personal but simply makes doctrinal or other propositional points.

God further occurs in *The Fathers According to Rabbi Nathan* as a person, engaged in conversation with other persons. But where God plays a personal part, it is not a very nuanced one, and God does not emerge as an amply described figure at all. In the following, God as person gives an order and wins an argument, without emerging as a significant protagonist in the story. It is Moses who has the leading part, with God as the loyal straight man yet again:

ARNA XII:II.2

A. At that time [the Holy One, blessed be he] said to the angel of death, "Go bring me the soul of Moses."

B. The angel of death went and stood before him, saying to him, "Moses, give me your soul."

C. Moses grew angry with him and said to him, "Where I am sitting you have no right even to stand, yet you have said, 'Give me your soul'!" He threw him out with outrage.

D. Then the Holy One, blessed be he, said to Moses, "Moses, you have had enough of this world, for lo, the world to come is readied for you, for a place is prepared for you from the first six days of creation."

E. For it is said, *And the Lord said, Behold a place by me, and you shall stand upon the rock* (Ex. 33:21).

F. The Holy One, blessed be he, took the soul of Moses and stored it away under the throne of glory.

G. And when he took it, he took it only with a kiss, as it is said, *By the mouth of the Lord* (Deut. 34:5).

Moses is the center of interest; he is the one who acts, God merely responds. God's action is not a means of setting forth God as a vivid person.

PERSONALITY

Nothing in *The Fathers According to Rabbi Nathan* undertakes the description of God as a vivid personality. What we noted in the treatment of God's presence—a rather enigmatic atmosphere of restrained discourse—has prepared us for this conclusion.

CONCLUSION

The Fathers According to Rabbi Nathan differs from *The Fathers* in one aspect so fundamental as to change the face of the base document completely. While the earlier authorship took slight interest in lives and deeds of sages, the later one contributed in a systematic and orderly manner the color and life of biography to the named but faceless sages of *The Fathers*. The stories about sages make points that correspond to positions taken in statements of viewpoints particular to *The Fathers According to Rabbi Nathan*. The stories also contain those fresh points that differentiate the later from the earlier document. There are two sides to the matter. First is the national-eschatological interest of the later document, with its focus on living only in the Land of Israel. Then there is the contrast between this age, possessed by the Gentiles, and the age to come, in which redeemed Israel will enjoy a paramount position. Without counterpart in the earlier composition, that contrast emerges not only in sayings but also in stories about the critical issue. That is the destruction of Jerusalem and the loss of the Temple, along with the concomitant matter, repentance and how it is achieved at this time. When we consider the contents of those stories, we see time and again that same national-salvific and eschatological teleology that eludes discovery in *The Fathers*. Yet a further point of development lies in the notion that study of the Torah combined with various virtues, for example, good deeds, fear of sin, suffices, with a concomitant assurance that making a living no longer matters. Here too the new medium of the later document—the stories about sages—bears the new message. That conviction emerges not only explicitly—for example, in the sayings of Hananiah about the power of Torah-study to take away many sources of suffering, Judah b. Ilai's that one should treat words of the Torah as the principal, earning a living as trivial, and so on—but also in the detail that both Aqiba and Eliezer began poor but through their mastery of Torah ended rich.

The Fathers presents an ideal of the sage as model for the everyday life of the individual, who must study the Torah and also work, and through the good life prepare now for life after death, while *The Fathers According to Rabbi Nathan* has a different conception of the sage, of the value and meaning of the study of the Torah, and of the center of interest—and also has selected a new medium for the expression of its distinctive conception. To spell this out: (1) The sage is now—in *The Fathers According to Rabbi Nathan*—not a judge and teacher alone but also a supernatural figure. (2) Study of the Torah in preference to making a living promises freedom from the conditions of natural life. (3) Israel as the holy people seen as a supernatural social entity takes center stage. *And these innovative points are conveyed not only in sayings but in stories about sages.*

What follows is that the medium not only carries a new message but forms a component of that new message. The sage as a supernatural figure now presents Torah-teachings through what he does, not only through what he says. Therefore, telling stories about what sages did and the circumstances in which they made their sayings forms part of the Torah in a way in which in the earlier document it clearly did not. The interest in stories about sages proves therefore not merely literary or formal; it is more than a new way of conveying an old message. Stories about the sages are told because sages stand for a message that can emerge only in stories and not in sayings alone. So we turn to a close reading of the stories themselves to review that message and find out why through stories in particular the message now emerges. For what we see is nothing short of a new mode of revelation, that is, of conveying and imparting God's will in the Torah. Judaism (our term and category) requires stories because the Torah (their term and category) reaches Israel through not merely what the sage says but what he is and does. The stories about sages portray a burden of values distinct from those expressed in the sayings of *The Fathers*. Those stories commonly are attached to portions of *The Fathers According to Rabbi Nathan* that serve as exegeses of sayings in *The Fathers* on the one side, or in Scripture on the other. The framers of *The Fathers According to Rabbi Nathan* in this way imputed to *The Fathers* (as well as to Scripture) the messages that, in fact, they themselves proposed to deliver. The importance of this fact for our search for the incarnation of God is self-evident. Once the sage gets his biography, God could not be denied one too. In the concluding document in the formative canon of the Judaism of the dual Torah, the Talmud of Babylonia, God, like the sage, gained that characterization through stories that would render God incarnate: like woman and man, in attitude and action— only God. And yet that final qualification—like humanity, yet God—will in the end signal the fundamental genius of the sages of the dual Torah. They took for granted that they were like God. Therefore God was like them. Yet the climactic statement of their system concerning the profoundly human character of divinity— the statement in the form of a story of the incarnation of God— will differ radically and fundamentally from all stories about sages (which I call "sage-stories").

That ultimate incarnation of God will register the point that God is not (merely) a sage. God is God. With that fundamental story told, God attains that full personality of incarnation that the Judaism of the dual Torah would know and encounter through all time. The incarnation of God will be accomplished through the differentiation, in the story in particular, of the story of God from the story of the sage. Given sages' conception of the Torah and of themselves as the living Torah, that point of differentiation will proclaim a sublime statement. To specify the message very simply: we are in the image and likeness, but we are not the same. To be like something is not to be that something. It is merely to be like it. The incarnation of God in the imagination of the sages of the dual Torah yields not the banality of God like us, but the sublimity of us like God—but not God. God alone is God. In pointing toward that ultimate conclusion of the Judaic version of the incarnation of God, I have moved well beyond this stage in my argument. First, let us turn to the Bavli and its repertoire of sayings and stories on the character of divinity. Then we shall return to the comparison of the incarnation of the Torah in the sage, effected through sayings and stories, with the incarnation of God, also expressed through allusions and stories. Then, in the concluding chapter, I shall spell out in detail how and why the ultimate message of the Judaism of the dual Torah on the incarnation of God is that simple statement I offered just now: incarnate, God is always God, the one and only God.

PART FOUR

From Personality to Incarnation: The Bavli's Classic Statement of the Dual Torah, 500–600

9

The Bavli and the Incarnation of God

INCARNATION: GOD AS MAN

The portrayal of God as a man—that is, of man as the image of God on earth—did not begin with the Bavli. We have already encountered a stunning and explicit statement of the matter in *Genesis Rabbah*, fully two hundred years before the closure of the Bavli. Here we find the simple claim that the angels could not discern any physical difference whatever between man—Adam—and God:

1.A. Said R. Hoshaiah, "When the Holy One, blessed be he, came to create the first man, the ministering angels mistook him [for God, since man was in God's image,] and wanted to say before him, 'Holy, [holy, holy is the Lord of hosts].'

B. "To what may the matter be compared? To the case of a king and a governor who were set in a chariot, and the provincials wanted to greet the king, 'Sovereign!' But they did not know which one of them was which. What did the king do? He turned the governor out and put him away from the chariot, so that people would know who was king.

C. "So too when the Holy One, blessed be he, created the first man, the angels mistook him [for God]. What did the Holy One, blessed be he, do? He put him to sleep, so everyone knew that he was a mere man.

D. "That is in line with the following verse of Scripture: 'Cease you from man, in whose nostrils is a breath, for how little is he to be accounted' (Is. 2:22)."

(*Gen. R.* VIII:X)

A view such as the present one invites precisely the development fully exposed in the pages of the Talmud of Babylonia. The reason that framers of prior documents in the Land of Israel did not follow the inner logic of the idea expressed here and produce concrete allusions to, and stories about, the incarnation of God derives from the specific character of the Christian challenge.[1] In Iranian Babylonia there was no reason not to move to the inexorable conclusion; consequently, it was in the Bavli in particular that God became man. There we see in a variety of dimensions the single characterization of God as incarnate. The incarnation, moreover, was not merely a matter of pointing to spiritual or other nonmaterial traits shared by God and humanity. God's physical traits and attributes are represented as identical to those of a human being. That is why the character of the divinity may accurately be represented as incarnational: God in the flesh, God represented as a person consubstantial in indicative physical traits with the human being.

Telling stories provides the means by which theological traits are portrayed as personalities of God who is like a human being. It is one thing to hypostatize a theological abstraction, for example, "The quality of mercy said before the Holy One, blessed be he. . . ." It is quite another to construct a conversation between God and, for example, David with a complete argument and a rich interchange in which God's merciful character is spelled out as the trait of a specific personality. And that is what we find in the Bavli and, so far as my survey suggests, not in any prior document. It is in the Bavli that the specification of an attribute of God, such as being long-suffering, is restated by means of narrative. God then emerges not as an abstract entity with theological traits but as a fully exposed incarnate person, a personality. God is portrayed as engaged in conversation with human beings because God and humanity can understand one another within the same rules of discourse. When we speak of the incarnation of God, traits of a corporeal, emotional, and social nature form the repertoire of appropriate characteristics. To begin with, we consider the particular means by which, in the pages of the Talmud of Babylonia or Bavli in particular, these traits are set forth.

---

1. Above, chapter 7, pp. 103ff.

The following story shows us the movement from the abstract and theological to the concrete and narrative mode of discourse about God:

A. "And Moses made haste and bowed his head toward the earth and worshipped" (Ex. 34:8):

B. What did Moses see?

C. R. Hanina b. Gamula said, "He saw [God's attribute of] being long-suffering [Ex. 34:7]."

D. Rabbis say, "He saw [the attribute of] truth [Ex. 34:7]." It has been taught on Tannaite authority in accord with him who has said, "He saw God's attribute of being long-suffering."

E. For it has been taught on Tannaite authority:

F. When Moses went up on high, he found the Holy One, blessed be he, sitting and writing, "Long-suffering."

G. He said before him, "Lord of the world, 'Long-suffering for the righteous'?"

H. He said to him, "Also for the wicked."

I. [Moses] said to him, "Let the wicked perish."

J. He said to him, "Now you will see what you want."

K. When the Israelites sinned, he said to him, "Did I not say to you, 'Long-suffering for the righteous'?"

L. [111b] He said to him, "Lord of the world, did I not say to you, 'Also for the wicked'?"

M. That is in line with what is written, "And now I beseech you, let the power of my Lord be great, according as you have spoken, saying" (Num. 14:17). [M. Freedman, *The Babylonian Talmud. Sanhedrin* (London: Soncino Press, 1948), 764 n. 7: What called forth Moses' worship of God when Israel sinned through the Golden Calf was his vision of the Almighty as long-suffering.]

(*b. San* 111a–b, VI)

The statement at the outset, A–D, is repeated in narrative form at F–M. Once we are told that God is long-suffering, then it is in particular narrative form that that trait is given definition. God then emerges as a personality, specifically because Moses engages in argument with God. He reproaches God, questions God's actions and judgments, holds God to a standard of consistency—and receives appropriate responses. God in heaven does not argue with humanity on earth. God in heaven issues decrees, forms the premise of the earthly rules, constitutes a presence, may even take the form of a "you" for hearing and answering prayers. But all of this is in accord with established reasons and laws. When God argues, discusses, defends and explains actions, emerges as a personality etched in words, then God attains that incarnation that imparts to God the status of a being consubstantial with humanity. It is in particular through narrative that that transformation of God from person to personality, the incarnation of God, takes place. Since incarnation, as I have defined matters, involves physical traits, attitudes of mind, emotion, and intellect consubstantial with those of human beings, and the doing of the deeds people do in the way in which they do them, I have now to demonstrate that all three modes of incarnation come to full expression in the Bavli. This we do in sequence, ending with a clear demonstration that God incarnate takes the particular form of a sage. And that will yield the problem of the final chapter, namely, the difference between God and all (other) sages.

INCARNATION: THE PHYSICAL
ATTRIBUTES OF GOD

The claim that the character of God is shaped in the model of a human being requires substantiation, first of all, in quite physical traits, such as are taken for granted in the passage just now cited. Incarnation means precisely that: representation of God in the flesh, as a human being, in the present context, as a man. We begin with a clear statement that has God represented as a man,[2] seen in the interpretation of the vision of the prophet Zechariah:

A. And said R. Yohanan, "What is the meaning of the verse of Scripture, 'I saw by night, and behold a man riding upon a red horse, and he stood among the myrtle trees that were in the bottom' (Zech. 1:8)?

B. "What is the meaning of, 'I saw by night'?

C. "The Holy One, blessed be he, sought to turn the entire world into night.

D. "'And behold a man riding'—'man' refers only to the Holy One, blessed be he, as it is said, 'The Lord is a man of war, the Lord is his name' (Ex. 15:3).

E. "'On a red horse'—the Holy One, blessed be he, sought to turn the entire world to blood.

---

2. I cannot point to a single representation of God in the feminine in the literature under survey, but, of course, the potentiality was present from scriptural writings onward.

F. "When, however, he saw Hananiah, Mishael, and Azariah, he cooled off, as it is said, 'And he stood among the myrtle trees that were in the deep.'"

(b. San. 1:1, XLII[93A])

The passage in *Pesiqta deRab Kahana* has prepared us for the citation of Ex. 15:3 as proof that God makes the appearance of a human being. We recall the explicit statement in this same regard:

B. [it was necessary for] the Holy One, blessed be he, to say to them, "You see me in many forms. But I am the same one who was at the sea, I am the same one who was at Sinai, *I [anokhi] am the Lord your God who brought you out of the land of Egypt* (Ex. 20:2)."

Scripture of course knows that God has a face, upon which human beings are not permitted to gaze. But was that face understood in a physical way, and did God enjoy other physical characteristics? An affirmative answer emerges clearly in the following:

A. "And he said, 'You cannot see my face'" (Ex. 33:20).
B. It was taught on Tannaite authority in the name of R. Joshua b. Qorha, "This is what the Holy One, blessed be he, said to Moses:
C. "'When I wanted [you to see my face], you did not want to, now that you want to see my face, I do not want you to.'"
D. This differs from what R. Samuel bar Nahmani said R. Jonathan said.
E. For R. Samuel bar Nahmani said R. Jonathan said, "As a reward for three things he received the merit of three things.
F. "As a reward for: 'And Moses hid his face' (Ex. 3:6), he had the merit of having a glistening face.
G. "As a reward for: 'Because he was afraid to' (Ex. 3:6), he had the merit that 'They were afraid to come near him' (Ex. 34:30).
H. "As a reward for: 'To look upon God' (Ex. 3:6), he had the merit: 'The similitude of the Lord does he behold' (Num. 12:8)."

A. "And I shall remove my hand and you shall see my back" (Ex. 33:23).
B. Said R. Hana bar Bizna said R. Simeon the Pious, "This teaches that the Holy One, blessed be he, showed Moses [how to tie] the knot of the phylacteries."

(b. Ber. 7A, LVI)

That God is able to tie the knot indicates that God has fingers and other physical gifts. God furthermore is portrayed as wearing phylacteries as well. It follows that God has an arm and a forehead. There is no element of a figurative reading of the indicated traits. That is why, when God is further represented as having eyes and teeth, we have no reason to assign that picture to the status of (mere) poetry:

A. "His eyes shall be red with wine, and his teeth white with milk" (Gen. 49:12):
B. R. Dimi, when he came, interpreted the verse in this way: "The congregation of Israel said to the Holy One, blessed be he, 'Lord of the Universe, wink to me with your eyes, which gesture will be sweeter than wine, and show me your teeth, which gesture will be sweeter than milk.'"

(b. Ket. 111b)

The attribution of physical traits is explicit and no longer general or possibly figurative. Another such representation assigns cheeks to God:

A. R. Joshua b. Levi, "What is the meaning of the verse, 'His cheeks are as a bed of spices' (Song 5:13)?
B. "At every act of speech which went forth from the mouth of the Holy One, blessed be he, the entire world was filled with the fragrance of spices."
C. But since at the first act of speech, the world was filled, where did the second act of speech go?
D. The Holy One, blessed be he, took from his treasures a strong wind, which removed the first draft of fragrance in sequence.

(b. Shab. 88b)

Joining speech, which is not material, to fragrance, cheeks, and the like, will not have surprised the authorship of *Pesiqta deRab Kahana,* as we have already noted. From eyes and teeth and cheeks, we move on to the physical attributes of having arms and the like. In the following passage, God is given hands and palms:

E. Further, [the congregation of Israel] made its request in an improper manner, "O God, set me as a seal on your heart, as a seal on your arm" (Song 8:6).
F. [But the Holy One, blessed be he, responded in a proper way.] Said the Holy One, blessed be he, to [the congregation of Israel,] "My daughter, now you are asking for something which sometimes can be seen and sometimes cannot be seen. But I shall give you something which can always be seen.
G. "For it is said, 'Behold, I have graven you on the palms of my hands' (Is. 49:16) [and the palms are always visible, in a way in which the heart and arm are not]."

(b. Ta. 4a)

Hands are attached to arms, and it is implicit that God has arms as well. That God has arms is shown again by the claim that God puts on phylacteries just as Moses does:

A. Said R. Abin bar Ada said R. Isaac, "How do we know on the basis of Scripture that the Holy One, blessed be he, puts on phylacteries? As it is said, 'The Lord has sworn by his right hand, and by the arm of his strength' (Is. 62:8).
B. "'By his right hand' refers to Torah, as it is said, 'At his right hand was a fiery law for them' (Deut. 33:2).
C. "'And by the arm of his strength' refers to phylacteries, as it is said, 'The Lord will give strength to his people' (Ps. 29:11).
D. "And how do we know that phylacteries are a strength for Israel? For it is written, 'And all the peoples of the earth shall see that the name of the Lord is called upon you and they shall be afraid of you' (Deut. 28:10)."
E. And it has been taught on Tannaite authority:
F. R. Eliezer the Great says, "This [Deut. 28:10] refers to the phylacteries that are put on the head."

(b. Ber. 6A, XXXVIII)

Once more we find clear evidence of a corporeal conception of God. We have no basis on which to assume the authorship at hand meant a (merely) poetic characterization, or, indeed, what such a more spiritual interpretation would have required. Assuming that the words mean precisely what they say, we have to conclude that God is here portrayed as incarnate. Later on we shall be told what passages of Scripture are written in the phylacteries that God puts onto his right arm and forehead.

We shall presently review the range of God's emotions, which appear to be pretty much the same as human ones. But first let us treat the matter of God's doing what people do, in the way in which they do them. In the Bavli's stories God not only looks like a human being but also does the acts that human beings do. For example, God spends the day much as does a mortal ruler of Israel, at least as sages imagine such a figure. That is, he studies the Torah, makes practical decisions, and sustains the world (meaning administers public funds for public needs)—just as (in their picture of themselves) sages do. What gives us a deeply human God is that for the final part of the day, God plays with his pet, leviathan. Some correct that view and hold that God spends the rest of the day teaching youngsters. In passages such as these we therefore see the concrete expression of a process of the incarnation of God:

A. Said R. Judah said Rab, "The day is twelve hours long. During the first three, the Holy One, blessed be he, is engaged in the study of the Torah.

B. "During the next three God sits in judgment on the world and when he sees the world sufficiently guilty to deserve destruction, he moves from the seat of justice to the seat of mercy.

C. "During the third he feeds the whole world, from the horned buffalo to vermin.

D. "During the fourth he plays with the leviathan, as it is said, 'There is leviathan, whom you have made to play with' (Ps. 104:26)."

E. [Another authority denies this final point and says,] "What then does God do in the fourth quarter of the day?

F. "He sits and teaches school children, as it is said, 'Whom shall one teach knowledge, and whom shall one make to understand the message? Those who are weaned from milk' (Is. 28:9)."

G. And what does God do by night?

H. If you like, I shall propose that he does what he does in daytime.

I. Or if you prefer: he rides a light cherub and floats in eighteen thousand worlds . . .

J. Or if you prefer: he sits and listens to the song of the heavenly creatures, as it is said, "By the day the Lord will command his lovingkindness and in the night his song shall be with me" (Ps. 42:9).

(*b. A.Z.* 3b)

Other actions of God that presuppose a physical capacity are indicated in the following, although the picture is not so clearly one of concrete physical actions as in the earlier instances:

A. Said R. Judah said Rab, "Everything that Abraham personally did for the ministering angels the Holy One, blessed be he, personally did for his children, and everything that Abraham did through servants the Holy One, blessed be he, carried out also through ministering angels.

B. "'And Abraham ran to the herd' (Gen. 18:7). 'And a wind went forth from the Lord' (Num. 11:31).

C. "'And he took butter and milk' (Gen. 18:8). 'Behold, I will rain bread from heaven for you' (Ex. 16:4).

D. "'And he stood by them under the tree' (Gen. 18:8). 'Behold, I will stand before you there upon the rock'" (Ex. 17:6).

(*b. B.M.* 86b)

The passage proceeds to point out further examples of the same parallels. The various actions of God in favor of Israel correspond to the concrete actions of Abraham for God or the angels. The comparison of Abraham's actions to those of God invites the notion that God is represented as incarnate. But in this instance we are not compelled to a reading of God as an essentially corporeal being. The actions God does can be accomplished in some less material or physical way. In the balance, however, we do find evidence to suggest that the authorship of the Bavli understood that God looks like a human being, specifically, like a man, and that God does what human beings of a particular order or class do.

INCARNATION: THE EMOTIONS
AND ATTITUDES OF GOD

The incarnation of God encompassed not only physical but also emotional or attitudinal traits. In the final stage of the Judaism of the dual Torah God emerged as a fully exposed personality. The character of divinity, therefore, encompassed God's virtue, the specific traits of character and personality that God exhibited above and here below. Above all, humility, the virtue sages most often asked of themselves, characterized the divinity. God wanted people to be humble, and God therefore showed humility.

A. Said R. Joshua b. Levi, "When Moses came down from before the Holy One, blessed be he, Satan came and asked [God], 'Lord of the world, Where is the Torah?'

B. "He said to him, 'I have given it to the earth . . .' [Satan ultimately was told by God to look for the Torah by finding the son of Amram].

C. "He went to Moses and asked him, 'Where is the Torah which the Holy One, blessed be he, gave you?'

D. "He said to him, 'Who am I that the Holy One, blessed be he, should give me the Torah?'

E. "Said the Holy One, blessed be he, to Moses, 'Moses, you are a liar!'

F. "He said to him, 'Lord of the world, you have a treasure in store which you have enjoyed every day. Shall I keep it to myself?'

G. "He said to him, 'Moses, since you have acted with humility, it will bear your name: "Remember the Torah of Moses, my servant" (Mal. 3:22).'"

(b. Shab 89a)

God here is represented as favoring humility and rewarding the humble with honor. What is important is that God does not here cite Scripture or merely paraphrase it; the conversation is an exchange between two vivid personalities. True enough, Moses, not

God, is the hero. But the personality of God emerges in a vivid way. The following passage shows how traits imputed to God also define proper conduct for sages, not to mention other human beings.

At issue once again is humility, and as we see, arrogance—the opposite—is treated as denial of God, humility, the imitation of God:

P. And R. Yohanan said in the name of R. Simeon b. Yohai, "Whoever is arrogant is as if he worships idolatry.

Q. "Here it is written, 'Everyone who is arrogant in heart is an abomination to the Lord' (Prov. 16:5), and elsewhere it is written, 'You will not bring an abomination into your house' (Deut. 7:26)."

R. And R. Yohanan on his own account said, "He is as if he denied the very Principle [of the world],

S. "as it is said, 'Your heart will be lifted up and you will forget the Lord your God' (Deut. 8:14)."

T. R. Hama bar Hanina said, "He is as if he had sexual relations with all of those women forbidden to him on the laws of incest.

U. "Here it is written, 'Everyone who is arrogant in heart is an abomination to the Lord' (Prov. 16:5), and elsewhere it is written, 'For all these abominations . . .' (Lev. 18:27)."

V. Ulla said, "It is as if he built a high place,

W. "as it is said, 'Cease you from man, whose breath is in his nostrils, for wherein is he to be accounted of' (Is. 2:22).

X. "Do not read, 'wherein,' but rather, 'high place.'"

(b. Sot. 5b, XVI)

A. Whence [in Scripture] do we derive an admonition against the arrogant?

B. Said Raba said Zeiri, "'Listen and give ear, do not be proud' (Jer. 13:15)."

C. R. Nahman bar Isaac said, "From the following: 'Your heart will be lifted up, and you will forget the Lord your God' (Deut. 8:14).

D. "And it is written, 'Beware, lest you forget the Lord your God' (Deut. 8:11)."

E. And that accords with what R. Abin said R. Ilaa said.

F. For R. Abin said R. Ilaa said, "In every place in which it is said, 'Beware lest . . . that you not . . . ,' the meaning is only to lay down a negative commandment [so that one who does such a thing violates a negative admonition]."

(b. Sot. 5b, XVIII)

A. "With him also who is of a contrite and humble spirit" (Is. 57:15).

B. R. Huna and R. Hisda:

C. One said, "I [God] am with the contrite."

D. The other said, "I [God] am the contrite."

E. Logic favors the view of him who has said, "I [God] am with the contrite," for lo, the Holy One, blessed be he, neglected all mountains and heights and brought his Presence to rest on Mount Sinai,

F. and he did not raise Mount Sinai upward [to himself].

G. R. Joseph said, "A person should always learn from the attitude of his Creator, for lo, the Holy One, blessed be he, neglected all mountains and heights and brought his Presence to rest on Mount Sinai,

H. "and he neglected all valuable trees and brought his Presence to rest in the bush."

(b. Sot. 5b XX)

A. Said R. Eleazar, "Whoever is arrogant is worthy of being cut down like an asherah [a tree that is worshipped].

B. "Here it is written, 'The high ones of stature shall be cut down' (Is. 10:33),

C. "and elsewhere it is written, 'And you shall hew down their Asherim' (Deut. 7:5)."

D. And R. Eleazar said, "Whoever is arrogant—his dust will not be stirred up [in the resurrection of the dead].

E. "For it is said, 'Awake and sing, you that dwell in the dust' (Is. 26:19).

F. "It is stated not 'you who lie in the dust' but 'you who dwell in the dust,' meaning, one who has become a neighbor to the dust [by constant humility] even in his lifetime."

G. And R. Eleazar said, "For whoever is arrogant the Presence of God laments,

H. "as it is said, 'But the haughty he knows from afar' (Ps. 138:6)."

(b. Sot. 5b XXI)

A. R. Avira expounded, and some say it was R. Eleazar, "Come and take note of the fact that not like the trait of the Holy One, blessed be he, is the trait of flesh and blood.

B. "The trait of flesh and blood is that those who are high take note of those who are high, but the one who is high does not take note of the one who is low.

C. "But the trait of the Holy One, blessed be he, is not that way. He is high, but he takes note of the low,

D. "as it is said, 'For though the Lord is high, yet he takes note of the low' (Ps. 138:6)."

(b. Sot. 5b XXII)

A. Said R. Hisda, and some say it was Mar Uqba, "Concerning whoever is arrogant said the Holy One, blessed be he, he and I cannot live in the same world,

B. "as it is said, 'Whoever slanders his neighbor in secret—him will I destroy; him who has a haughty look and a proud heart I will not endure' (Ps. 101:5).

C. "Do not read, 'him [I cannot endure]' but 'with him [I cannot endure].'"

D. There are those who apply the foregoing teaching to those who slander, as it is said, "Whoever slanders his neighbor in secret—him will I destroy" (Ps. 101:5).

(*b. Sot.* 5b XXIII)

A. Said R. Joshua b. Levi, "Come and take note of how great are the humble in the sight of the Holy One, blessed be he.

B. "For when the sanctuary stood, a person would bring a burnt-offering, gaining thereby the reward for bringing a burnt-offering, or a meal-offering, and gaining the reward for a meal-offering.

C. "But a person who is genuinely humble does Scripture treat as if he had made offerings of all the sacrifices,

D. "as it is said, 'The sacrifices [plural] of God are a broken spirit' (Ps. 51:19).

E. "And not only so, but his prayer is not rejected, as it is said, 'A broken and contrite heart, O God, you will not despise' (Ps. 51:19)."

(*b. Sot.* 5b XXIX)

The repertoire shows clearly that sages impute to God those traits of personality that are recommended and claim that God favors personalities like God's own. The clear implication is that God and the human being are consubstantial as to attitudes, emotions, and other aspects of virtue.

God laughs just as does a human being. The attribution to God of a sense of humor portrays the divinity once more as incarnate, the model by which the human being was made not only in physical form but also in personality traits.

A. [In a dispute between R. Eliezer and R. Joshua, a heavenly voice stated, "Why do you argue with R. Eliezer, since in all matters, the law is in accord with his position. R. Joshua stood and exclaimed, 'It is not in heaven' (Deut. 30:12)," [meaning that decisions of the law are made by sages and not by divine intervention]. R. Nathan met Elijah and asked him, "What did the Holy One, blessed be he, do then?"

B. He said to him, "He laughed out loud, saying, 'My children have won over me, my children have won over me.'"

(*b. B.M.* 59b)

God's laughter is not only because of delight. It may also take on a sardonic character, for instance, as ridicule:

A. Said R. Yose, "In the age to come idolators will come and convert [to Judaism] . . . and will put phylacteries on their foreheads and arms, place show-fringes on their garments and a *mezuzah* on their doorposts. When, however, the battle of Gog and Magog takes place, they will be asked, 'Why have you come?'

B. "They will reply, 'Against God and his anointed . . .' (Ps. 2:1).

C. "Then each of the converts will toss off the religious emblems and leave . . . and the Holy One, blessed be he, will sit and laugh,

D. "as it is said, 'He who sits in heaven laughs . . .' (Ps. 2:4)."

(*b. A.Z.* 3b)

The repertoire of God's emotions encompasses not only desirable but also undesirable traits. God not only exhibits and favors humility and has the capacity to laugh out of both joy and ridicule. God also becomes angry and performs acts that express that anger:

A. And said R. Yohanan in the name of R. Yose, "How do we know that one should not placate a person when he is angry?

B. "It is in line with the following verse of Scripture: 'My face will go and then I will give you rest' (Ex. 33:14).

C. "Said the Holy One, blessed be he, to Moses, 'Wait until my angry countenance passes, and then I shall give you rest.'"

D. But does the Holy One, blessed be he, get angry?

E. Indeed so.

F. For it has been taught on Tannaite authority:

G. "A God that is angry every day" (Ps. 7:12).

H. And how long is this anger going to last?

I. A moment.

J. And how long is a moment?

K. It is one fifty-eight thousand eight hundred and eighty-eighth part of an hour.

L. And no creature except for the wicked Balaam has ever been able to fix the moment exactly.

M. For concerning him it has been written, "He knows the knowledge of the Most High" (Num. 24:16).

N. How if Balaam did not even know what his beast was thinking, was he likely to know what the Most High is thinking?

O. But this teaches that he knew exactly how to reckon the very moment that the Holy One, blessed be he, would be angry.

P. That is in line with what the prophet said to Israel, "O my people, remember now what Balak, king of Moab, devised, and what Balaam, son of Beor, answered him . . . that you may know the righteous acts of the Lord" (Mic. 6:5).

Q. Said R. Eleazar, "The Holy One, blessed be he, said to Israel, 'Know that I did any number of acts of righteousness with you, for I did not get angry in the time of the wicked Balaam. For had I gotten angry, not one of (the enemies of) Israel would have survived, not a remnant.'

R. "That is in line with what Balaam said to Balak, 'How shall I curse whom God has not cursed, and how shall I execrate whom the Lord has not execrated?' (Num. 23:8).

S. "This teaches that for that entire time [God] did not get mad."

T. And how long is God's anger?

U. It is a moment.

V. And how long is a moment?

W. Said R. Abin, and some say, R. Abina, "A moment lasts as long as it takes to say 'a moment.'"

X. And how do we know that a moment is how long God is angry?

Y. For it is said, "For his anger is but for a moment, his favor is for a lifetime" (Ps. 30:6).

Z. If you like, you may derive the lesson from the following: "Hide yourself for a little while until the anger be past" (Is. 26:20).

AA. And when is God angry?

BB. Said Abayye, "It is during the first three hours of the day, when the comb of the cock is white, and it stands on one foot."

CC. But it stands on one foot every hour.

DD. To be sure, it stands on its foot every hour, but in all the others it has red streaks, and in the moment at hand there are no red streaks [in the comb of the cock].

(b. Ber. 7A, LI)

What is striking in this sizable account is the characterization of God's anger in entirely corporeal terms. God not only becomes angry, God also acts in anger. For one example, in anger God loses his temper:

A. Said R. Judah said Rab, "When the Holy One, blessed be he, proposed to create the world, he said to the angelic prince of the sea, 'Open your mouth and swallow all the water in the world.'

B. "He said to him, 'Lord of the world, it is quite sufficient if I stick with what I already have.'

C. "Forthwith he kicked him with his foot and killed him.

D. "For it is written, 'He stirs up the sea with his power, and by his understanding he smites through Rahab' (Job 26:12)."

(b. B.B. 74b)

Like a human being, God thus can lose his temper. God's anger derives not only from ill-temper but deeper causes. God is dissatisfied with the world as it is and so expresses anger with the present condition of humanity, on account of Israel:

F. For it has been taught on Tannaite authority:

G. R. Eliezer says, "The night is divided into three watches, and [in heaven] over each watch the Holy One, blessed be he, sits and roars like a lion,

H. "as it is said, 'The Lord roars from on high and raises his voice from his holy habitation, roaring he does roar because of his fold' (Jer. 25:30).

I. "The indication of each watch is as follows: at the first watch, an ass brays, at the second, dogs yelp, at the third, an infant sucks at its mother's breast or a woman whispers to her husband."

(b. Ber. 3a, VI)

A. Said R. Isaac bar Samuel in the name of Rab, "The night is divided into three watches, and over each watch, the Holy One, blessed be he, sits and roars like a lion.

B. "He says, 'Woe to the children, on account of whose sins I have wiped out my house and burned my palace, and whom I have exiled among the nations of the world.'"

(b. Ber. 3a, VII)

A. It has been taught on Tannaite authority:

B. Said R. Yose, "Once I was going along the way, and I went into one of the ruins of Jerusalem to pray. Elijah, of blessed memory, came and watched over me at the door until I had finished my prayer. After I had finished my prayer, he said to me, 'Peace be to you, my lord.'

C. "And I said to him, 'Peace be to you, my lord and teacher.'

D. "And he said to me, 'My son, on what account did you go into this ruin?'

E. "And I said to him, 'To pray.'

F. "And he said to me, 'You would have done better to pray on the road.' . . .

J. "And he said to me, 'My son, what sound did you hear in this ruin?'

K. "I said to him, 'I heard the sound of an echo moaning like a pigeon and saying, "Woe to the children, on account of whose sins I have wiped out my house and burned my palace and whom I have exiled among the nations of the world."'

L. "He said to me, 'By your life and the life of your head, it is not only at this moment that the echo speaks in such a way, but three times daily, it says the same thing.

M. "'And not only so, but when Israelites go into synagogues and schoolhouses and respond, "May the great name be blessed," the Holy One shakes his head and says, "Happy is the king, whom they praise in his house in such a way! What does a father have, who has exiled his children? And woe to the children who are exiled from their father's table!"'"

(b. Ber. 3a, VIII)

God's anger and mourning form emotions identical to those of human beings, as is made explicit. Israel are God's children, and God mourns for them as a parent mourns for children who have suffered. The incarnation of God therefore takes the form of representing God's attitudes as the same as those of human beings, though of a cosmic order. But God's anger derives from broader causes than Israel's current condition.

INCARNATION: THE SOCIAL ATTRIBUTES OF GOD

The humanity of God emerges in yet another way. God enters into transactions with human beings and accords with the rules that govern those relationships. So God exhibits precisely the social attributes that human beings do. A number of stories, rather protracted and detailed, tell the story of God as a social being, living among and doing business with mortals. These stories provide extended portraits of God's relationships, in particular arguments, with important figures, such as angelic figures, as well as Moses, David, and Hosea. In them God negotiates, persuades, teaches, argues, exchanges reasons. The incarnation of God therefore comes to expression in a variety of portraits of how God will engage in arguments with human beings and angels, and so enters into the existence of ordinary people. These disputes, negotiations, transactions yield a portrait of God who is reasonable and capable of give and take, as in the following:

F. Rabbah bar Mari said, "What is the meaning of this verse: 'But they were rebellious at the sea, even at the Red Sea; nonetheless he saved them for his name's sake' (Ps. 106:7)?

G. "This teaches that the Israelites were rebellious at that time, saying, 'Just as we will go up on this side, so the Egyptians will go up on the other side.' Said the Holy One, blessed be he, to the angelic prince who reigns over the sea, 'Cast them [the Israelites] out on dry land.'

H. "He said before him, 'Lord of the world, is there any case of a slave [namely, myself] to whom his master [you] gives a gift [the Israelites], and then the master goes and takes [the gift] away again? [You gave me the Israelites, now you want to take them away and place them on dry land.]'
I. "He said to him, 'I'll give you one and a half times their number.'
J. "He said before him, 'Lord of the world, is there a possibility that a slave can claim anything against his master? [How do I know that you will really do it?]'
K. "He said to him, 'The Kishon brook will be my pledge [that I shall carry out my word. Nine hundred chariots at the brook were sunk, [Jud. 4:13] while Pharaoh at the sea had only six hundred, thus a pledge one and a half times greater than the sum at issue.]'
L. "Forthwith [the angelic prince of the sea] spit them out onto dry land, for it is written, 'And the Israelites saw the Egyptians dead on the sea shore' (Ex. 14:30)."

(b. Ar. 15A–B)

God is willing to give a pledge to guarantee his word. He furthermore sees the right claim of the counterpart actor in the story. Hence we see how God obeys precisely the same social laws of exchange and reason that govern other incarnate beings.

Still more interesting is the picture of God's argument with Abraham. God is represented as accepting accountability, by the standards of humanity, for what God does.

A. Said R. Isaac, "When the temple was destroyed, the Holy One, blessed be he, found Abraham standing in the Temple. He said to him, 'What is my beloved doing in my house?'
B. "He said to him, 'I have come because of what is going on with my children.'
C. "He said to him, 'Your children sinned and have been sent into exile.'
D. "He said to him, 'But wasn't it by mistake that they sinned?'
E. "He said to him, 'She has wrought lewdness' (Jer. 11:15).
F. "He said to him, 'But wasn't it just a minority of them that did it?'
G. "He said to him, 'It was a majority' (Jer. 11:15).
H. "He said to him, 'You should at least have taken account of the covenant of circumcision [which should have secured forgiveness despite their sin]!'
I. "He said to him, 'The holy flesh is passed from you' (Jer. 11:15).
J. "'And if you had waited for them, they might have repented!'
K. "He said to him, 'When you do evil, then you are happy' (Jer. 11:15).
L. "He said to him, 'He put his hands on his head, crying out and weeping, saying to them, "God forbid! Perhaps they have no remedy at all!"'

M. "A heavenly voice came forth and said, 'The Lord called you "a leafy olive tree, fair with excellent fruit"' (Jer. 11:16).

N. "'Just as in the case of an olive tree, its future comes only at the end [that is, it is only after a long while that it attains its best fruit], so in the case of Israel, their future comes at the end of their time.'"

(b. Men. 53b)

God relates to Abraham as to an equal. That is shown by God's implicit agreement that he is answerable to Abraham for what has taken place with the destruction of the Temple. God does not impose silence on Abraham, saying that that is a decree not to be contested but only accepted. God as a social being accepts that he must provide sound reasons for his actions, as must any other reasonable person in a world governed by rules applicable to everyone. Abraham is a fine choice for the protagonist, since he engaged in the argument concerning Sodom. His complaint is expressed at B: God is now called to explain himself. At each point, then, Abraham offers arguments in behalf of sinning Israel, and God responds, item by item. The climax, of course, has God promising Israel a future worth having. God emerges as both just and merciful, reasonable but sympathetic. The transaction attests to God's conformity to rules of reasoned transactions in a coherent society.

The same picture is drawn in still greater detail when God engages Hosea in discussion. Here, however, Hosea complains against Israel, and God takes the part of Abraham in the earlier account. God's social role is defined in the model of the sage or master, a role we shall presently find prominent in the repertoire of portraits of incarnation. God teaches Hosea by providing an analogy, for Hosea, of what Hosea proposes that God do.

I.A. Said the Holy One, blessed be he, to Hosea, "Your children have sinned."

B. He should have said to him, "They are your children, children of those to whom you have shown grace, children of Abraham, Isaac, and Jacob. Send your mercy to them."

C. It is not enough that he did not say the right thing, but he said to him, "Lord of the world, the entire world is yours. Trade them in for some other nation."

D. Said the Holy One, blessed be he, "What shall I then do with that elder? I shall tell him, 'Go, marry a whore and have children of prostitution.' Then I'll tell him, 'Divorce her.' If he can send her away, then I'll send away Israel."

E. For it is said, "And the Lord said to Hosea, Go, take a whore and have children of prostitution" (Hos. 1:1).

II.A. After he had two sons and a daughter, the Holy One, blessed be he, said to Hosea, "Should you not have learned the lesson of your master Moses? Once I had entered into discourse with him, he separated from his wife. So you too, take your leave of her."

B. He said to him, "Lord of the world, I have children from her, and I simply cannot drive her out or divorce her."

C. Said to him the Holy One, blessed be he, "Now if you, married to a whore, with children of prostitution, and you don't even know whether they're yours or whether they come from some other fathers, are in such a state, as to Israel, who are my children, children of those whom I have tested, the children of Abraham, Isaac and Jacob . . .

D. ". . . how can you say to me, 'Trade them in for some other nation'?"

E. When [Hosea] realized that he had sinned, he arose to seek mercy for himself. Said the Holy One, blessed be he, to him, "Instead of seeking mercy for yourself, seek mercy for Israel, against whom I have on your account issued three decrees [exile, rejection, and without compassion, reflecting the names of his children]."

F. He went and sought mercy and [God] annulled [the decrees] and gave them this blessing: "Yet the number of the children of Israel shall be as the sand of the sea . . . and instead of being called 'You are not my people,' they will be called 'You are the children of the living God.' And the children of Judah and the children of Israel shall be gathered together. . . . And I will sow her to me in the land, and have compassion on her who was not treated with compassion and say to those who were not my people, 'You are my people' (Hos. 2:1–2, 25)."

(b. Pes. 87a)

Hosea negotiates with God, proposing that God reject Israel for some other nation. God's reply is that of an experienced teacher. He puts the disciple through a concrete lesson, which imparts to the disciple the desired experience and leads to the disciple's drawing the right conclusion. The social transaction, then, is worked out in accord with rules of reason. Just as experience teaches Hosea the lesson that one does not reject, but forgives, sinful relations, so Hosea draws the correct conclusion. The story then portrays God in a social transaction that is governed by accepted laws of orderly conduct.

God's relationships with David, a paramount theme in the story of David's sin with Bath Sheba, yield the picture of how God responds in a reasonable way to a reasonable proposal. Then, to be sure, God teaches a lesson of right conduct. But, throughout, God's role remains the same: a social and rational being, like mortals. What is important for my argument is the representation of God as engaged in negotiation in accord with rules that apply to heaven and earth alike. God then enters into society as a full participant in the world of humanity and plays a role that forms the counterpart to that of any just person. The incarnation of God here takes the now-well-established form of God as fully engaged in social transactions with counterparts on earth. We consider only those portions of the protracted story that pertain to our topic:

A. Said R. Judah said Rab, "One should never put himself to the test, for lo, David, king of Israel, put himself to the test and he stumbled.

B. "He said before him, 'Lord of the world, on what account do people say, "God of Abraham, God of Isaac, and God of Jacob," but they do not say, "God of David"?'

C. "He said to him, 'They endured a test for me, while you have not endured a test for me.'

D. "He said before him, 'Lord of the world, here I am. Test me.'

E. "For it is said, 'Examine me, O Lord, and try me' (Ps. 26:1).

F. "He said to him, 'I shall test you, and I shall do for you something that I did not do for them. I did not inform them [what I was doing], while I shall tell you what I am going to do. I shall try you with a matter having to do with sexual relations.'

G. "Forthwith: 'And it came to pass in an eventide that David arose from off his bed' (2 Sam. 11:2)."

(*b. San.* 107a)

The opening passage represents God in conversation with David and responsive to David's reasoning. This is more than the presence of God familiar in the earliest strata of the canon, and God in conversation with David forms a personality, not the mere "you" of prayer familiar in the initial writings of the Judaism of the dual Torah. Where God cites Scripture, it is not merely to prove a point but to make a statement particular to the exchange at hand. So it is not a conventional portrait of God's serving as the voice of an established text. It is, to the contrary, the picture of God engaged in a social transaction with a sentient being.

We skip the description of David's relationship with Bath Sheba and move directly to David's plea of forgiveness. In the passages that follow, God serves merely as audience for David's statements:

A. Raba interpreted Scripture, asking, "What is the meaning of the following verse: 'To the chief musician, a Psalm of David. In the Lord I put my trust, how do you say to my soul, Flee as a bird to your mountain?' (Ps. 11:1)?

B. "Said David before the Holy One, blessed be he, 'Lord of the world, Forgive me for that sin, so that people should not say, "The mountain that is among you [that is, your king] has been driven off by a bird."'"

C. Raba interpreted Scripture, asking, "What is the meaning of the following verse: 'Against you, you alone, have I sinned, and done this evil in your sight, that you might be justified when you speak and be clear when you judge' (Ps. 11:1)?

D. "Said David before the Holy One, blessed be he, 'Lord of the world. It is perfectly clear to you that if I had wanted to overcome my impulse to do evil, I should have done so. But I had in mind that people not say, "The slave has conquered the Master [God, and should then be included as 'God of David']."'"

E. Raba interpreted Scripture, asking, "What is the meaning of the following verse: 'For I am ready to halt and my sorrow is continually before me' (Ps. 38:18)?

F. "Bath Sheba, daughter of Eliam, was designated for David from the six days of creation, but she came to him through anguish."

G. And so did a Tannaite authority of the house of R. Ishmael [teach], "Bath Sheba, daughter of Eliam, was designated for David, but he 'ate' her while she was yet unripe."

H. Raba interpreted Scripture, asking, "What is the meaning of the following verse: 'But in my adversity they rejoiced and gathered themselves together, yes, the abjects gathered themselves together against me and I did not know it, they tore me and did not cease' (Ps. 35:15)?

I. "Said David before the Holy One, blessed be he, 'Lord of the world, it is perfectly clear to you that if they had torn my flesh, my blood would not have flowed [because I was so embarrassed].

J. "'Not only so, but when they take up the four modes of execution inflicted by a court, they interrupt their Mishnah-study and say to me, "David, he who has sexual relations with a married woman—how is he put to death?"

K. "'I say to them, "He who has sexual relations with a married woman is put to death through strangulation, but he has a share in the world to come, while he who humiliates his fellow in public has no share in the world to come."'"

(b. San. 107a)

Now God emerges once more and plays the role of antagonist to David's protagonist:

A. R. Dosetai of Biri interpreted Scripture, "To what may David be likened? To a gentile merchant.
B. "Said David before the Holy One, blessed be he, 'Lord of the world, "Who can understand his errors?" (Ps. 19:13).'
C. "He said to him, 'They are remitted for you.'
D. "'"Cleanse me of hidden faults" (Ps. 19:13).'
E. "'They are remitted to you.'
F. "'"Keep back your servant also from presumptuous sins" (Ps. 19:13).'
G. "'They are remitted to you.'
H. "'"Let them not have dominion over me, then I shall be upright" (Ps. 19:13), so that the rabbis will not hold me up as an example.'
I. "'They are remitted to you.'
J. "'"And I shall be innocent of great transgression" (Ps. 19:13), so that they will not write down my ruin.'
K. "He said to them, 'That is not possible. Now if the Y that I took away from the name of Sarah [changing it from Sarai to Sarah] stood crying for so many years until Joshua came and I added the Y [removed from Sarah's name] to his name, as it is said, "And Moses called Oshea, the son of Nun, Jehoshua" (Num. 13:16), how much the more will a complete passage of Scripture [cry out if I remove that passage from its rightful place]!'"

(b. San. 107a)

God once more emerges as a fully formed personality. For God's role here is not merely to cite Scripture. K forms the centerpiece. God can do just so much, but no more, and this detail is the contribution not of Scripture but of the storyteller. The incarnation of God once more takes shape in the notion of God as bound by rules of procedure and conduct. God enters into civil and rational transactions with human beings and conforms to the same rules, with the result that is expressed here.

A. "And I shall be innocent from great transgression" (Ps. 19:13):
B. He said before him, "Lord of the world, forgive me for the whole of that sin [as though I had never done it]."
C. He said to him, "Solomon, your son, even now is destined to say in his wisdom, 'Can a man take fire in his bosom, and his clothes not be burned? Can one go upon hot coals, and his feet not be burned? So he who goes in to his neighbor's wife, whoever touches her shall not be innocent' (Prov. 6:27–29)."
D. He said to him, "Will I be so deeply troubled?"

E. He said to him, "Accept suffering [as atonement]."
F. He accepted the suffering.

A. Said R. Judah said Rab, "For six months David was afflicted with saraat, and the Presence of God left him, and the sanhedrin abandoned him.
B. "He was afflicted with saraat, as it is written, 'Purge me with hyssop and I shall be clean, wash me and I shall be whiter than snow' (Ps. 51:9).
C. "The Presence of God left him, as it is written, 'Restore to me the joy of your salvation and uphold me with your free spirit' (Ps. 51:14).
D. "The sanhedrin abandoned him, as it is written, 'Let those who fear you turn to me and those who have known your testimonies' (Ps. 119:79).
E. "How do we know that this lasted for six months? As it is written, 'And the days that David ruled over Israel were forty years: [107b] Seven years he reigned in Hebron, and thirty-three years he reigned in Jerusalem' (1 Kgs. 2:11).
F. "Elsewhere it is written, 'In Hebron he reigned over Judah seven years and six months' (2 Sam. 5:5).
G. "So the six months were not taken into account. Accordingly, he was afflicted with saraat [for such a one is regarded as a corpse].
H. "He said before him, 'Lord of the world, forgive me for that sin.'
I. "'It is forgiven to you.'
J. ""'Then show me a token for good, that they who hate me may see it and be ashamed, because you, Lord, have helped me and comforted me" (Ps. 86:17).'
K. "He said to him, 'While you are alive, I shall not reveal [the fact that you are forgiven], but I shall reveal it in the lifetime of your son, Solomon.'
L. "When Solomon had built the house of the sanctuary, he tried to bring the ark into the house of the Holy of Holies. The gates cleaved to one another. He recited twenty-four prayers [Freedman, 734 n. 4: in 2 Chron. 6 words for prayer, supplication and hymn occur twenty-four times], but was not answered.
M. "He said, 'Lift up your head, O you gates, and be lifted up, you everlasting doors, and the King of glory shall come in. Who is this King of glory? The Lord strong and mighty, the Lord mighty in battle' (Ps. 24:7).
N. "And it is further said, 'Lift up your heads, O you gates, even lift them up, you everlasting doors' (Ps. 24:7).
O. "But he was not answered.
P. "When he said, 'Lord God, turn not away the face of your anointed, remember the mercies of David, your servant' (2 Chron. 6:42), forthwith he was answered.

Q. "At that moment the faces of David's enemies turned as black as the bottom of a pot, for all Israel knew that the Holy One, blessed be he, had forgiven him for that sin."

(b. San. 106b–107a, CCXLVI–CCLI)

As we see, our hero is not God but David. The story is not told to characterize God, who plays a supporting part, if not a mere straight man. Nonetheless, the portrayal of God justifies the claim that we have here an incarnate God, consubstantial with humanity not only in physical and emotional traits but also, and especially, in the conformity to the social laws of correct transactions that, in theory at least, make society possible.

GOD AS SAGE

Among the available models for the incarnation of God, such as those introduced in Pesiqta deRab Kahana's authorships' repertoire—warrior, teacher, young man—the one that predominated entailed representation of God as sage. We recall that God is represented as a schoolmaster:

F. "He sits and teaches school children, as it is said, 'Whom shall one teach knowledge, and whom shall one make to understand the message? Those who are weaned from milk' (Is. 28:9)."

(b. A.Z. 3b)

But this is not the same thing as God as a master-sage teaching mature disciples, that is, God as rabbi and sage. That representation emerges in a variety of ways and proves the single most important mode of the incarnation of God. God's personality merged throughout with the Bavli's authorships' representation of the personality of the ideal master or sage. That representation in the Bavli proved detailed and specific. A sage's life—Torah learned, then taught, through discipleship—encompassed both the correct modes of discourse and ritual argument on the one side, and the recasting of all relationships in accord with received convention of courtesy and subservience on the other. God then is represented in both dimensions—as a master requiring correct conduct of his disciples, and as a teacher able to hold his own in arguments conducted in accord with the prevailing ritual. For one example, a master had the right to demand an appropriate greeting, and God, not receiving that greeting, asked why:

A. Said R. Joshua b. Levi, "When Moses came up on high, he found the Holy One, blessed be he, tying crowns onto the letters of the Torah. He said to him, 'Moses, don't people say hello in your town?'
B. "He said to him, 'Does a servant greet his master [first]?'
C. "He said to him, 'You should have helped me [at least by greeting me and wishing me success].'
D. "He said to him, 'Now I pray you let the power of the Lord be great, just as you have said' (Num. 14:17)."

(b. Shab. 89a)

Moses here plays the role of disciple to God the teacher, a persistent pattern throughout. Not having offered the appropriate greeting, the hapless disciple is instructed on the matter. Part of the ritual of "being a sage" thus comes to expression. Yet another detail of that same ritual taught how to make a request—and how not to do so. A request offered in humility is proper; one made in an arrogant or demanding spirit is not. Knowing what to ask is as important as knowing how. The congregation of Israel shows how not to do so, and God shows, nonetheless, the right mode of response in the following:

A. The congregation of Israel made its request in an improper way, but the Holy One, blessed be he, responded in a proper way.
B. For it is said, [the congregation of Israel said to God,] "And let us know, eagerly strive to know, the Lord, the Lord's going forth is sure as the morning, and the Lord shall come to us as the rain" (Hos. 6:3).
C. Said the Holy One, blessed be he, to [the congregation of Israel,] "My daughter, now you are asking for something which sometimes is wanted and sometimes is not really wanted. But I shall give you something which is always wanted.
D. "For it is said, 'I will be as dew to Israel' (Hos. 14:6)."
E. Further, [the congregation of Israel] made its request in an improper manner, "O God, set me as a seal on your heart, as a seal on your arm" (Song 8:6).
F. [But the Holy One, blessed be he, responded in a proper way.] Said the Holy One, blessed be he, to [the congregation of Israel,] "My daughter, now you are asking for something which sometimes can be seen and sometimes cannot be seen. But I shall give you something which can always be seen.

G. "For it is said, 'Behold, I have graven you on the palms of my hands' (Is. 49:16) [and the palms are always visible, in a way in which the heart and arm are not]."

(*b. Ta.* 4a)

Dew is always wanted, rain not. To be a seal on the heart or arm is to be displayed only occasionally. But the hands are always visible. Consequently, God as sage teaches Israel as disciple how to make a proper request.

The status of sage, expressed in rituals of proper conduct, is attained through knowing how to participate in argument about matters of the Torah, particularly the law. Indeed, what makes a sage an authority is knowledge of details of the law. Consequently, my claim that God is represented as a particular sort of human being, namely, as a sage, requires evidence that God not only follows the arguments (as above, "My sons have conquered me!"), and even has opinions which he proposes to interject, but also himself participates in debates on the law. Ability to follow those debates and to contribute forcefully to them forms the chief indicator. That that ability joins some men to God is furthermore explicit. So the arguments in the academy in heaven, over which God presides, form the exact counterpart to the arguments on earth—with the result that God emerges as precisely consubstantial, physically and intellectually, with the particular configuration of the sage:

A. In the session in the firmament, people were debating this question: if the bright spot came before the white hair, the person is unclean. If the white hair came before the bright spot, he is clean. What about a case of doubt?
B. The Holy One, blessed be he, said, "Clean."
C. And the rest of the fellowship of the firmament said, "Unclean."
D. They said, "Who will settle the matter?"
E. It should be Rabbah b. Nahmani, for he is the one who said, "I am an expert in the laws of plagues and in the effects of contamination through the overshadowing of a corpse." . . .
F. A letter fell down from the sky to Pumbedita: "Rabbah b. Nahmani has been called up by the academy of the firmament. . . ."

(*b. B.M.* 86a)

God in this story forms part of the background of action. Part of a much longer account attached to the academy of Pumbedita of how

Rabbah b. Nahmani was taken up to heaven, the story shows us how God is represented in a heavenly session of the heavenly academy studying precisely those details of the Torah, here Leviticus 13 as restated in Mishnah-tractate *Negaim,* as were mastered by the great sages of the day. That the rest of the heavenly court would disagree forms an essential detail, because it verifies the picture and validates the claim, to come, that heaven required the knowledge of the heroic sage. That is the point of B–C–D. Then Rabbah b. Nahmani is called to heaven—that is, killed and transported upward—to make the required ruling. God is not the centerpiece of the story. The detail that a letter was sent from the heavenly academy to the one on earth at Pumbedita then restates the basic point of the story, the correspondence of earth to heaven on just this matter.

Though in the image of the sage, God towers over other sages, disposes of their lives, and determines their destinies. Portraying God as sage allowed the storytellers to state vividly convictions on the disparity between sages' great intellectual achievements and their this-worldly standing and fate. But God remains within the model of other sages, takes up the rulings, follows the arguments, participates in the sessions that distinguish sages and mark them off from all other people:

A. Said R. Judah said Rab, "When Moses went up to the height, he found the Holy One, blessed be he, sitting and tying crowns to the letters [of the Torah]."

B. "He said to him, 'Lord of the universe, why is this necessary?'

C. "He said to him, 'There is a certain man who is going to come into being at the end of some generations, by the name of Aqiba b. Joseph. He is going to find expositions to attach mounds and mounds of laws to each point [of a crown].'

D. "He said to him, 'Lord of the universe, show him to me.'

E. "He said to him, 'Turn around.'

F. "[Moses] went and took his seat at the end of eight rows, but he could not understand what the people were saying. He felt weak. When discourse came to a certain matter, one of [Aqiba's] disciples said to him, 'My lord, how do you know this?'

G. "He said to him, 'It is a law revealed by God to Moses at Mount Sinai.'

H. "Moses' spirits were restored.

I. "He turned back and returned to the Holy One, blessed be he. He said to him, 'Lord of the universe, now if you have such a man available, how can you give the Torah through me?'

J. "He said to him, 'Be silent. That is how I have decided matters.'

K. "He said to him, 'Lord of the universe, you have now shown me his mastery of the Torah. Now show me his reward.'

L. "He said to him, 'Turn around.'

M. "He turned around and saw people weighing out his flesh in the butcher shop.

N. "He said to him, 'Lord of the universe, such is his mastery of Torah, and such is his reward?'

O. "He said to him, 'Be silent. That is how I have decided matters.'"

(b. Men. 29b)

This is the single most important narrative in the Bavli's repertoire of allusions to, and stories about, the incarnation of God. For God's role in the story finds definition as hero and principal actor. He is no longer the mere interlocutor, nor does he simply answer questions of the principal voice by citing Scripture. Quite to the contrary, God makes all the decisions and guides the unfolding of the story. Moses then appears as the straight man. He asks the questions that permit God to make the stunning replies. Why do you need crowns on the letters of the Torah? Aqiba will explain them, by tying laws to these trivial and opaque details. What are these laws? I cannot follow them. Aqiba will nonetheless attribute them to you. Why then give the Torah through me instead of him, since he understands it and I do not? It is my decree. Finally, comes the climax: what will this man's reward be? His flesh will be weighed out in butcher shops. The response remains the same. Moses who is called "our rabbi" and forms the prototype and ideal of the sage does not understand. God then tells him to shut up and accept his decree. God does what he likes, with whom he likes. Perhaps the storyteller had in mind a polemic against rebellious brilliance, as against dumb subservience. But that does not seem to me the urgent message, which rather requires acceptance of God's decrees, whatever they are, when the undeserving receive glory, when the accomplished come to nothing. That God emerges as a fully formed personality—the model for the sage—hardly requires restatement.

INCARNATION IN HEAVEN AND ON EARTH: GOD AND ISRAEL

The paramount trait of the sage in the Bavli is his profound engagement with the life of Israel, God's people. The sage conducts an

ongoing love affair with Israel, just as does God, caring for everything that Jews say and do, the sanctity of their community, the
holiness of their homes. Israel, unique among nations and holy to
God, forms on earth a society that corresponds to the retinue and
court of God in heaven. No surprise, then, that just as Israel glori-
fies God, so God responds and celebrates Israel. In the passages at
hand the complete incarnation of God, in physical, emotional, and
social traits, comes to expression. God wears phylacteries, an indication of a corporeal sort. God further forms the correct attitude
toward Israel, which is one of love, an indication of an attitude on
the part of divinity corresponding to right attitudes on the part of
human beings. Finally, to close the circle, just as there is a "you" to
whom humanity prays, so God too says prayers—to God—and the
point of these prayers is that God should elicit from himself forgiveness for Israel:

A. Said R. Nahman bar Isaac to R. Hiyya bar Abin, "As to the phylacteries of the Lord of the world, what is written in them?"

B. He said to him, "'And who is like your people Israel, a singular nation
on earth' (1 Chron. 17:21)."

C. "And does the Holy One, blessed be he, sing praises for Israel?"

D. "Yes, for it is written, 'You have avouched the Lord this day . . . and
the Lord has avouched you this day' (Deut. 26:17, 18).

E. "Said the Holy One, blessed be he, to Israel, 'You have made me a
singular entity in the world, and I shall make you a singular entity in
the world.

F. "'You have made me a singular entity in the world,' as it is said, 'Hear
O Israel, the Lord, our God, the Lord is one' (Deut. 6:4).

G. "'And I shall make you a singular entity in the world,' as it is said, 'And
who is like your people, Israel, a singular nation in the earth' (1
Chron. 17:21)."

H. Said R. Aha, son of Raba to R. Ashi, "That takes care of one of the
four subdivisions of the phylactery. What is written in the others?"

I. He said to him, "'For what great nation is there . . . And what great
nation is there . . .' (Deut. 4:7, 8), 'Happy are you, O Israel . . .'
(Deut. 33:29), 'Or has God tried . . . ,' (Deut. 4:34). And 'To make
you high above all nations' (Deut. 26:19)."

J. "If so, there are too many boxes!

K. "But the verses, 'For what great nation is there' and 'And what great
nation is there,' which are equivalent, are in one box, and 'Happy are
you, O Israel' and 'Who is like your people Israel' are in one box, and
'Or has God tried . . . ,' in one box, and 'To make you high' in one box.

L. "And all of them are written in the phylactery that is on the arm."

(b. Ber. 6a–b XXXIX)

A. Said R. Yohanan in the name of R. Yose, "How do we know that the Holy One, blessed be he, says prayers?

B. "Since it is said, 'Even them will I bring to my holy mountain and make them joyful in my house of prayer' (Is. 56:7).

C. "'Their house of prayer' is not stated, but rather, 'my house of prayer.'

D. "On the basis of that usage we see that the Holy One, blessed be he, says prayers."

E. What prayers does he say?

F. Said R. Zutra bar Tobiah said Rab, "May it be my will that my mercy overcome my anger, and that my mercy prevail over my attributes, so that I may treat my children in accord with the trait of mercy and in their regard go beyond the strict measure of the law."

(b. Ber. 7a. XLIX)

A. It has been taught on Tannaite authority:

B. Said R. Ishmael b. Elisha, "One time I went in to offer up incense on the innermost altar, and I saw the crown of the Lord, enthroned on the highest throne, and he said to me, 'Ishmael, my son, bless me.'

C. "I said to him, 'May it be your will that your mercy overcome your anger, and that your mercy prevail over your attributes, so that you treat your children in accord with the trait of mercy and in their regard go beyond the strict measure of the law.'

D. "And he nodded his head to me."

E. And from that story we learn that the blessing of a common person should not be negligible in your view.

(b. Ber. 7a. L)

The corporeal side to the incarnation of God is clear at the outset, God's wearing phylacteries. The consubstantial traits of attitude and feeling—just as humanity feels joy, so does God; just as humanity celebrates God, so does God celebrate Israel—are made explicit. The social transactions of incarnation are specified as well. Just as Israel declares God to be unique, so God declares Israel to be unique. And just as Israel prays to God, so God says prayers. What God asks of himself is that he transcend himself—which is what, in prayer, humanity asks for as well.

THE THIRD PHASE OF THE JUDAISM OF THE DUAL TORAH: WHY IN IRANIAN BABYLONIA IN PARTICULAR?

The process of the incarnation of God which we have traced item by item in the Bavli culminates in the portrait of God as Israel's

counterpart, trait by trait, and in all relationships: God unique in
heaven, Israel unique on earth, the one like the other and matched
only by the other—and both finding ultimate embodiment in the
sage. Since that process clearly had brought forth concrete statements that God "in our image and likeness" is to be portrayed in
incarnate form, with the powerful story of *Genesis Rabbah* about the
angels' not knowing the difference between God and the first man,
we wonder why it was in the Bavli, not in the Yerushalmi and its
associated writings, that the stories before us came to redaction.
Once we frame the question in that simple way, the obvious difference between Roman-Byzantine-Christian Palestine, that is, the
Land of Israel, and Iranian-Zoroastrian Babylonia comes to the
fore. The Land of Israel was also Roman-Christian Palestine. Babylonia was part of the Iranian Empire under Sasanian rule. Christianity posed a considerable challenge to Judaism on the Roman
side of the international frontier, but constituted itself a minority
cult on the other.[3]

With the Christians pointing to Jesus Christ as God incarnate,
the conception of the incarnation of God for sages became both
plausible and also problematical.[4] Scripture had long provided
ample occasions for offering to Judaic system-builders a character
of divinity that encompassed accessible human traits. *Genesis Rabbah* and *Pesiqta DeRab Kahana* have given us sufficient reason to
affirm that fact for the Judaism of the dual Torah. But the crisis of
the age threatened the foundations of Judaism as it then flour-
ished. Christian theologians maintained that the political triumph
of Christ's church, now in charge of the Roman Empire, had validated the representation of Jesus as Christ and also as the union of
humanity and divinity. Christian iconography left little to the
imagination in the representation of Christ as union of God and
man. Christian theologians carefully explained in detail how the
union realized in (that one) man the traits of God. For the Judaic
sages political conditions in the Land of Israel, which is to say, in

3. I have presented the main facts of the matter in my summary of earlier
findings, reprinted as *Judaism, Christianity, and Zoroastrianism in Talmudic Babylonia,* Studies in Judaism (Lanham, Md: University Press of America, 1986).
4. The reason that Christianity in the fourth century, but not earlier, struck
sages as a serious challenge is spelled out in my *Judaism and Christianity in the Age of
Constantine* (Chicago: University of Chicago Press, 1987).

Roman and Christian Palestine, rendered acute and dangerous the formerly chronic dispute with Christianity. With the conception of the incarnation of God a considerable component of the Christian position, sages in the documents of the Land of Israel clearly treated with reticence, and mainly through allusion, the perfectly available conception of God as incarnate. While the politics of Christian Rome posed an obstacle to the realization of the incarnation of God in stories and allusions, on the Iranian and Zoroastrian side there was no counterpart consideration.

The Judaic writings redacted in Sasanian Iran contain slight evidence that the challenge of Christian success in Rome required a response. The pressing issues of interreligious dispute came from the state-religion, the worship of Mazda, and from the sages in the line of Zoroaster. Whatever the substance of these issues, the character of divinity as incarnate did not frame one of them. I know of no statement deriving from the fifth, sixth, or seventh centuries of a Zoroastrian critique of Judaism. The one systematic Zoroastrian apologia in hand, *Shkand Gumanik Vicar*, comes to us from the ninth century.[5] At issue in that statement are rather philosophical arguments, for example, concerning whether God's essence was light or darkness, against the notion of *creatio e nihilo*, and—pertinent to our problem—against the corporeality of God. The author of the *Shkand* ridicules the notion that the Lord grew tired in making the world. Why was he tired? Why, then, did God make Adam and Eve and give them commands that they could not naturally carry out? God is shown to be confused, unreasonable, malicious, in favor of ignorance and against knowledge. God is furthermore represented by Judaism as vengeful, angry, harsh, possessed of unpleasant physical qualities, warlike, cruel, capricious, mean. The sheer anthropomorphism and incarnationalism of Judaism is ridiculed.

We do not know that Mazdean critics of Judaism in the centuries in which the Bavli took shape addressed to Judaism a similar critique of its corporeal conception of God, and we also cannot necessarily assign to Mazdean thinkers of the period in which the Bavli

---

5. I have reprinted my translation, from the Pazend, of the pertinent chapters of the *Shkand* in *Judaism, Christianity, and Zoroastrianism*, 175–98.

was forming that powerful rationalism that characterized the ninth-century apologetic (against Islam, as a matter of fact). All we can do is propose that if out of Zoroastrian theology in the later Sasanian period emerged no powerful tendency to accomplish the incarnation of God, sages will have found no motive to avoid saying what they wished. And if the later critique echoed earlier arguments (as many scholars suppose), then sages will have had every reason to affirm precisely what their critics in the Mazdean world will have condemned. The incarnation of God in stories concerning God's wisdom and love will then have faced the challenge—not a crisis at all—head-on: God indeed takes human form, but it is in love and wisdom, not in hatred and stupidity, as the other side maintains. The polemical charge in the incarnation of God on the part of Judaic sages then contains both a negative and a positive: the positive is to affirm what the other side condemned, the negative to deny the traits alleged by the other side and to impute instead the ones all sides could affirm.[6] Why, then, Babylonia, and not the Land of Israel? Because there was no reason not to and every reason to represent as incarnate the character of divinity.

---

6. But in so stating, I seem to have wandered back from the sixth and seventh centuries in Iranian Babylonia to the nineteenth and twentieth centuries in Europe and America, where the same exchange repeated itself. With Christians affirming God's incarnation, Jews denied that incarnation found a place in the Judaic portrait of the character of divinity. They, moreover, claimed that such a conception of God was incompatible with the heritage of the Hebrew Scriptures, and that all representation of God as a human being in those Scriptures was "merely figurative" or otherwise spiritual, whatever these things can have meant. With Christians condemning the Jews' God as vindictive and (merely) just, Judaic apologists (both Jewish and Christian) restated the obvious fact that the character of divinity in Judaism, like that in Christianity, portrayed God as loving and compassionate. The requirements of interreligious dialogue therefore appear to play a more considerable role in the inner logic of religious reflection than may have been fully appreciated.

PART FIVE

Narrative and
the Incarnation of God

10

Sage-Story, God-Story: Incarnation through Narrative

THE ISSUE OF INCARNATION

The issue of incarnation in the formative centuries of the Judaism of the dual Torah concerns not the invention of an essentially new conception of God but the recovery of what was among other Judaisms an entirely conventional one. What requires explanation is not an innovation but the resort to an available option. What concerns us is not so much why, in light of the prior Judaic systems and their statements, the Judaism of the dual Torah represented God in incarnate form. It is, rather, how the incarnation of God attained realization. As we have seen, in the earlier stages of the unfolding of the canon of the Judaism of the dual Torah, we have no hint of an incarnation of God, and it is only in the final and complete statement of that Judaism that we confront, in full and whole realization, the notion of God with an individuality, a personality, a corporeal character. The answer to that question requires us to pursue two distinct lines of inquiry. The first concerns incarnation—treating as human and fleshly and corporeal what is, to begin with, either an object or an abstraction—as a mode of thought, not with special reference to God. Here we want to know the point at which, in the unfolding of the canon of the Judaism of the dual Torah, the conception of incarnation serves as a mode of presenting as a human person or personality some thing or some idea. Within this inquiry, further, we want to know precisely how the conception of incarnation comes to expression. The second addresses the issue now fully exposed, namely, why is it that in the pages of the Bavli in particular the process of incarnation reaches the person of God. The next three sections work out the first of the two lines of investigation; the last section, the latter.

THE SAGE AND THE INCARNATION
OF THE TORAH

The incarnation of not God but the Torah in the person of the sage marked the beginning of the process fully realized, for the divinity, in the Bavli. The process of turning an object or an abstract conception into a human being—representing what in fact was not human as a sentient and human being, consubstantial with human persons and capable of human discourse, thus incarnation as corporeal, consubstantial in emotion and virtue, fleshly in action—got under way, for the Judaism of the dual Torah, when the Torah was made flesh. In the Talmud of the Land of Israel or Yerushalmi, the Torah came to be represented in the person of the sage, who was, in himself, the Torah incarnate. Before the process of incarnation had reached God, therefore, in the Judaism of the dual Torah, the Torah itself had attained human form and representation in the person of the sage. The pages of the Talmud of the Land of Israel show us in statement and in story the process by which the sage came to be represented as the living Torah. Precisely how the incarnation of the Torah in the person of the sage, who is represented as the Torah incarnate, came to full expression will require a protracted survey of the way in which the first of the two Talmuds portrays the incarnation of an object, the Torah, or the abstraction, revelation.

The reason that the Torah was made flesh was that the Torah was the source of salvation. When the sage was transformed into a salvific figure through his mastery of the Torah, it was an easy step to regard the sage as the living Torah. That step most certainly was taken by the time of the authorship of the Yerushalmi, which set it forth in rich detail as an established fact of life. That is why we begin with the basic doctrine of the relationship between the figure of the sage and the salvation of Israel. In the Talmud of the Land of Israel, the rule of heaven and the learning and authority of the rabbi on earth turned out to be identified with one another. The first stage in the incarnation of the Torah in the person of the sage is marked by that identification. Salvation for Israel depended upon adherence to the sage and acceptance of his discipline. *Both God's will in heaven and the sage's words on earth constituted Torah.* And Israel would be saved through Torah, so the sage was the savior, as much as he embodied the Torah in the here and now as a kind of living and breathing Torah. The vastly expanded definition of the symbol of "Torah" stood behind the process of incarnation. For it was now deemed appropriate to compare or apply that symbol to a remarkable range of things. Incarnation, however, was far more specific and concrete. *It is represented by the claim that a sage himself was equivalent to a scroll of the Torah—a material, legal comparison, not merely a symbolic metaphor.* Here are expressions of that conception in the Talmud of the Land of Israel.

A. He who sees a disciple of a sage who has died is as if he sees a scroll of the Torah that has been burned.

(*y. M.Q.* 3:7.X)

I. R. Jacob bar Abayye in the name of R. Aha: "An elder who forgot his learning because of some accident which happened to him—they treat him with the sanctity owed to an ark [of the Torah]."

(*y. M.Q.* 3:1.XI)

At this stage we find the sage represented as equivalent to the scroll of the Torah, and, turning the statement around, the scroll of the Torah is realized in the person of the sage. The conception is not merely figurative or metaphorical, for, in both instances, actual behavior was affected.

Still more to the point, what the sage *did* had the status of law; the sage was the model of the law, thus once again enjoyed the standing of the human embodiment of the Torah. Since the sage exercised supernatural power as a kind of living Torah, his very deeds served to reveal law as much as his words expressed revelation. That is a formidable component of the argument that the sage embodied the Torah, another way of saying that the Torah was incarnated in the person of the sage. The capacity of the sage himself to participate in the process of revelation is illustrated in two types of materials. First of all, tales told about rabbis' behavior on specific occasions immediately are translated into rules for the entire community to keep. Accordingly, he was a source not merely of good example but of prescriptive law.

X. R. Aha went to Emmaus, and he ate dumpling [prepared by Samaritans].

Y. R. Jeremiah ate leavened bread prepared by them.

Z. R. Hezekiah ate their locusts prepared by them.

AA. R. Abbahu prohibited Israelite use of wine prepared by them.

(y. A.Z. 5:4:III)

These reports of what rabbis had done enjoyed the same authority, as statements of the law on eating what Samaritans cooked, as did citations of traditions in the names of the great authorities of old or of the day. What someone did served as a norm, if the person was a sage of sufficient standing.

Far more common in the Talmud are instances in which the deed of a rabbi is adduced as an authoritative precedent for the law under discussion. It was everywhere taken for granted that what a rabbi did, he did because of his mastery of the law. Even though a formulation of the law was not in hand, a tale about what a rabbi actually did constituted adequate evidence on how to formulate the law itself. So from the practice of an authority, a law might be framed quite independently of the person of the sage. The sage then functioned as a lawgiver, like Moses. Among many instances of that mode of generating law are the following:

A. Gamaliel Zuga was walking along, leaning on the shoulder of R. Simeon b. Laqish. They came across an image.

B. He said to him, "What is the law as to passing before it?"

C. He said to him, "Pass before it, but close [your] eyes."

D. R. Isaac was walking along, leaning on the shoulder of R. Yohanan. They came across an idol before the council building.

E. He said to him, "What is the law as to passing before it?"

F. He said to him, "Pass before it, but close [your] eyes."

G. R. Jacob bar Idi was walking along, leaning upon R. Joshua b. Levi. They came across a procession in which an idol was carried. He said to him, "Nahum, the most holy man, passed before this idol, and will you not pass by it? Pass before it but close your eyes."

(y. A.Z. 3:11.II)

FF. R. Aha had chills and fever. [They brought him] a medicinal drink prepared from the phallus of Dionysian revelers. But he would not drink it. They brought it to R. Jonah, and he did drink it. Said R. Mana, "Now if R. Jonah, the patriarch, had known what it was, he would never have drunk it."

GG. Said R. Huna, "That is to say, 'They do not accept healing from something that derives from an act of fornication.'"

(y. A.Z. 2:2.III)

What is important is GG, the restatement of the story as a law. The example of a rabbi served to teach how one should live a truly holy life. The requirements went far beyond the measure of the law, extending to refraining from deeds of a most commonplace sort. The example of rabbinical virtue, moreover, was adduced explicitly to account for the supernatural or magical power of a rabbi. There was no doubt in people's imagination, therefore, that the reason rabbis could do the amazing things people said they did was that they embodied the law and exercised its supernatural or magical power. This is stated quite openly in what follows.

C. There was a house that was about to collapse over there [in Babylonia], and Rab set one of his disciples in the house, until they had cleared out everything from the house. When the disciple left the house, the house collapsed.

D. And there are those who say that it was R. Adda bar Ahwah.

E. Sages sent and said to him, "What sort of good deeds are to your credit [that you have that much merit]?"

F. He said to them, "In my whole life no man ever got to the synagogue in the morning before I did. I never left anybody there when I went out. I never walked four cubits without speaking words of Torah. Nor did I ever mention teachings of Torah in an inappropriate setting. I never laid out a bed and slept for a regular period of time. I never took great strides among the associates. I never called my fellow by a nickname. I never rejoiced in the embarrassment of my fellow. I never cursed my fellow when I was lying by myself in bed. I never walked over in the marketplace to someone who owed me money.

G. "In my entire life I never lost my temper in my household."

H. This was meant to carry out that which is stated as follows: "I will give heed to the way that is blameless. Oh when wilt thou come to me? I will walk with integrity of heart within my house" (Ps. 101:2).

(y. Ta. 3:11.IV)

The correlation between learning and teaching, on the one side, and supernatural power or recognition, on the other, is explicit in the following:

A. R. Yosa fasted eighty fasts in order to see R. Hiyya the Elder [in a dream]. He finally saw him, and his hands trembled and his eyes grew dim.

B. Now if you say that R. Yosa was an unimportant man, [and so was unworthy of such a vision, that is not the case]. For a weaver came before R. Yohanan. He said to him, "I saw in my dream that the heaven fell, and one of your disciples was holding it up."

C. He said to him, "Will you know him [when you see him]?"

D. He said to him, "When I see him, I shall know him." Then all of his disciples passed before him, and he recognized R. Yosa.

E. R. Simeon b. Laqish fasted three hundred fasts in order to have a vision of R. Hiyya the Elder, but he did not see him.

F. Finally he began to be distressed about the matter. He said, "Did he labor in learning of Torah more than I?"

G. They said to him, "He brought Torah to the people of Israel to a greater extent than you have, and not only so, but he even went into exile [to teach on a wider front]."

H. He said to them, "And did I not go into exile too?"

I. They said to him, "You went into exile only to learn, but he went into exile to teach others."

(y. Ket. 12:3.VII)

This story shows that the storyteller regarded as a fact of life the correlation between mastery of Torah sayings and supernatural power—visions of the deceased, in this case. That is why Simeon b. Laqish complained, E–F, that he had learned as much Torah as the other, and so had every right to be able to conjure the dead. The greater supernatural power of the other then was explained in terms of the latter's superior service to "Torah." It seems to me pointless to distinguish supernatural power from magic. The upshot is that the sage was made a magician by Torah-learning and could save Israel through Torah, source of the most powerful magic of all.

The special position of the sage as supernaturally favored figure also imposed on Israelite society the requirement to accord him special dignity. The disciple of a sage himself had to exemplify what was required by his behavior toward his own master, who taught him Torah. The disciple's acts of respect for the master, devotion to his standing and honor, ongoing concern for his comfort were principal expressions of the respect for Torah upon which the entire system rested. *Accordingly, the respect paid to the Torah also was due to the sage, a view quite natural in light of the established identification of sage and Torah.*

Seeing Scripture in their own model, sages took the position that the (written) Torah of old, its supernatural power and salvific promise, in their own day continued to endure—among themselves and in their persons. In consequence, the promise of salvation contained in every line of Scripture was to be kept in every deed of learning and obedience to the law effected under their auspices. So while they projected backward the things they cherished in an act of (to us) extraordinary anachronism, in their eyes they carried forward, to their own time, the promise of salvation for Israel contained within the written Torah. In finding sages in the (written) Torah, the Talmud's sages implicitly stated a view of themselves as the continuation of the sanctified way of life of the written Torah. It followed that the pattern and promise of salvation contained therein lay within their way of life. The sage rules uncontingently, with perfect certainty to begin with, meaning confidence in his authority. So the Judaism of the dual Torah invents Scripture as source of certainty (something of which the Mishnah scarcely dreamed) and at the same time makes the sage authority and arbiter of what is true and certain. So the Talmud effects an astonishing parallelism between Scripture and sage. The Yerushalmi brings forth the sage as Scripture incarnate, and out of the union of the Torah and the person of the rabbi, the Judaism of the dual Torah was begotten.

When that union is fully realized, then the literary expression will prove striking. We are able, moreover, to show that precisely the same modes of explanation and interpretation found suitable for the Mishnah and the Scripture served equally well for the sayings and doings of sages. That fact may be shown in three ways. First, just as Scripture supplied proof texts, so deeds or statements of sages provided proof texts. Second, just as a verse of Scripture or an explicit statement of the Mishnah resolved a disputed point, so what a sage said or did might be introduced into discourse as ample proof for settling a dispute. And third, it follows that just as Scripture or the Mishnah laid down Torah, so what a sage did or said laid down Torah. In the dimensions of the applied and practical reason by which the law unfolded, the sage found a comfortable place in precisely the taxonomic categories defined, to begin with, by both the Mishnah and Scripture.

Specifically, we shall now see that what a sage says is treated precisely as statements in Scripture and the Mishnah are received. That is to say, the same modes of exegetical inquiry pertaining to the Mishnah and Scripture apply without variation to statements made by rabbis of the contemporary period themselves. Indeed, precisely the same theological and exegetical considerations come to bear both upon the Mishnah's statements and opinions expressed by talmudic rabbis. Since these were not to be distinguished from one another in the requirement that opinion be suitably grounded in Scripture, they also should be understood to have formed part of precisely the same corpus of Torah truths. What the Mishnah and the later rabbi said expressed precisely the same kind of truth: revelation—whether through the medium of Scripture, or that contained in the Mishnah, or that given in the opinion of the sage himself. The way in which this search for proof texts applies equally to the Mishnah and to the rabbi's opinion is illustrated in the following passage:

A. The party of Korah has no portion in the world to come, and will not live in the world to come [*m. San.* 10:4].

B. What is the scriptural basis for this view?

C. "So they and all that belonged to them went down alive into Sheol; and the earth closed over them, and they perished from the midst of the assembly" (Num. 16:33).

D. "The earth closed over them"—in this world.

E. "And they perished from the midst of the assembly"—in the world to come [*m. San.* 10:4D–F].

F. It was taught: R. Judah b. Batera says, "The contrary view is to be derived from the implication of the following verse:

G. "'I have gone astray like a lost sheep; seek thy servant and do not forget thy commandments' (Ps. 119:176).

H. "Just as the lost object which is mentioned later on in the end is going to be searched for, so the lost object which is stated herein is destined to be searched for" [*t. San.* 13:9].

I. Who will pray for them?

J. R. Samuel bar Nahman said, "Moses will pray for them."

K. [This is proved from the following verse:] "'Let Reuben live, and not die, [nor let his men be few]' (Deut. 33:6)."

L. R. Joshua b. Levi said, "Hannah will pray for them."

M. This is the view of R. Joshua b. Levi, for R. Joshua b. Levi said, "Thus did the party of Korah sink ever downward, until Hannah went and prayed for them and said, 'The Lord kills and brings to life; he brings down to Sheol and raises up' (1 Sam. 2:6)."

(*y. San.* 10:4.I)

We have a striking sequence of proof texts, serving (1) the cited statement of the Mishnah, A–C, then (2) an opinion of a rabbi in the Tosefta, F–H, then (3) the position of a rabbi, J–K and L–M. The process of providing proof texts, therefore, is central; the nature of the passages requiring the proof texts, a matter of indifference. We see that the search for appropriate verses of Scripture vastly transcends the purpose of studying the Mishnah and Scripture, the exegesis of their rules, or the provision of adequate authority for the Mishnah and its laws. In fact, any proposition that is to be taken seriously, whether in the Mishnah, in the Tosefta, or in the mouth of a talmudic sage himself, will elicit interest in scriptural support.

Why does the quest in Scripture for proof texts matter here? It is because we see that the real issue turns out to have been not the Mishnah at all, nor even the vindication of its diverse sayings, one by one. Why not? Once the words of a sage, not merely a rule of the Mishnah, are made to refer to Scripture for proof, it must follow that, in the natural course of things, a rule of the Mishnah or of the Tosefta will likewise be asked to refer to Scripture. That the living sage validated his own words through Scripture explains why the sage in the fourth century validated also the words of the (then) ancient sages of the Mishnah and Tosefta through verses of Scripture. It is one undivided phenomenon. Distinctions are not made among media—(1) oral, (2) written, or (3) living—of the Torah. The Torah—in our language, the canon of revealed truth—is in three media, not two. Scripture, the Mishnah, the sage—the three spoke with equal authority. True, one had to come into alignment with the other, the Mishnah with Scripture, the sage with the Mishnah. But it was not the case that one component of the Torah, of God's Word to Israel, stood within the sacred circle, another beyond. Interpretation and what was interpreted, exegesis and text, belonged together.

While Scripture and the Mishnah govern what the sage knows, in the Yerushalmi (as in the Bavli) it is the sage who authoritatively speaks about them. What sages were willing to do to the Mishnah in the Yerushalmi and Bavli is precisely what they were prepared to do in Scripture—impose upon it their own judgment of its meaning. It is the source of the authority of the sage himself that turns out to pose the fundamental question. With the answer to that question we also know, first, the status, as to revelation, of the things the sage says, whether he speaks of the Mishnah or of Scripture; second, we know the standing of the books he writes, whether these are tractates of the Yerushalmi or the Bavli or the compositions of exegeses of Scripture. The sage speaks with authority about the Mishnah and the Scripture. As much as they, he therefore has authority deriving from revelation. He himself may participate in the process of revelation. There is no material difference. Since that is so, the sage's book, whether the Yerushalmi or the Bavli to the Mishnah or Midrash to Scripture, is Torah—that is, revealed by God. It also forms part of the Torah, a fully canonical document. The reason, then, is that the sage is like Moses, "our rabbi," who received torah and wrote the Torah. So while the canon was in three parts— Scripture, Mishnah, sage—the sage, in saying what the other parts meant and in embodying that meaning in his life and thought, took primacy of place. If no document organized itself around sayings and stories of sages, it was because that was superfluous. Why so? Because all documents equally, whether Scripture, whether Mishnah, whether Yerushalmi, gave full and complete expression of deeds and deliberations of sages, beginning, after all, with Moses, our rabbi. The important point is simple. The sage forms a living Torah, a Torah become flesh. To state my prospective argument quite simply: first came the incarnation of the sage, in the Yerushalmi and related writings, then—as we shall see presently— came God in the Bavli. It follows that an account of how the story came to serve as the chosen medium for the statement of the proposition of incarnation of the sage will provide a model for our review of the character and use of the story, in the Bavli, for the statement of the incarnation of God.

THE SAGE-STORY AND ITS TRAITS

Among the three media in which the Judaic system of the dual Torah took shape—the written Torah and its exegesis, the oral

Torah and its exegesis, the person of the sage—it is the figure of the sage that now attracts our attention. The reason is that when an authorship wished to present the picture of the Torah as a human being, that authorship appealed to the figure of the sage. It would be quite natural later on to resort to the same medium, namely, the story, to represent the incarnation of God as well, and that is, in the main, what happened. So let us consider the stories about sages, then the ones that present the incarnation of God (henceforward: sage-stories).[1]

Among the modes of conveying thought available to an authorship within the Judaism at hand that we have considered—commentary to the Mishnah and secondary expansion of its statements, commentary to Scripture, telling stories about sages—it was that third mode of expression that predominated. Accordingly, the representation of the sage as the incarnation of the Torah is expressed principally in stories about the sage and his deeds. The importance of that fact for our larger inquiry into the representation of God in the form of a human being will become clear in the next section. What we shall see is that when an authorship wished to accomplish the incarnation of God, the authorship appealed to the story as the medium for its message of incarnation, its Judaic "gospel" of the Holy One, blessed be he, walking among human beings, arguing with them, teaching them, performing miracles for them, expressing love of them. One reason is that the work of incarnation to begin with had dealt with the sage, and portrayals of the sage as the incarnation of the Torah made use of the medium of the story. Consequently, the medium of story for the message of incarnation would in due course serve yet another topic.

The document I have chosen for the present analysis is *The Fathers According to Rabbi Nathan,* a document whose closest affinities place it in the circle of the authorship of the Talmud of Babylonia, ca. sixth century. I chose that compilation for two reasons. First, the base document upon which *The Fathers According to Rabbi Nathan* is built, namely, *The Fathers,* a mid-third-century collection

---

1. I review the argument of my *Judaism and Story: The Evidence of the Fathers According to Rabbi Nathan* (Chicago: University of Chicage Press, 1988).

of aphorisms attributed to sages of the late-second-century Mishnah, does not tell stories about its sages. Second, *The Fathers According to Rabbi Nathan* provides a remarkably apt opportunity to investigate in the context of religious literature the entry of the story as an important medium for presenting a message in Judaism, since that document contains an unusually rich selection of stories about sages. For, as we have seen in the sample in hand, *The Fathers,* like the Mishnah and the Tosefta, contains no sustained narratives about sages and has very few narratives of other types. The narrative level pertaining to apophthegms set in a "dramatic" framework is reached by "One day he saw . . . and said . . . ," with the "one day" serving to establish the episodic character in which the saying is presented. Had the apophthegm stated simply "Whenever he saw a skull, he said . . . ," it would have obviated the need for the (pseudo-) narrative setting in which it presently appears. In the movement from *The Fathers* to *The Fathers According to Rabbi Nathan,* therefore, we are able to see how the framers of the later work of exegesis of an earlier writing found a place in their composition for a genre of materials not found appropriate for use as a paramount medium among prior framers or authorships of canonical documents. Following this development for the incarnation of the Torah in sage in *The Fathers According to Rabbi Nathan* provides guideposts in our examination of the parallel development for the incarnation of God—also very much in the model of the sage—in the Bavli.

Drawing the parallel at hand between the sage-story and the God-incarnate-story proves apt for yet another reason. We have already noticed that before the Bavli, the document of the canon of the Judaism of the dual Torah rarely endowed God with a personality. Only in the Bavli do we find a rich representation of God as a human person. The same pattern unfolds for the telling of tales about sages. Until the Yerushalmi, the components of the same canon rarely tell detailed stories about sages; when they do, moreover, these stories principally illustrate points of law or doctrine and contain remarkably slight representation of the sage's individual traits of personality and character, let alone deed. The Judaism portrayed in the writings of the sages, or rabbis, of late antiquity, from the first to the seventh century, in the beginning took slight interest in the lives and persons of those sages. The use of the sage-story as a principal mode of communication, furthermore, will have surprised the compilers of earlier compositions in the unfolding canon of the Judaism of the Dual Torah. For the authorship of the Mishnah, to which *The Fathers* had itself been attached as the first and most important apologetic, took slight interest in telling stories about sages.

That is not to say the authorship of the Mishnah did not include narratives, for it assuredly did so, particularly for the purpose of a precedent of a law or the illustration of the law on the one side, or of providing a setting for the presentation of a saying on the other. But many centuries later, the authorship of *The Fathers According to Rabbi Nathan* made remarkably extensive use of the story about the sage, his origins, sagacity, historical importance, and mode of dying. In doing so, they supplied *The Fathers,* a tractate attached to the Mishnah and congruent, in its judgment of narrative, to the Mishnah, with a layer of narrative in the genre of the story about the sage. By the end of the period at hand, by contrast, the canonical writings of Judaism, represented first by the Yerushalmi and then by the Bavli, drew upon a rich corpus of stories about the beginnings (meaning of Torah-study), sagacity, historical power, and endings (meaning death while engaged in Torah-study) of those same figures. The story of an important event in the life of a sage told, for example, in the Talmud of the Land of Israel in the end of the fourth century, and its successor two centuries later, took an important role in the presentation of the message of the Torah.

Here an important qualification is required. While the two Talmuds present stories about sages, neither one contains anything we might call a "gospel" of a sage or even a chapter of a gospel. There is no sustained biography of any sage, and the stories we do have remain episodic and ad hoc. In the two Talmuds, serving as exegesis of the Mishnah, and in the contemporary Midrash-compilations, providing exegesis of Scripture, the sage-story does not play a prominent role. This may be seen in a simple fact. While both Talmuds resort for their fundamental redactional structure to the Mishnah, and while, in addition, the Bavli appeals to sustained passages of Scripture as the basis for organizing its materials,[2] neither of the two Talmuds formulates stories about a given authority as a continuous, more than merely episodic, narrative.

What is important for our study of the incarnation of God through the medium of storytelling requires a brief survey of one trait of the sage-story. The survey concerns its narrative qualities. In my analysis of the diverse narratives in *The Fathers According to Rabbi Nathan* I was able to accomplish a taxonomy of narrative, generated by the document under close analysis here. I found five kinds of narrative, or to put it differently, five species of the genus narrative. I classified these species as (1) parable, (2) precedent, (3) narrative setting for a saying, (4) scriptural story, and (5) sage-story. In the section following this one we discuss how the stories they serve as the medium for the incarnation of God (God-story) compare to the sage-stories. I seek to set into the broader taxonomic framework the particular stories that serve as a medium for the message of God as a human being. The reason that we can accomplish such a comparison between the sage-story and the stories before us is simple. It is that formal, not merely thematic, differences generate the taxonomy at hand. A story about a scriptural hero differs in its narrative qualities from a story about a sage-hero.

The difference is simple. The conventions exhibited in the stories about sages but not in other types of narratives in *The Fathers According to Rabbi Nathan* require movement. The narrator requires that something actually happen, so that a problem and its solution are recorded through an account of what people not only said but also did (sometimes, to be sure, stated implicitly and not through detailed description). So I understand by "sage-story" a narrative with these distinctive and indicative (but by no means unique) traits:

1. a beginning, middle, and end,
2. tension and resolution,
3. characterization accomplished through an account of motivation,
4. about a particular person,

---

2. An important point, to be considered in the next section of this chapter.

5. concerning what that person said and did on a distinct and important, one-time occasion.
6. A sage-story rarely cites verse of Scripture and it differs from a scriptural story in its omission of close attention to citations of verses of Scripture as a main focus of discourse.

I derived the foregoing catalogue of those indicative traits of the sage-story from an inductive analysis of those sage-stories in *The Fathers According to Rabbi Nathan* that exhibit no parallels or counterparts in other writings. In comparing the version of the origin of Aqiba, which is unique to *The Fathers According to Rabbi Nathan,* and the version of the origin of Eliezer, which appears both in *The Fathers According to Rabbi Nathan* and elsewhere, for example, as well as the two stories of the destruction of Jerusalem, the one in *The Fathers According to Rabbi Nathan,* the other in the Talmud of Babylonia, both of them involving Yohanan ben Zakkai, I was able to distinguish our document's sage-stories from counterpart narratives elsewhere by resort to the stated criteria for the definition of a story, meaning a sage-story. For these distinctive and indicative traits do not characterize other stories, for example, ones about scriptural heroes, let alone parables, settings for sayings (in which nothing much happens), or legal precedents and illustrations of the law through concrete accounts of circumstance.

Other kinds of narratives, precedents and illustrations of the law, parables, narrative settings for stationary sayings, and stories told as part of the exegesis of Scripture (e.g., about scriptural heroes), do not conform to these traits at all. None of the other kinds of narratives tells us about motivation and characterization, none of them portrays a situation with movement provided by tension and resolution, and, therefore, none has beginning, middle, and end. Ordinarily, the narrative other than the sage-story portrays a stationary tableau. The one exception, the parable, speaks of paradigms, not persons, illustrating a teaching in a rhetorically similar, if more affecting way as does a narrative setting for a saying. It is in *The Fathers According to Rabbi Nathan* that the story about the sage, with its stylistically indicative traits, forms the largest proportion of narratives of any document among the principal writings in the canon of Judaism in late antiquity. All the others resort to narratives of various kinds in the service of making diverse points. But our authorship is the one to employ the story about the sage to make its two new and critical points, the one about the supernatural character of the Torah-sage, the other about the eschatological character of the teleology of the Judaism of the dual Torah contained within the canonical writings before us. The new messages of *The Fathers According to Rabbi Nathan*, concerning the nation enduring this age and waiting for the age to come, occur not only in sayings but also in stories. A medium not utilized in *The Fathers* but extensively used in *The Fathers According to Rabbi Nathan* carries a new message.

Let me now spell out in a concrete way the indicative traits of the sage-story. A story may share the tasks of an illustration in that it presents a narrative: such and such is what happened. It is also alike in its interest in the concrete and specific way of framing a point. But it is different in one fundamental and definitive way. Its importance requires emphasis:

While meaning to provide a good example of how one should behave, the teller of a story always deals with a concrete person and a particular incident.

The person is concrete in that he (in *The Fathers According to Rabbi Nathan* there is not a single story about a woman) is always specified by name. It concerns a particular incident in that the viewpoint of the narrator makes clear the one-timeness and specificity of the event that is reported. The story always happens in historical time, and the point it wishes to make is subordinate to the description of action, the development of a point of tension, at which the story commences, and its resolution, at which the story concludes: beginning, middle, and end. The sage-storyteller, moreover, is never bound by the requirements of a larger redactional purpose and intent. While we cannot say that the story is told "for its own sake," since I cannot define the traits of a story told "for its own sake," we must conclude that the generative and definitive power of the story derives from internal and intrinsic tensions and interests and not extrinsic ones. That is, the storyteller wishes to compose the narrative along lines required by the generative tension of the story at hand, not those imposed by the redactional purpose supplied by the (planned) setting of the story. The power of the story—its definitive function—is intrinsic to the narrative and self-evident within the narrative. Any further point that the story serves to prove or illustrate lies outside of the imaginative framework.

The medium bears a very particular message. Stories on sages in *The Fathers According to Rabbi Nathan* yield a single message: people may begin study of the Torah at any point in life, and, if they work hard, they will achieve success, riches, and fame. If they cut off their ties from their family, they will end up inheriting their family's estate, and if their wives tolerate their long absences and support them and their family, their wives will share in their success, riches, and fame. It follows that the stories on the common theme of the origins of great masters, as preserved in *The Fathers According to Rabbi Nathan*, address the question of the breakup of the families of mature men who choose to study the Torah and respond by promising success, riches, and fame for those who in mature years do convert to study of the Torah. The lesson of the origins of the great masters is to give up home and family in favor of the Torah. The subject matter—sages—generates its own narrative literary conventions that differ from those that guide writers of stories about scriptural figures. We furthermore find propositions emerging from stories on sages. The distinctive narrative conventions make one cogent and critical point: The sage learns through study of the Torah, which is accomplished solely by service of the master, to be patient and affable and forebearing. The story about a sage has a beginning, middle, and end, and the story about a sage also rests not only on verbal exchanges ("he said to him . . . , he said to him . . .") but on (described or implicit) action; the story about a sage unfolds from a point of tension and conflict to a clear resolution and remission of the conflict; the story about a sage rarely invokes a verse of Scripture. That means that where a distinct subject comes into view, the narrator of stories about sages will nonetheless follow a fixed set of everywhere-applicable narrative conventions. The point of differentiation among stories derives from the contrast between the topic sage and the topic Scripture and its heroes and other topics. Stories are told in one way for the one topical category, in another for the other.

The general remarks about the characteristics of the sage-story takes on concreteness in a single example. I choose a brief story, on the death of two sages (boldface = citation of tractate *Avot,* that is, *The Fathers*):

A. **A sword comes into the world because of the delaying of justice and perversion of justice, and because of those who teach the Torah not in accord with the law.**

(ARNA XXXVIII:V.1)

A. When they seized Rabban Simeon b. Gamaliel and R. Ishmael on the count of death, Rabban Simeon b. Gamaliel was in session and was perplexed, saying, "Woe is us! For we are put to death like those who profane the Sabbath and worship idols and practice fornication and kill."

C. Said to him R. Ishmael b. Elisha, "Would it please you if I said something before you?"

D. He said to him, "Go ahead."

E. He said to him, "Is it possible that when you were sitting at a banquet, poor folk came and stood at your door, and you did not let them come in and eat?"

F. He said to him, "By heaven [may I be cursed] if I ever did such a thing! Rather, I set up guards at the gate. When poor folk came along, they would bring them in to me and eat and drink with me and say a blessing for the sake of Heaven."

G. He said to him, "Is it possible that when you were in session and expounding [the Torah] on the Temple mount and the vast populations of Israelites were in session before you, you took pride in yourself?"

H. He said to him, "Ishmael my brother, one has to be ready to accept his failing. [That is why I am being put to death, the pride that I felt on such an occasion.]"

I. They went on appealing to the executioner for grace. This one [Ishmael] said to him, "I am a priest, son of a high priest, kill me first, so that I do not have to witness the death of my companion."

J. And the other [Simeon] said, "I am the patriarch, son of the patriarch, kill me first, so that I do not have to witness the death of my companion."

K. He said to him, "Cast lots." They cast lots, and the lot fell on Rabban Simeon b. Gamaliel.

L. The executioner took the sword and cut off his head.

M. R. Ishmael b. Elisha took it and held it in his breast and wept and cried out:"Oh holy mouth, oh faithful mouth, oh mouth that brought forth beautiful gems, precious stones and pearls! Who has laid you in the dust, who has filled your mouth with dirt and dust.

N. "Concerning you Scripture says, *Awake, O sword, against my shepherd and against the man who is near to me* (Zech. 13:7)."

O. He had not finished speaking before the executioner took the sword and cut off his head.

P. Concerning them Scripture says, *My wrath shall wax hot, and I will kill you with the sword, and your wives shall be widows, and your children fatherless.* (Ex. 22:23).

(ARNA XXXVIII:V.2)

The story establishes the tension at the outset: why do we die as do sinners? This question is resolved in the colloquy at C–H, at which the first act concludes. The sequence of tension and resolution is exceedingly important for our analysis of the God-story, as we shall presently see. The second act, I–L, has the sages appeal to the executioner to spare the one the sight of the martyrdom of the other. The third and final component has Ishmael's lament: the mouth that taught the Torah will be avenged. The sage who dies in peace addresses his lessons to the Torah-community: the decline of the great tradition because of the failure of the sages and their disciples. The sage who dies as a martyr teaches a lesson of hope to Israel at large: God will ultimately exact justice of those who sin by persecuting Israel, just as God exacts strict justice even for the peccadillo of pride.

The lessons imparted are these: XXXVIII:V.1: Sages suffer the death penalty for the sin of pride; XXXVIII:V.2: Sages are martyred but know that, in due course, God will punish those who have sinned against them. If I had to single out the main point sages wished through the topic at hand to underline, it is God's perfect justice. Sages' deaths, therefore, are so portrayed as to bring that comfort that is contained within the conviction of divine vengeance for injustice and divine faithfulness in exacting justice on sinners and evildoers, Israelite and Gentile alike. For if the sage is punished for mere pride, there can be no limit to the matter. Sage-stories—with their beginnings, middles, and endings, their actions whether described or merely implied within verbal exchanges, their tensions and resolutions—follow the pattern familiar within the earlier categories. That positive trait is joined to a negative one. The story about a sage never serves to prove a proposition concerning the meaning of a verse of Scripture. With this example in hand, we may turn back to the Bavli's stories that accomplish the incarnation of God.

FROM ALLUSION TO REALIZATION:
THE STORY AS THE MEDIUM OF
THE INCARNATION OF GOD

As we review the stories that represent God as a human being, we notice that many of those I collected allude to the incarnation of God. For the purpose of demonstrating the development among the authorship(s) represented in the Bavli of an interest in portraying God as a man, those stories required attention. But most of them allude to God as incarnate, and only a few show us precisely where and how the incarnation of God comes to expression in detailed pictures of action and movement. These latter stories form the focus of interest. Merely alluding to God as incarnate— for example, having arms or legs, engaging in set-piece dialogue based on verses of Scripture or exchanges of theological positions—hardly draws us close to the orbit of the moving tales of the sage as Torah incarnate. Stories that tell us the tale of God moving among (some) human beings, working among them, engaging in argument with them, transacting exchanges among them form a tiny but critical corpus. For they permit us to address what I think is the fundamental question before us. When sages in the authorship of the Bavli represent God as a human being, do they point us toward God as essentially in the model of the sage? Or do the stories about the incarnation of God carry us beyond that model and into an entirely other realm of being and of meaning? That is what forms the question at hand.

To specify my criterion for answering the question at hand, our task is now to ask whether a story that accomplishes the representation of God as a human person, that is, the incarnation of God, carries forward the narrative policies of the sage-story, or whether the Bavli's pictures of God as a human being (which we shall henceforward call God-incarnate-stories) follow their own program and conventions. Recall the criteria for the sage-story, as distinct from all other narratives in *The Fathers According to Rabbi Nathan:* (1) a beginning, middle, and end, (2) tension and resolution, (3) characterization accomplished through an account of motivation, (4) about a particular person, and (5) concerning what that person said and did on a distinct and important, one-time occasion. A sage story (6) rarely cites verses of Scripture and it differs from a scriptural story in its omission of close attention to citations of verses of Scripture as a main focus of discourse.

A survey of the stories in *The Fathers According to Rabbi Nathan* yields in detail ample justification for the claim that, as the medium is different, so too is the message. On the surface we come across numerous obvious differences in narrative convention dictating the technique of telling stories about sages in particular. Three, among the six just now listed, seem to me definitive:

1. The story about a sage has a beginning, middle, and end, and the story about a sage also rests not only on verbal exchanges ("he said to him . . . , he said to him . . ."), but on (described) action.
2. The story about a sage unfolds from a point of tension and conflict to a clear resolution and remission of the conflict.
3. The story about a sage rarely invokes a verse of Scripture and never serves to prove a proposition concerning the meaning of a verse of Scripture.

These traits prove distinctive. For, when I analyzed, in the same compilation, the traits of stories about scriptural figures and themes (surveyed in my book but not cited here), they proved quite the opposite:

1. In the story about a scriptural hero there is no beginning, middle, and end, and little action. The burden of the narrative is carried by "he said to him . . . , he said to him. . . ." Described action is rare and plays slight role in the unfolding of the narrative. Often the narrative consists of little more than a setting for a saying, and the point of the narrative is conveyed not through what is told but through the cited saying.
2. The story about a scriptural hero is worked out as a tableau, with description of the components of the stationary tableau placed at the center. There is little movement, no point of tension that is resolved.
3. The story about a scriptural hero always invokes verses from Scripture and makes the imputation of meaning to those verses the center of interest.

We therefore can differentiate the sage-story from the Scripture-story of *The Fathers According to Rabbi Nathan*. With the specified traits before us, we may now revert to a brief review of the stories presented in chapter 9. For the purpose of the present analysis I take one example among several. We begin with the representation, through mere allusions to accepted traits or facts, of God as man. The single most striking statement that God looks like a man is in the following:

1.A. Said R. Hoshaiah, "When the Holy One, blessed be he, came to create the first man, the ministering angels mistook him [for God, since man was in God's image,] and wanted to say before him, 'Holy, [holy, holy is the Lord of hosts].'

B. "To what may the matter be compared? To the case of a king and a governor who were set in a chariot, and the provincials wanted to greet the king, 'Sovereign!' But they did not know which one of them was which. What did the king do? He turned the governor out and put him away from the chariot, so that people would know who was king.

C. "So too when the Holy One, blessed be he, created the first man, the angels mistook him [for God]. What did the Holy One, blessed be he, do? He put him to sleep, so everyone knew that he was a mere man.

D. "That is in line with the following verse of Scripture: 'Cease you from man, in whose nostrils is a breath, for how little is he to be accounted' (Is. 2:22)."

(*Gen. R.* VIII:X)

This is not a story about God, for example, things God did, arguments God conducted, God's behavior in a given circumstance and how it solved a problem, and the like. It is the statement of the abstract proposition, in the form of a story, that, since man looked like God, God had to show the difference. This God did simply by putting man to sleep—with the further implication, I think, that death marks the difference. Here we have a kind of narrative. But in the numerous other pericopes that impute physical attributes to God, we have no narratives at all. In proposing to show that a sizable document imputed corporeal form to God, I had of course to assemble a variety of genres of writing. But none of those items can be classified as a story.

Not only so, but in stories that represent God's emotional structure and other virtues, God rarely serves as the hero of the story or plays the role of protagonist. Showing that it is a virtue to be humble, the storyteller provides a narrative of how God showed humility.

A. Said R. Joshua b. Levi, "When Moses came down from before the Holy One, blessed be he, Satan came and asked [God], 'Lord of the world, Where is the Torah?'

B. "He said to him, 'I have given it to the earth . . .' [Satan ultimately was told by God to look for the Torah by finding the son of Amram.]

C. "He went to Moses and asked him, 'Where is the Torah which the Holy One, blessed be he, gave you?'

D. "He said to him, 'Who am I that the Holy One, blessed be he, should give me the Torah?'

E. "Said the Holy One, blessed be he, to Moses, 'Moses, you are a liar!'

F. "He said to him, 'Lord of the world, you have a treasure in store which you have enjoyed every day. Shall I keep it to myself?'

G. "He said to him, 'Moses, since you have acted with humility, it will bear your name: "Remember the Torah of Moses, my servant" (Mal. 3:22).'"

(*b. Shab* 89a)

God is not the protagonist of this story; God is only the straight man. Satan is the principal actor, setting up the circumstance for Moses' stunning saying. In the drama, God speaks the critical line—but as a bit player. The same critical—yet tangential—role is assigned to God in the story about Eliezer's and Joshua's argument. When heaven's intervention is rejected, God enters the story—only to underline the main point of the story, which is made through the actions and dramatic dialogue assigned to others:

B. He said to him, "He laughed out loud, saying 'My children have won over me, my children have won over me.'"

(*b. B.M.* 59b)

At the risk of taxing the reader's patience, I give yet a third example of how stories in which God is represented as incarnate, indeed, as a sage, treat God as a mere straight man:

A. In the session in the firmament, people were debating this question: if the bright spot came before the white hair, the person is unclean. If the white hair came before the bright spot, he is clean. What about a case of doubt?

B. The Holy One, blessed be he, said, "Clean."

C. And the rest of the fellowship of the firmament said, "Unclean."

D. They said, "Who will settle the matter?"

E. It should be Rabbah b. Nahmani, for he is the one who said, "I am an expert in the laws of plagues and in the effects of contamination through the overshadowing of a corpse." . . .

F. A letter fell down from the sky to Pumbedita: "Rabbah b. Nahmani has been called up by the academy of the firmament . . ."

(b. B.M. 86a)

God plays a role here as an ordinary sage. But God's part in the story is minimal and even the representation of God as incarnate is tangential. It is a story about the sage in the heavenly academy; the sage is like God, doing the things that (by the way) God is represented as doing. God is not the hero, nor even part of the detail; God is a mere backdrop.

Other descriptions of things God says and does follow suit. People refer to God, but God does not emerge richly characterized as the centerpiece of narrative. One last example of the numerous allusions to God, whether in the form of narrative or in other forms altogether:

A. Said R. Isaac bar Samuel in the name of Rab, "The night is divided into three watches, and over each watch, the Holy One, blessed be he, sits and roars like a lion.

B. "He says, 'Woe to the children, on account of whose sins I have wiped out my house and burned my palace, and whom I have exiled among the nations of the world.'"

(b. Ber. 3a, VII)

K. "I said to him, 'I heard the sound of an echo moaning like a pigeon and saying, "Woe to the children, on account of whose sins I have wiped out my house and burned my palace and whom I have exiled among the nations of the world'" . . .

M. "'And not only so, but when Israelites go into synagogues and schoolhouses and respond, "May the great name be blessed," the Holy One shakes his head and says, "Happy is the king, whom they praise in his house in such a way! What does a father have, who has exiled his children? And woe to the children who are exiled from their father's table!"'"

(b. Ber. 3a, VIII)

While represented as a fully formed personality in these stories, God nonetheless does not enter into the narrative as an actor, a person who walks and talks among human beings. We may say very simply that when the authorships at hand wished to make their points about God as a personality, they found no strong reason to tell stories about God as they told stories about sages. To state matters in our own, secular terms, the narrative role of God in these stories does not conform to that of the sage in sage-stories.

That is not to suggest that God appears only as a straight man. When God is represented in negotiations with mortals, engaged in exchanges and gaining his wishes through give and take, God enjoys a more active role in the narrative. Unlike the foregoing pericopes, in the following one we have God as a hero and principal actor:

F. Rabbah bar Mari said, "What is the meaning of this verse: 'But they were rebellious at the sea, even at the Red Sea; nonetheless he saved them for his name's sake' (Ps. 106:7)?

G. "This teaches that the Israelites were rebellious at that time, saying, 'Just as we will go up on this side, so the Egyptians will go up on the other side.' Said the Holy One, blessed be he, to the angelic prince who reigns over the sea, 'Cast them [the Israelites] out on dry land.'

H. "He said before him, 'Lord of the world, is there any case of a slave [namely, myself] to whom his master [you] gives a gift [the Israelites], and then the master goes and takes [the gift] away again? [You gave me the Israelites, now you want to take them away and place them on dry land.]'

I. "He said to him, 'I'll give you one and a half times their number.'

J. "He said before him, 'Lord of the world, is there a possibility that a slave can claim anything against his master? [How do I know that you will really do it?]'

K. "He said to him, 'The Kishon brook will be my pledge [that I shall carry out my word. Nine hundred chariots at the brook were sunk [Jud. 4:13] while Pharaoh at the sea had only six hundred, thus a pledge one and a half times greater than the sum at issue.]'

L. "Forthwith [the angelic prince of the sea] spit them out onto dry land, for it is written, 'And the Israelites saw the Egyptians dead on the sea shore' (Ex. 14:30)."

(*b. Ar.* 15A–B)

The pericope is a story, not merely an allusion to a fact or a syllogistic proposition or an exegesis. From G forward, the narrative takes its own course. It starts with a crisis, the problem of the Israelites at the sea. God intervenes as the hero to solve the crisis. The tension in the story derives from H and is worked out at the exchanges of H–I, then J–K. We have a beginning, middle, and end. There is a point of tension and conflict, ending in a resolution. But there is a very considerable point of difference between this narrative and the sage-story, and it is in the critical role, beginning and end, of verses of Scripture. The story is spun out to explain Ps. 106:7. Its climactic moment is Jud. 3:23, then Ex. 14:30. In no way does this story, in which God plays the role of protagonist, conform to the pattern established for sage-stories in *The Fathers According to Rabbi Nathan*.

The same reversion to Scripture as the critical source for narrative movement, on the one side, and the propositions for narrative statement, on the other, also characterizes stories of conflict between God and other personalities. To show that the pattern persists, I give a further illustration:

A. Said R. Isaac, "When the temple was destroyed, the Holy One, blessed be he, found Abraham standing in the Temple. He said to him, 'What is my beloved doing in my house?'

B. "He said to him, 'I have come because of what is going on with my children.'

C. "He said to him, 'Your children sinned and have been sent into exile.'

D. "He said to him, 'But wasn't it by mistake that they sinned?'

E. "He said to him, 'She has wrought lewdness' (Jer. 11:15).

F. "He said to him, 'But wasn't it just a minority of them that did it?'

G. "He said to him, 'It was a majority' (Jer. 11:15).

H. "He said to him, 'You should at least have taken account of the covenant of circumcision [which should have secured forgiveness despite their sin]!'

I. "He said to him, 'The holy flesh is passed from you' (Jer. 11:15).

J. "'And if you had waited for them, they might have repented!'

K. "He said to him, 'When you do evil, then you are happy' (Jer. 11:15).

L. "He said to him, 'He put his hands on his head, crying out and weeping, saying to them, "God forbid! Perhaps they have no remedy at all!"'

M. "A heavenly voice came forth and said, 'The Lord called you "a leafy olive tree, fair with excellent fruit"' (Jer. 11:16).

N. "'Just as in the case of an olive tree, its future comes only at the end [that is, it is only after a long while that it attains its best fruit], so in the case of Israel, their future comes at the end of their time.'"

(*b. Men.* 53b)

On the one side, the tension established between God and Abraham generates a compelling story. The issue is worked out with a beginning, middle, and end. There is surely a clear resolution at N.

But the unfolding of the story, on God's part, is simply through statements God has already made—in Scripture. In fact, we have little more than a dramatization, to good effect, of Jer. 11:15–16. No sage-story unfolds through the citations, in the mouths of sages, of verses of Scripture. The reason for the difference is not difficult to find. The author of this story (Isaac) has simply taken what God said to Jeremiah and recast the matter into statements God made to Abraham when the Temple was destroyed. Isaac has not given God language that, so far as Scripture is concerned, God did not say anyhow. Isaac has merely reframed God's statements in Scripture into a dramatic story. It follows that in the point at which a sage-story and a God-story differ, it is for a reason we can specify. But while the representation of God in God-stories works itself out in a narrative model different from that of the sage-story, the difference is still more profound. For, as we shall presently see, while God forms the model of the sage, God is not represented as merely another, more perfect sage. In the God-story as compared to the sage-story, God is truly wholly other: alike but essentially unlike.

We may go a step further and offer the hypothesis that, where we have a true story about God in incarnate form, it will ordinarily end with the climax of a verse of Scripture, being pointed toward that goal. A rather routine story shows us the central role played by the cited verse:

A. Said R. Joshua b. Levi, "When Moses came up on high, he found the Holy One, blessed be he, tying crowns onto the letters of the Torah. He said to him, 'Moses, don't people say hello in your town?'

B. "He said to him, 'does a servant greet his master [first]?'

C. "He said to him, 'You should have helped me [at least by greeting me and wishing me success].'

D. "He said to him, 'Now I pray you let the power of the Lord be great, just as you have said' (Num 14:17)."

(*b. Shab.* 89a)

The point of the story is made at C–D. God's message then derives from the cited verse of Scripture, which tells us how to greet the Master.

Up to this point, we have found out a simple fact. When stories treat God as incarnate, they are unlike sage-stories at a critical point. Sage-stories do not reach their climax in the citation of verses of Scripture and do not serve to amplify the meaning or application of those stories. God-stories do. But does that definitive trait place God-stories into the classification of stories about scriptural figures and themes, as these appear in *The Fathers According to Rabbi Nathan*? We recall that three traits characterize Scripture-stories: (1) these lack beginning, middle, and end, and convey little movement; (2) they tend to form a tableau in stasis; (3) the climax will come with verses of Scripture, exegesis of which forms the center of interest. We shall now see that it is only at that third point at which stories about God and stories about scriptural heroes intersect.

That leaves for reconsideration one profound and evocative story, among the repertoire surveyed in chapter 8. It is the story that represents God as a critical actor, that unfolds from beginning to middle and end, that involves action, that sets up a point of tension and then resolves that tension, and that does not invoke a verse of Scripture or provide a proposition concerning the meaning of such a verse. In all its indicative traits, the following story treats the incarnation of God in accord with the conventions characteristic of sage-stories in *The Fathers According to Rabbi Nathan*:

A. Said R. Judah said Rab, "When Moses went up to the height, he found the Holy One, blessed be he, sitting and tying crowns to the letters [of the Torah]."

B. "He said to him, 'Lord of the universe, why is this necessary?'

C. "He said to him, 'There is a certain man who is going to come into being at the end of some generations, by the name of Aqiba b. Joseph. He is going to find expositions to attach mounds and mounds of laws to each point [of a crown].'

D. "He said to him, 'Lord of the universe, show him to me.'

E. "He said to him, 'Turn around.'

F. "[Moses] went and took his seat at the end of eight rows, but he could not understand what the people were saying. He felt weak. When discourse came to a certain matter, one of [Aqiba's] disciples said to him, 'My Lord, how do you know this?'

G. "He said to him, 'It is a law revealed by God to Moses at Mount Sinai.'

H. "Moses' spirits were restored.

I. "He turned back and returned to the Holy One, blessed be he. He said to him, 'Lord of the universe, now if you have such a man available, how can you give the Torah through me?'

J.   "He said to him, 'Be silent. That is how I have decided matters.'
K.   "He said to him, 'Lord of the universe, you have now shown me his mastery of the Torah. Now show me his reward.'
L.   "He said to him, 'Turn around.'
M.   "He turned around and saw people weighing out his flesh in the butcher shop.
N.   "He said to him, 'Lord of the universe, such is his mastery of Torah, and such is his reward?'
O.   "He said to him, 'Be silent. That is how I have decided matters.'"

(*b. Men.* 29b)

This story in every detail but one conforms to the indicative traits of the sage-story. Verses of Scripture play no role. God is the protagonist of the story; Moses the straight man. The story unfolds with a marked beginning, the tension created by Moses' question about the details of the letters in which the Torah is written. The middle is worked out at D–H. There is then a second point of tension—Moses cannot understand the message—and then comes a resolution. Everything Aqiba says begins with Moses. But that produces the third and most intense point of tension, leading to the story's real point, which unfolds at I–O. So we move in stages: conflict, resolution, then to a higher level of conflict.

But at one stunning point the story that expresses the incarnation of God takes its leave of the sage-story. What we lack is the resolution of the final point of conflict; it is open-ended. *Be silent. That is how I have decided matters.* That statement hardly marks a happy ending, and it assuredly does not answer the question with which the passage commences. The story merely restates the question in a more profound way. So the one truly striking story about God in the form of not a human being in general but a sage in particular, a sage engaged in debate and argument, turns out to make precisely the opposite of the point of every other sage-story. All other such stories tell us how sages resolve points of tension and sort out conflict, bringing to a happy resolution whatever problem has generated the action of the story. But this story tells us the precise opposite, which is that God decrees and even the sage—even our rabbi, Moses, the sage of all sages—must maintain humble silence and accept the divine decree. Turning matters around in a secular direction, we may state the proposition in this way: the sage is like God, but, like all other human beings, subject to God's ultimately autocephalic decree.

A story built on the premise of the incarnation of God—fully exposing God's traits of personality and portraying God like a sage, engaged in argument with a man as master engages in argument with a disciple—serves a stunning purpose, which contradicts its academic form. It is to show that God, while like a sage, is more than a sage—much more. And, even in this deeply human context, that "more" is to be stated only in the submission expressed through silence. This I take to be the final statement of the incarnation of God of the Judaism of the dual Torah. God incarnate remains God ineffable. When the Judaism of the dual Torah wishes to portray the character of divinity, it invokes in the end the matter of relationship and not tactile quality and character. If we wish to know God, it is through our *relationship* to God, not through our (entirely legitimate and welcome) act of the incarnation of God in heart and mind and soul, deliberation and deed. And the way to engage with, relate to God in the face of (in the suggestive instance at hand) the Torah and torture of Aqiba is silence.

In an age struck dumb by horror and Holocaust, in anguish seeking God's face in a time of the hiding of the face, incarnation takes its unanticipated forms, just as at the Sea, just as at Sinai. In response to God's self-revelation, whether at the Sea, whether at Sinai, whether in sickness or in health, whether in moments of despair and disappointment or in an hour of exultation and ecstacy, what is to be said?

"He said to him, 'Be silent. That is how I have decided matters.'"
"And Abram put his faith in the Lord, and the Lord counted that faith in him as righteousness."

Index of Subjects

Index of Biblical and Talmudic References